WASHINGTON
ICE
A CLIMBING GUIDE

WASHINGTON
ICE
A CLIMBING GUIDE

JASON D. MARTIN & ALEX KRAWARIK

THE MOUNTAINEERS BOOKS

Published by
The Mountaineers Books
1001 SW Klickitat Way, Suite 201
Seattle, WA 98134

First edition, 2003

Published simultaneously in Great Britain by Cordee, 3a DeMontfort Street, Leicester, England, LE1 7HD

Manufactured in the United States of America

Aquisitions and Project Editor: Christine Hosler
Copyeditor: Julie Van Pelt
Cover and Book Design: The Mountaineers Books
Layout: Mayumi Thompson
Cartography: Moore Creative Designs
Illustrator: Brian D. Metz

Front cover photograph: *Andreas Schmidt climbing Flight to Mars near Snoqualmie Pass/Alpental* (photo by Sean Courage)
Back cover photograph: *Dan Erickson climbing on Drury Falls, Leavenworth* (photo by Alex Krawarik)
Frontispiece: *Mark Shipman climbing Shipman's Slippery Tongue near Leavenworth* (photo by Bruce White)

Library of Congress Cataloging-in-Publication Data
Martin, Jason D., 1972-
  Washington ice : a climbing guide / by Jason D. Martin and Alex Krawarik.— 1st ed.
      p. cm.
Includes bibliographical references and index.
  ISBN 0-89886-946-3 (paperback)
  1. Snow and ice climbing—Washington (State)—Guidebooks. 2. Washington (State)—Guidebooks. I. Krawarik, Alex, 1971- II. Title.
  GV200.3.M27 2003
  917.97—dc21
                                        2003010788

CONTENTS

SOUTH CASCADES

OUTLYING AREAS OF WASHINGTON

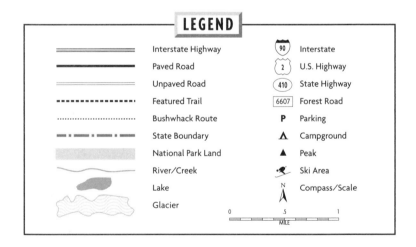

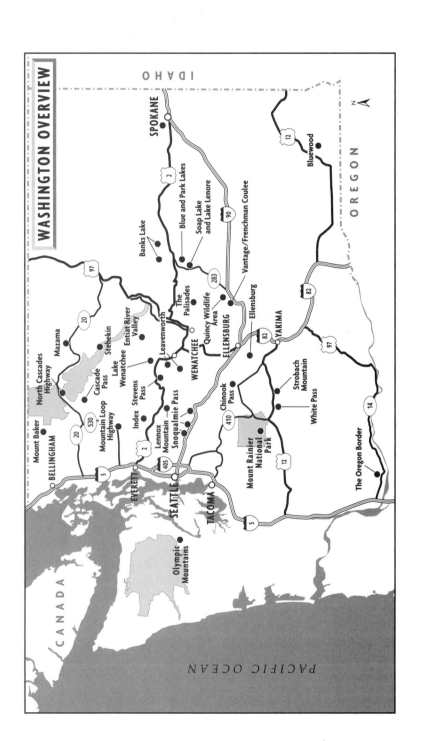

SPECIAL THANKS

This book would have been impossible without the help of the climbing community. Thanks to the following people and organizations:

Krista Eytchison, Erik Snyder, Mark Shipman, John Eminger, Larry Nevers Jr., David Zulinke, Gene Pires, Kevin Pogue, Dunham Gooding and the staff at the American Alpine Institute, Dan Smith, Sean McCabe, Paul Butler and the staff of North Cascade Mountain Guides, Mike Layton, Tim Crawford and the staff of *cascadeclimbers.com,* Geof Childs, Doug Littauer, Dave Burdick, Phil Fortier, Brett Bergeron, Darryl Cramer, Rolf Larson, William Robins, Ade Miller, Matt Perkins, Mike Maude, Jim Nelson, Paul Detrick, Karel Ziken, Eli Holmes, Stephen Karney, A. J. Ritter, Ryland Moore, Gregory Mueller, Casey Klahn, Andy Bourne, Dallas Kloke, Scott Bingen, Robert McGown, the staff of Second Ascent, Larry Goldie, Mike Gauthier, Len Kannapel, Alex Van Steen, Mark Houston, Craig John, Steve House, Paul Werner, Jeff Street, Tim Matsui, Mitch Merriman, Dale Remsberg, Laura J. James, Greg Child, Steve Swenson, Joseph Catellani, Paul Soboleski, Fred Beckey, Peter Potterfield, Tom Dancs, Jeremy Allyn, Joseph Puryear, Viktor Kramar, Geordie Romer, Steve Reynolds, Don Brooks, Matt Robertson, Alan Kearney, Coley Gentzel, Eric Simonson, Dave Leahey, Paul Klenke, Jay Hack, Justin Thibault, Andrew Shipley, Mike Palmer, Dan Cauthorn, Debbie Martin, Brien Sheedy, David Butler, Justin Busch, Jens Klubberud, Matt Kerns, Roger Strong, Blair Williams, Loren Campbell, Colin Haley, Freeman Keller, Bruce White, Laurel White, Doug Klewin, Pat Timson, Leavenworth Mountain Sports, Glen Frese, and Sean Isaac.

INTRODUCTION: THE ELUSIVE BEAST

"There's no ice in Washington!"

This is a common cry from the nonbelievers, those who would prefer to hide in the warm confines of their homes during the nastiest parts of the winter. Indeed they are wrong. There is ice in Washington, quite a bit of it. In fact, by watching the weather closely it's possible to have quite a decent season in this state. This is a bold statement in such a warm and wet region and it is not surprising that many questions may arise from it.

Yes, the ice is hard to get to. Yes, the approaches are long. Yes, patience is required to wait for the right conditions. And yes, there are many first ascents out there still waiting.

The ice in this state is pretty amazing. But getting to it takes an addiction to adventure beyond just ascending the ice. Generally speaking, climbs that are closest to roads require crossing a river or frozen reservoir and those not close to roads require a great deal of fortitude when it comes to winter travel in the mountains. Washington state ice climbing is an addiction to the journey.

This is not to say that there is never ice beside a road. In fact there are many areas where simple approaches to complex ice climbs can be found. However, many of these areas require climbers to be vigilant because conditions change so rapidly. Watch the weather, watch the conditions, and when the time is right, many of these sweet fruits will be ripe for the picking.

This guide is an attempt to create a comprehensive look at the sport of

Glen Frese on the first ascent of Byram Left and Right in the Palisades (photo by Mark Shipman)

ice climbing in Washington state. By no means is it complete. Areas that were long ago popular are continually being rediscovered and new areas are constantly coming to light as well.

Within this book climbers will find information on many waterfall ice-climbing routes as well as a few notable alpine ice routes. Included is comprehensive information on climbs that are not listed in other popular guidebooks. And lastly, information is included about possible ice climbs that may or may not have yet been completed.

Ice climbing in Washington state is indeed an elusive beast. By creating this guide we hope to help climbers capture and climb it.

CLIMBING ICE IN WASHINGTON

In a state that boasts more climbing diversity and possibilities than any other in the lower forty-eight, water-ice climbing is a relatively unknown and unpracticed discipline that has only recently undergone a renaissance. The increased interest in ice climbing here in the Pacific Northwest is due to many factors. These include the increased availability of information, the migration of dedicated ice climbers to the area from other parts of the country, the close proximity of good and reliable ice climbing in the Canadian Rockies and the British Columbia Interior, and the recent publication of guidebooks to these areas.

Ice climbing in Washington can sometimes be characterized by thin, poorly bonded or wet ice, difficult protection, difficult retreat, avalanche hazard, extremely steep snow top-outs, and other distasteful and dangerous realities that are due mostly to our climate, geology, and geography. The heavy snowfall in the mountains routinely buries climbs completely, or makes the ice conditions very difficult with severe avalanche concerns. Encroaching trees and shrubs can often make a climb less appealing and topping out difficult.

Ice climbing conditions also change hourly. What was solid in the early morning may become unstable or dangerous with sun exposure or warming temperatures. This is true anywhere, but because temperatures are usually closer to freezing here in Washington, climbers must remain constantly aware of changing conditions and how they affect the approach, climb, and retreat.

Many Washington ice climbs are remote by East Coast and even by Rockies standards. Significant travel or approach time is required to reach many climbs in the mountains. In some cases, with normal snowpack, climbs will only be reasonably approachable with snowshoes, skis, or snowmobile. On the plus side, coupled with typically marginal, wet weather, long approaches mean that Washington is currently a very uncrowded place to climb during the winter months. Winter is also the most magical time to be in the mountains. The air is crisp and clear, sounds are muffled, the forest is silent under snow. Enjoy the solitude!

As this book attests, there are a fair number of reliable ice climbs to choose from in Washington, and an even larger number of climbs that can come into

Climber Phil Fortier scopes out Goat Basin on Lennox Mountain. (Photo by Dave Burdick)

shape if conditions are good. Climbs in Washington range from short, inconsequential drips to large and committing climbs equal to those in the Canadian Rockies. But while the season in Washington can be long, the ice season and the ice climbs are never as long, reliable, or predictable as those to the north or inland. However, as information becomes more available through the publication of this and other guidebooks and with the proliferation of information on the Internet, good climbing will become more accessible to more climbers. In turn, more climbers climbing and exploring new climbs can mean more information and greater opportunities for others. Keep the information flowing.

We understand that as this guidebook becomes accepted and more people try ice climbing, some areas will become more crowded. Additionally, land and access issues will arise where before there were none (see the "Climbing Ethics" section at the end of the Introduction). Other climbs will be discovered, and people tired of the crowds will disperse. This has always been the case with climbing.

More than any other mountaineering discipline, learning how to ice climb requires competent and thoughtful instruction, and a conservative approach. Indeed, even learning to cope with the winter environment can be challenging. The combination of cold, wet weather, avalanche hazard, and abundant sharp and pointy objects makes ice climbing hazardous even before a route is climbed.

Unlike the Canadian Rockies or East Coast, there are relatively few top-roping or beginner areas in Washington. Most climbs, even of moderate difficulty, must be led. Teaching the skills required to lead and protect water ice, and to assess avalanche hazards, weather, and other objective dangers is beyond the scope of this book. Seek instruction, know your limits, and climb safe. Appendix B discusses how to find instruction and evaluate its quality.

ICE CLIMBING IS DANGEROUS

Ice climbing is a dangerous sport. Climbers should do everything in their power to acquire appropriate training to climb the ice routes described in this guide. As noted above, climbing ice in Washington seldom affords the possibility of top-roping a climb—more often than not the ability to lead is required. Beyond

Kaia P. Turner practices at the indoor ice-climbing wall at Cascade Crags in Everett. (Photo by Mike Palmer)

the appropriate training, use common sense. Be conservative. Always wear a helmet. Always take an avalanche beacon. Pay attention to avalanche conditions. And lastly, listen to your gut. If you don't feel comfortable, don't do it. Arrogance will get you killed.

One experienced Washington climber states that the Pacific Northwest has a higher ice-climbing injury rate than any other place because of our conditions. On a day in which people in Banff would stay home and watch TV, people in Washington will go climbing. This is partly because in Banff climbers know that the conditions and the ice will eventually get better. In Washington, however, that's a gamble; the conditions and ice here can always get worse. Washington climbers may drive for 3 or 4 hours to find that the route they wanted to do is in marginal shape. But they might decide to climb it anyway, even though it's fragile and difficult to protect, because next weekend might be spring. This is a recipe for disaster. It is always better to cut the loss and look around for something in better shape to do, or to go skiing, go rock climbing, or go for a hike. A 3-hour drive to go hiking in the snow is better than a 3-hour drive that puts a climber in a wheelchair.

EMERGENCIES

Any emergency situation in the backcountry can be serious. Lately, rescues have become more easily coordinated through the use of cell phones. Unfortunately, not all climbing areas described in this book have cell phone coverage. People who choose to travel in the backcountry should be self sufficient and capable of dealing with any emergency—first aid or otherwise—that might arise.

First and foremost, know your surroundings. Where is the nearest phone? Where is the nearest hospital? Are there other people in the area who may help in the event of an emergency? What kind of first-aid training does the party have? What kind of rescue training? All of this information should be kept in mind before venturing into a backcountry situation.

First-Aid Instruction

There are a number of backcountry first-aid courses available. Any person who intends on spending a serious amount of time climbing in the backcountry should consider taking one. Backcountry first-aid in Washington can be broken into the following groups and certifications:

MOFA Certificate Course: MOFA stands for Mountaineering-Oriented First Aid. This is a course specifically taught by the Mountaineers Club of Washington state. It is a 30-hour course that covers the absolute basics of backcountry first aid. A MOFA certificate or equivalent training should be held by all backcountry travelers. Log onto *www.mountaineers.org* for more information.

Wilderness First Responder (WFR): WFR certification courses or their equivalent are held by guides, rangers, and other backcountry professionals. This

Pat Mc Nerthney on The Pencil (photo by Matt Kerns)

certification requires an 80- to 90-hour first-aid course presented by a professional wilderness medicine instructor. Every two to three years, outdoor professionals receive a 24-hour recertification. Though these courses are oriented toward those who make their living in the outdoors, the classes are open to all.

Wilderness Emergency Medical Technician (WEMT): This is the highest certification available in backcountry medicine. The WEMT certificate usually requires 180 hours of study. Like a front-country EMT, those who receive this training must also recertify every two years.

There are many companies and organizations that offer courses throughout the year at many different locations in the United States and Canada. See Appendix C for a list of companies that provide extensive first-aid training to the backcountry traveler.

Rescue

An emergency that requires a high-angle rescue in a backcountry environment is an unfortunate risk that all climbers take. Most of the guide services listed in Appendix B, Ice-Climbing Instruction, provide courses in high-angle rescue.

Helicopter rescues: Expensive helicopter rescues are becoming more and more common in the Northwest. This is not to say that these rescues are un-called for. However, you should have an understanding of what types of situations require a helicopter evacuation.

If a person is capable of walking out of the backcountry and the situation is not life-threatening, then a helicopter should not be called. On the other hand, if a person is in a life-threatening state, needs immediate surgery, or has some type of major injury that will be exacerbated by walking out, then a helicopter should be considered.

Any correspondence with rescue personal should indicate the level of injury. What is the urgency of the evacuation and will it improve the patient's condition? The person responsible for making the decision to send or not to send a helicopter will seriously weigh these two questions.

Depending on the geographical location of the injury and the rescue jurisdiction, a helicopter may or may not be immediately available. Some areas in the state will require an "expert opinion" on the subject before committing the resource of a helicopter. This opinion could come from a doctor, a ranger, a guide, or search and rescue personnel. Other areas will dispatch a helicopter based on the initial descriptions of the injury.

If the situation looks bad enough that the patient should be evacuated by helicopter, the following pieces of information should be clearly communicated via radio or cell phone to the person in charge of the evacuation:

- The reason for the helicopter request.
- The level of consciousness in the patient. Is he unconscious? Conscious? Does he know his name? Does he know what happened to him? Or if he's unconscious, is he responsive to pain?
- Identify the type of injury or illness.
- Identify the number of patients.
- Estimate the weight of the patient(s).
- Identify landmarks or elevation, or anything that may be used to locate the group.
- A pilot may not be familiar with the terrain; give Global Positioning System (GPS) coordinates if available.
- And lastly, identify the current or expected weather conditions, including wind speed and directions.

In the event of a whiteout, a helicopter rescue is unlikely. Be prepared for this type of situation in deteriorating weather, high winds, or waning daylight.

Once a helicopter has committed to the rescue, there are two possible scenarios that may arise. In the first, the helicopter will hover above the ground and rescue personnel will be lowered via a cable. The rescuer will put a harness on the patient and then both the rescuer and the patient will be raised back into the helicopter. In the second scenario, the helicopter will land.

A helicopter can land in a space as small as 60 feet by 60 feet. A space that is 100 feet by 100 feet is much better. If possible, put up streamers or plastic flagging on the downwind side of the landing zone long before the helicopter's arrival. If smoke grenades are available, these should be deployed in the same vicinity as the streamers while the helicopter makes a pass to check out the landing. This will allow the pilot to gauge the wind.

It is important to keep the patient and all onlookers at least 150 feet away from the landing zone. Additionally, all materials such as ski poles and jackets should be moved or fastened down, lest they get blown away in the wash from the rotors. And lastly, never go behind the helicopter while the blades are spinning.

Local hospitals: Sometimes your party will be able to self-evacuate, but a patient may still require a visit to a hospital. Appendix C lists hospitals in the cities and towns near the climbing areas described in this guide.

SEASON

The ice-climbing season in Washington is not very predictable, but in a normal year, ice starts forming in December and lasts until late February or into March. In good years the season can last from mid-November to late March, especially in high-alpine areas near the passes. In poor years, the season becomes harder to work with. Ice will still exist in various (usually more inaccessible) places, but good ice will be harder to get to and require more ingenuity to approach and climb; this means more work, more weather watching, and more time.

Still, the key to the ice-climbing season and to ice climbing in Washington in general is that there is usually good ice to be had somewhere! A good season just means that the good ice abounds in a lot of different areas at once, for a longer period of time. A bad season means that the good ice will be located only in one area for a few weeks, then in another area for another few weeks. What makes a season good or bad is the same in Washington as it is anywhere else, even in the Canadian Rockies.

Good or bad, there is no such thing as a normal year. Every year is different and so ice forms differently every year. That's one reason climbing ice is so exciting! It's never the same, even throughout a single season. (Contrast that with a favorite rock route!) However, some general patterns can be observed. In order for most climbs to form, there has to be adequate precipitation. There are only a few ice climbs fed by perennial streams in Washington; most are formed by snowmelt or groundwater flow. A drought year, like the winter of 2000–01, typically results in only a few main routes forming (and those are still temperature dependent). Strobach Mountain, southeast of Mount Rainier, was very thin that season, but Drury Falls near Leavenworth was in classic form! Conversely, an overly wet season, like the 150 percent snowpack during the winter of 2001–02, buries climbs that are normally exposed. And microclimate variations can produce surprising results: that winter, though several areas near the passes had fat ice (with some snow removal required), Drury Falls didn't form well . . . it was too warm in Tumwater Canyon for most of the winter.

One thing is for sure: because of the maritime climate here in the Pacific Northwest, including the large amount of snow that falls, ice can form very quickly; but because of rapidly changing temperatures, ice can disappear even

The Weeping Wall near the Bluewood Ski Area (photo by Kevin Pogue)

faster! In places like the Canadian Rockies and East Coast, ice takes a long time to form because of the low snowfall, but it stays around all season because of the cold temperatures. Throw in some Chinook winds and a midwinter snowfall, and the ice can sustain itself fairly easily. In the Cascades, the reverse is true. Large volumes of water result in poorly formed ice (often there is too much volume to allow a route to freeze adequately), and warm temperatures keep ice from lasting very long.

The perfect ingredients for good ice, then, are cold temperatures, mild precipitation, and controlled temperature fluctuations. This describes conditions just east of the Cascade crest: cold temperatures at elevation, reduced precipitation with slightly lower water content, and less radical temperature fluctuations in the mountains. It is no wonder that many ice-climbing areas east of the crest, such as Mazama, Lake Julius, Leavenworth, and Strobach Mountain, host the most reliable climbs in Washington.

The ice-climbing season for each area of the state is different. Ice located to the north near Mount Baker and to the south on Strobach Mountain tends to hang around a bit longer than in other areas. In the desert, a wet autumn and deep freezes help the climbs form. Desert temperatures can also be colder, helping routes form, but climbs are very susceptible to sun damage. For this reason ice near Banks Lake or Vantage is a difficult proposition: The weather may be just cold enough for routes to shape up, but the bright sun can cause them to decay. Pay very close attention to the conditions before spending hours upon hours driving to some distant location. In the mountains, on the east side of

Suiting up to attempt Falling Falls in the Palisades (photo by Matt Kerns)

the Cascades, the season can often last into March, especially around Leavenworth, White Pass, and Washington Pass. Finally, on the west side of the Cascades, including the Olympics and Mount Rainier, the season is invariably much shorter, as climbs are destroyed by warm temperatures and rain faster than they can form. These western areas are also the ones most accessible to the majority of climbers, giving Washington the undeserved reputation for having little or no ice climbing.

The most important weapon in any climber's arsenal for making the season a good one is a positive attitude and a genuine sense of adventure. The second most important weapon is the ability to dig up information from friends and on the Internet. Before leaving for a climb, find current information online about the conditions and see what other people are saying. After climbing, keep the information flowing by posting your own exploits. We as an ice climbing community have a wonderful resource in the Internet. Use this tool. It will help climbers tick some of the more elusive climbs in Washington state. Consider posting trip reports on the following Internet sites: *www.cascadeclimbers.com*, *www.mountaineers.org, www.summitpost.com,* and *www.boealps.org.*

WEATHER PATTERNS AND COMMON SENSE
by Jeff Renner

Even a brief look at a map of the United States and Canada shows something you won't find in Europe, Asia, or even Africa. The major mountain ranges run north-south. That's certainly true in Washington state, and has a major impact on both short-term weather patterns and long-term climate. North-south mountain ranges allow frigid, arctic air to slide far to the south, well away from the regions in which they originate. They also allow warm air from the south to migrate well to the north. The net effect can be abrupt changes in the weather. When such ranges block moist air from an ocean, the result can also be widely varying weather patterns over very short distances. That's what makes Washington's weather so complicated, and at no time of the year can it become as complicated as during the winter months.

THE BIG PICTURE

The question is straightforward: will the weather enhance ice formation and quality or detract from it? The answer is considerably more complicated. While there are certainly some large-scale patterns that have a major impact on freezing or melting, the complexity of terrain that makes our region both beautiful and fascinating also results in weather patterns that are as significant as they are localized. The small picture can and often does exceed the importance of the big picture in understanding Washington weather and how it will affect favorite ice climbing routes.

Understanding the big picture, however, makes the little one less elusive; that's where we'll begin. Keep in mind that the jet stream tends to steer disturbances at or near the ground as well as those higher up in the atmosphere. What is the jet stream? It's a fast-moving river of air in the upper atmosphere. The direction of either the jet stream or, in its absence, the winds aloft, has a major effect on weather. Let's look at several common patterns.

When the jet stream or winds aloft are generally moving out of the south to southwest (fig. 1), very warm air is being pumped into Washington. The result will be abnormally high freezing or snow levels, and

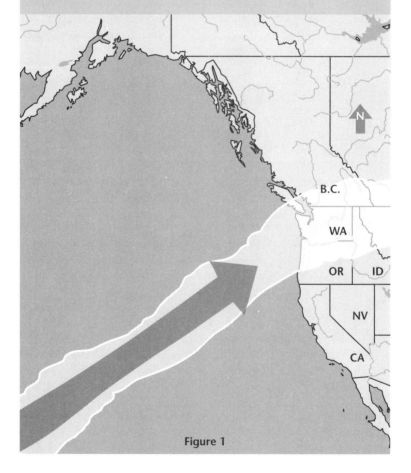

Figure 1

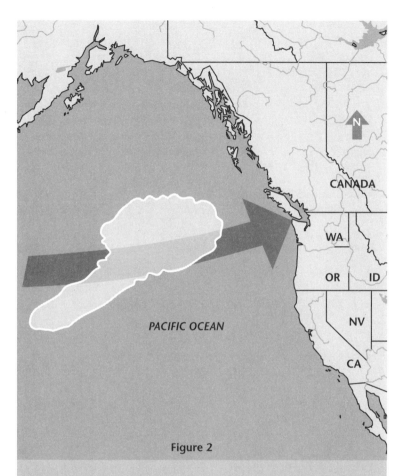

Figure 2

considerable melting of snow or ice. This pattern is what's called a "pine-apple express" and it can produce storms that are exceptionally strong. This pattern typically persists for days, whatever the strength of the storms may be. Put away the ice tools and head for the gym.

A southwesterly to westerly flow aloft (fig. 2) will also result in higher freezing or snow levels, but the pattern tends to be dynamic, not per-sisting nearly as long as a pineapple express. While temperatures in the mountains will warm considerably ahead of an approaching disturbance, they'll also drop after it passes through. The key strategy is to time out-ings for just after a cold front moves through in such a pattern, or to head east of the Cascades, which will usually be more insulated from such warming.

A northwesterly jet or flow aloft (fig. 3) typically results in rapidly

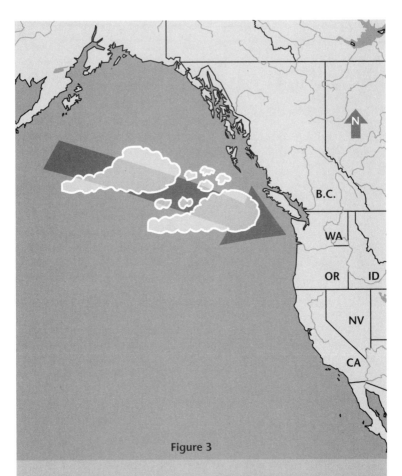

Figure 3

moving disturbances and low snow or freezing levels that are at or below pass elevations during the winter months. The key questions to consider in such a pattern is whether the winds forecast will be strong enough to compromise safety or the snowfall heavy enough to elevate avalanche conditions or degrade the climbing route. Western Cascade and Olympic routes will typically experience temperatures cold enough to result in freezing or improved ice condition.

The last pattern is a northerly jet or flow aloft (fig. 4). This typically brings an arctic outbreak, accompanied by very low snow levels (sometimes near sea level!) and followed by cold, dry, and often clear conditions. Ice conditions after the outbreak will usually be excellent; the biggest challenge may be navigating around city or suburban drivers panicked by slick roads!

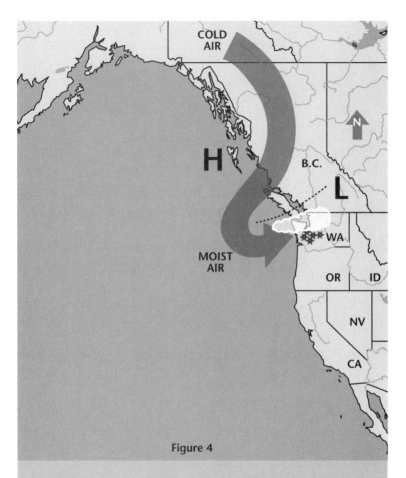

Figure 4

Two questions arise from this discussion: first, how can you determine the direction of the jet stream or winds aloft, and second, do temperatures at sea level offer any clues as to the likely freezing or snow level? The position of the jet stream is often shown on television weather presentations, either at the same time satellite pictures are shown, or shortly afterward. Some newspapers also show the jet stream's position on their weather page. Lacking those, you can get a general sense of the jet stream's movement by looking at the general direction of clouds on a satellite picture; an example is shown in Figure 5.

It is also possible to get a sense of where the freezing level is from surface air temperatures (as opposed to those higher in the atmosphere). This technique is only an estimate, using the average decrease of temperature with altitude, commonly called the lapse rate. In practice, the

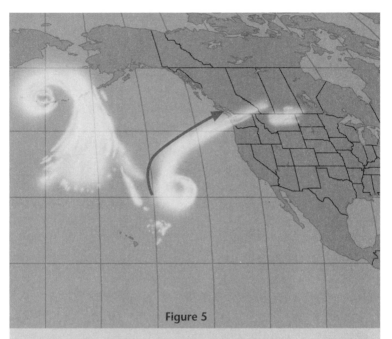

Figure 5

actual decrease of temperature with altitude can vary considerably. But in many cases, an estimate may be very helpful. Such an estimate requires you to know your elevation and the outside temperature; simply substitute those in the following equation:

Your Elevation + [(Outside Temperature - 32°) x 1000]/ 3.5° = Freezing Level

For example, if you're at 2000 feet and the temperature is 39 degrees:

2000 + [(39 - 32) x 1000]/3.5 = 2000 + 7000/3.5 = 2000 + 2000 = 4000 feet

Now, how do you use that to estimate the snow level? The snow level is usually 1000 feet below the freezing level. In the above case, a freezing level of 4000 feet should yield a snow level of 3000 feet. If there are heavy showers, the snow level may briefly descend to 2000 feet below the freezing level.

LOCALIZED WEATHER PATTERNS

Local weather can vary significantly from overall conditions, and knowing such patterns can mean the difference between a genuine suffer fest and a climb that ends in smiles and satisfaction. It's a matter of comparing the conditions that generate such patterns with the reported weather and your intended climb location. Let's examine such key patterns.

The Puget Sound Convergence Zone

Some of the heaviest precipitation in western Washington occurs not with a cold front, but after it crosses the Cascades and exits the state. If coastal winds shift to a direction ranging between southwest to northwesterly, the onshore winds typically split when they encounter the Olympics, moving either to the north through the Strait of Juan de Fuca, or south through the Chehalis gap. Because the Cascade range is such an effective north-south barrier, those eastward-moving winds are then forced to turn either north or south as the enter the Puget Sound area. As shown in the illustration (fig. 6), the winds turning south from the Strait collide with the winds turning north from the Chehalis gap, converging in the central parts of both Puget Sound and the Cascades. This results in increased cloud cover and usually increased precipitation, occasionally even thunderstorms. If a disturbance has passed through western Washington and coastal winds are becoming southwesterly or northwesterly, better visibility and higher cloud bases are likely north of Stevens pass or south of Snoqualmie pass. Certainly weather will be better on the east side of the Cascades.

Backdoor Cold Fronts

Backdoor what? Backdoor cold fronts. Keep in mind that most cold fronts move from the Pacific inland. However in this instance, the coldest air is to the east. Anyone who's spent much time in Washington during the winter knows the coldest air typically resides east of the Cascades. The air following a winter cold front moving inland from the Pacific toward the Cascades is often warmer than the air just to the east. This collision of air masses leads to a sort of atmospheric sumo wrestling match that has a major effect on freezing levels and by extension, climbing conditions.

As the low pressure system generating the front over the Pacific approaches the coast, air moves from the colder, higher pressure air east of the Cascades through the passes toward the west. As that cold air rises, the moisture in that air typically condenses just like your breath on a cold day. That typically leads to a low deck of stratus clouds through the passes, especially along the eastern approaches to the passes. Poor visibility and snow typically mark this area. As the clouds associated with the front moving inland reach the passes, snowfall intensifies in the passes, even though the snow level elsewhere may actually rise above pass elevations. This pattern is what's called the backdoor cold front. The colder air isn't moving from west to east, but from east to west.

As the cold front from the Pacific pushes over the Cascades (and this typically takes awhile), the layer of cold air beneath thins, often to the point

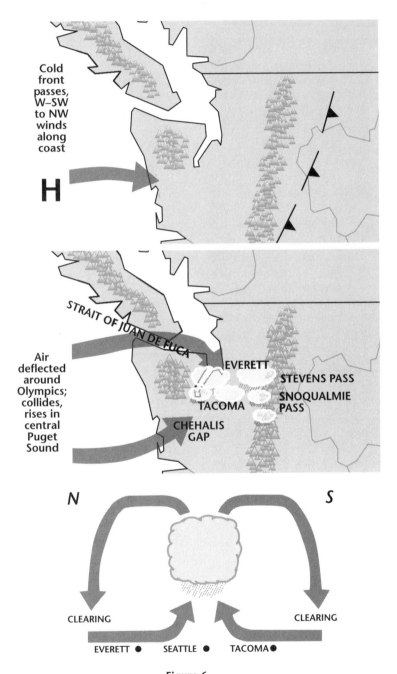

Cold front passes, W–SW to NW winds along coast

H

STRAIT OF JUAN DE FUCA

Air deflected around Olympics; collides, rises in central Puget Sound

EVERETT

STEVENS PASS

SNOQUALMIE PASS

TACOMA

CHEHALIS GAP

N   S

CLEARING   CLEARING

EVERETT ●   SEATTLE ●   TACOMA ●

Figure 6

that rain is falling through that cold air, resulting in either sleet or freezing rain within the passes. That will add a glaze of ice to favorite routes near and just east of the passes, though getting there may be difficult and unwise. Eventually, the Pacific air mass pushes through, changing the precipitation to rain in the passes and temperatures rise—one of the few situations where colder air doesn't follow a cold front.

Watch for such backdoor cold fronts when eastern Washington has been locked in bitter cold and the approaching front is moving across the Pacific. When this pattern is forecast, colder air and better climbing conditions will initially be found east of the Cascades (including the east slopes), though poor visibility will be found closest to the passes. The moderate to heavy snow that follows will be very localized within the passes and near the western approaches. Be vigilant for freezing rain, first to the west of the passes, then within the passes, and finally to the east of the passes.

SEASONAL PATTERNS

Understanding short-term patterns such as convergence zones and backdoor cold fronts can prevent wasted or even hazardous drives. Given the all-too-short nature of the ice-climbing season, alpinists begin anticipating conditions long before the first frost west or east of the Cascades. That leads to the inevitable question: will this be a good season?

Like any aspect of climbing, there's never any shortage of opinions about the prospects for the coming season. The foundation may range from the width of the black stripe on a woolly bear caterpillar to the *Farmer's Almanac*. Neither has particularly proven itself, at least here in the Northwest. Meteorologists know the hazards of medium- and especially long- range projections. A hot summer is certainly no guarantee of a cold winter. Here in Washington, forecasters tend to look for two different patterns: the El Niño–La Niña cycle, and what's called the PDO, the Pacific Decadal Oscillation.

The El Niño–La Niña cycle, simply put, is the impact of shifts in ocean circulation and sea surface temperatures on seasonal patterns. The arrival of either pattern is usually well documented in the news media. In an El Niño year, the jet stream tends to shift north of Washington or split and divert both to the north and south. The net effect in this state is a winter that tends to be warmer and drier. A La Niña winter produces the opposite effect: a cooler and wetter winter in Washington, which typically offers much better ice-climbing conditions. Keep in mind that there are weak and strong years for each type of pattern, and during any given winter, there are exceptions to the overall trend.

Pacific Decadal Oscillation. A rather long and obscure title. But the effects on Northwest weather are anything but obscure. What's the difference between a PDO event and an El Niño or La Niña? Keep in mind that all events are initially detected by changes in sea surface temperatures and all have an impact on weather. But while El Niño or La Niña events are mainly detected in sea surface temperatures in the tropics, PDO events are primarily detected in sea surface temperatures in the North Pacific just off North America. PDOs are also much longer lived than El Niño/La Niña events. The average PDO event lasts twenty to thirty years, while the duration of an El Niño or La Niña is much, much shorter—perhaps six to eighteen months.

A cool-phase PDO will generate below normal winter temperatures in Washington state and above average snowfall, while a warm phase PDO will have the opposite effect—above normal winter temperatures and below normal snowfall. While climate researchers are making great strides in understanding the PDO pattern, it's not well forecast in advance . . . yet. But when the news media does stories about our region being in the cold phase of a PDO, rejoice; it should be a good winter for ice climbing.

Climbers, like anyone who spends much time working or playing outside, will hear tales that a very warm summer will be followed by a cold, snowy winter or that a cool summer will lead to a mild winter. Don't believe the stories. At this point, there's no hard research to support such contentions. Short-term forecasts aren't perfect, and the reliability of long-range projections is at best mixed. Keep an eye on forecasts, on your environment, and keep asking questions.

EQUIPMENT

Numerous tools are critical for climbing ice in Washington. Besides your crampons, ice axe, and ice tools, essential gear includes a helmet, a recent avalanche forecast, an avalanche beacon (along with probe and shovel), V-thread material, and an adequate rack including short screws and pitons. More often than not climbers will be venturing into hazardous avalanche terrain, and should have the proper equipment and skills (see the Avalanche section later in the Introduction).

The climbs in Washington typically require at least several short screws on any given lead rack. Have several 10-centimeter screws and several 13-centimeter screws, in addition to standard 16- to 17-centimeter screws. Typically, 22-centimeter screws are sprinkled in for V-threads and belays.

Tool in Mazama ice (photo by Sean McCabe)

Ice hooks can be effective panic pieces and are often the only thing that will work in frozen mud or moss. Periodically these can also be substituted as pins in thin cracks.

Because there can be a fair amount of vegetation on routes near the passes and on the west side of the Cascade crest, long runners are recommended. Many climbs feature tree anchors or (less desirably) sagebrush anchors, where a long cordalette can come in handy.

The rock in the Cascades and in the desert is typically compact or even basaltic, and takes pitons and small rock protection well. Rock protection recommendations have been provided where possible in this guide. As a general rule, bring some rock protection when exploring new areas, especially in the desert; these climbs can be fantastic but thin, and are often protected with rock gear.

Bugaboo pitons are nice because they are durable and light, and they fit where small cams won't. For the most part Lost Arrows should be left at home, but a baby angle or two might be helpful. A small rack of cams and nuts should be carried on any thin ice climb. Keep in mind that rock in Washington can be highly fractured and unreliable, and artful and thoughtful rock protection skills are sometimes required.

There are many routes with walk-off descents, but a good number require rappels to get down. Unlike the Canadian Rockies or even climbs in the Lillooet, British Columbia, area, very few climbs in Washington have established descent routes or bolted rappel stations. Be ready to improvise, bring extra tied slings for descending from natural anchors, and V-thread materials. Be prepared to surrender gear, especially on obscure routes or first ascents.

> ### *The Mountaineers Ten Essentials:*
> ### *A Systems Approach*
>
> There are certain items that deserve space in every pack. A climber will not need every one of them on every trip, but they can be lifesavers in an emergency.
>
> 1. Navigation (map and compass)
> 2. Sun protection
> 3. Insulation (extra clothing)
> 4. Illumination (headlamp)
> 5. First-aid supplies
> 6. Fire (firestarter, matches, or lighter)
> 7. Repair kit and tools
> 8. Nutrition (extra food)
> 9. Hydration (extra water)
> 10. Emergency shelter
>
> *The Mountaineers Books*

V-THREAD (ABALAKOV SANDWICH)

The Abalakov Sandwich (or more simply, V-thread) has become the de facto standard rappel and retreat anchor for ice climbers everywhere. There are several detailed treatments currently in print (and several on the Internet), including those in *Mountaineering: The Freedom of the Hills*, *The Climbers Guide to West Coast Ice*, *Waterfall Ice: Climbs in the Canadian Rockies*, and *Climbing* magazine issue 124, among others. The V-thread plays a very important role in climbing water ice safely, so it is covered here briefly.

V-threads are fashioned by boring two holes toward each other in good ice, at roughly 60-degree angles to the surface of the ice. Modern ice screws, like Smileys, Black Diamond, and Grivel screws, all leave cleanly bored holes the length of the screw where they are placed. Since the strength of the anchor corresponds directly with the strength of the ice that it is placed in, it is important to locate good ice and use good, sharp screws to minimize fracturing of the ice and to create clean cores. The second hole drilled should meet the first hole, to create a triangular anchor in the ice.

Once the holes are bored, feed and fiddle a length of 5-millimeter or 6-millimeter perlon or thin webbing into one side and fish it out the other side with a small length of wire, sharpened coat hanger, or commercially available V-thread hooker.

Use the longest screw possible when drilling V-threads: A 22-centimeter screw will create a stronger anchor than a 17-centimeter screw when drilled in the same ice, because the size of the triangle (and therefore the amount of ice supporting the anchor) is greater. When in doubt or on poor ice, don't hesitate to create a double V-thread. For those climbers who really are nervous on V-threads, or just don't believe in betting it all on a single anchor, no matter how strong it's purported to be, a double V-thread provides peace of mind and only takes slightly more time to drill.

Back up ice anchors with a screw or another V-thread for everyone but the last person who rappels. It is also important that this extra safety anchor *not* be equalized with the V-thread: The idea is to test the V-thread and build confidence in it with some margin of error—an equalized anchor does not achieve this goal. The last person (typically the lightest person) to leave the rap station cleans the backup screw.

Be careful when using pre-existing V-thread anchors. Ice changes constantly and the anchor may or may not be as strong as it was when it was first drilled. Also, the perlon used for the anchor may have been weakened by the friction created by repeated pulling on rappel ropes. On some rare occasions it is possible to find a V-thread with rap rings. Don't trust these anchors any more than the others: the perlon may be in better shape but there is no guarantee that that ice is good.

It is important not to get too stingy: there are situations when a V-thread will not serve your purposes and screws, pitons, or other protection will have to be left in order to retreat. Thin and poorly bonded ice is common on Cascade climbs, including popular routes like *Hubba Hubba* (near Leavenworth), and sometimes the ice will be too thin to create adequate V-threads but rapping off a short screw or piton might work. Consider it part of the price of climbing to safely retreat from a route. Make a pact with your climbing partner to split the cost should these situations arise. Hopefully, this will provide the financial peace of mind needed to get to solid ground safely.

HOW TO USE THIS BOOK

This guide is structured to make it easy for the climber to understand what climbing in Washington is like, and to help identify climbs of interest across the state. We have had an enormous amount of fun researching and compiling this guide, and in the process have reaffirmed that ice climbing in Washington is nothing if not an adventure.

This introduction is meant to introduce climbers already familiar with the process of ice climbing to the nature of climbing in the Washington desert and mountains. Climbing in Washington offers unique challenges, and we hope the information in this book will get climbers a little bit more prepared than we were when we first started.

The climbing areas in this book are arranged first from north to south, and then typically from west to east. Both waterfall ice climbs and some selected alpine ice climbs are described throughout the state. While some chapters are bursting at the seams with climbs, other chapters report on isolated areas with only a few routes. Each climb description provides the climber with approach, route, and descent information. Each route also has expected avalanche hazard information in a typical snowpack year. Routes include suggested equipment information where possible: long ropes, or rock protection where ice climbs are typically thin or have mixed sections.

What Do Ardenvoirs Eat? at Eniat (photo by Mitch Merriman)

The process of reaching some of these routes may involve fairly complicated routefinding. Because of this, we have provided latitude and longitude coordinates for many routes to make planning easier. We have made every effort to ensure accuracy, *but not all climbs have been field-checked by the authors.*

Where possible, photographs and maps are provided, especially for areas in which climbs are closely grouped together, like Leavenworth, Banks Lake, and Strobach Mountain. The maps in this book are meant to introduce you to the locations of ice climbs, but you'll often need more detailed maps as well. At the start of each chapter we've listed the names of the U.S. Geological Survey (USGS) 7.5-minute topographic maps for that region.

The photographs that appear in this guide are provided by Washington activists who have been putting up hard routes in this state since the 1970s. The images lend a truly historical perspective to the routes, and this guide would be an incomplete work without them.

Lastly, we have included short sections called Rumors of Ice for many climbing areas. In some cases these are potential routes and in others they are things that we have first-hand knowledge about or that have been mentioned in interviews with local activists. Some of the routes have been climbed, and others are simply . . . rumors. These tempting suggestions, above all else, should inspire those who have an urge to become first ascentionists and those who have a thirst for adventure.

A plethora of routes are not covered in this guidebook. There are still more routes that have not yet seen an ascent. We hope that this book will inspire climbers to explore Washington's ice potential. We also hope that upon the discovery of new areas and routes, the information learned will be shared with others who have a common interest. Local climbers who have kept the information flowing have allowed this book to come to fruition.

ROUTE NAMES AND NEW ROUTE INFORMATION

As many of the routes in this guide were unnamed upon early compilation of them, unnamed climbs have been named after features in a given area. An unnamed route above Hidden Lake becomes the *Hidden Lake Route*. If there are a number of unnamed climbs in an area, a letter has been included to identify them. As a result, an unnamed route surrounded by unnamed routes becomes *Soap Lake A*. In some areas, such as Pee Wee's Playground at Banks Lake, whole collections of climbs have remained unnamed. If anyone has any information on the correct route names, please feel free to contact us. Additionally, you can send any information about new routes or route corrections to us at *wastateice@yahoo.com*.

RATINGS

Rating a frozen waterfall is a difficult thing to do. Routes go through phases, and may be easier or much more difficult depending on conditions. A route

may form from M5 in early season, through difficult and steep chandeliered WI 4 to fat WI 3 during just a few weeks. Route conditions can change hourly. What was solid brittle ice in the morning might turn to mush in the sun or with warming temperatures and rain. In Washington, routes are seldom in perfect condition. Because of each route's variabilty, we often give the rating as a type of range. For example, WI 3+/4 means that the route is generally WI 3+ *or* WI 4, depending on conditions; WI 3–4 means that a route is generally WI 3 *to* 4, depending on the exact line followed. In other cases where the rating is unknown, we specify WI or M to indicate the type of route, but follow the water-ice or mixed designation with a question mark.

In this guidebook the water-ice ratings reflect the following:

WI 1: What a climber slips on when leaving the bar. Most Washington ice climbers have taken a few whippers on this. Others will tell you that this is ice that doesn't exceed 60 degrees.

WI 2: Relatively easy ice with good protection. Generally considered the first grade where a second ice tool is required, though many purists will use only one. The route is generally sustained in the 60- to 70-degree range, but may have some steeper steps. Good examples of WI 2 in Washington are *Devil's Punch Bowl* (left side) and *Hubba Hubba* when it is in fat shape.

WI 3: These routes tend to be sustained up to 80 degrees. Protection is usually easy and there are decent rests. There may be short sections of vertical ice. Good examples of classic WI 3 climbs in Washington include *Sad Ce'bu* at Strobach, Alpental Falls, and the first two pitches of Drury Falls (which are a nice route on their own).

WI 4: At this grade, expect sustained 75- to 85-degree climbing, or shorter sections of vertical ice. Protection is usually easy to find, but frequently must be placed while standing on front points. Many classic and commonly climbed lines in Washington are solid WI 4. Drury Falls, many Strobach classics, as well as Pan Dome Falls are all good examples of the grade.

WI 5: These climbs require commitment and skill; they are the 5.11s of the ice-climbing world. Often the ice is not very good and protection is hard to find. Usually these routes are long, vertical, and strenuous. Some perfect examples of pure WI 5 routes include *The Emerald* and *The Cable* at Banks Lake, many lines at Strobach, and the *Source Lake Line* in Alpental Valley.

WI 6: These routes tend to be extremely technical climbs with vertical and even overhanging ice. The protection is difficult to find and perhaps even more difficult to place. There are usually few rests and thin, often questionable ice.

Beyond these water-ice ratings, we use the Yosemite Decimal System (5.0–5.15) to indicate rock grades when needed. On some of the more extreme routes, aid-climbing grades are also indicated.

Ice climbing on The Cable at Banks Lake (photo courtesy of the Greg Mueller Collection)

Mitch Merriman climbing Children of the Sun near Blue Lake. (Photo courtesy of the Mitch Merriman collection)

The confines of ice climbing are constantly being tested. A new grading system has recently been developed for those climbs that require a lot of rock climbing with ice tools, or what has recently been defined as drytooling. (Jim Dinonni says this is not climbing, it's what a male teenager without a girlfriend does.) This information is provided when the first ascensionist has indicated it within his or her grades.

M4: Real mixed climbing starts at this grade. Strong climbers should be okay. Equivalent to 5.8 climbing.

M5: Placements are not necessarily great. Drytooling requires some real thought. Equivalent to 5.9 climbing.

M6: A great deal of drytooling. Falling is a major consideration. Equivalent to 5.10 climbing.

M7: Equivalent to 5.11 climbing.

M8–M10: Really, really, really hard, sketchy climbing. Not only that, but it is difficult to define these ratings as grades. Equivalent to 5.11–5.13 climbing.

In this book, a rating of WI? or M? means that the rating of the climb in unknown.

This guide also covers a few interesting alpine ice and mixed routes. These routes are graded according to the (somewhat nebulous) Alpine Commitment Grade system, which indicates the overall grade, difficulty, and time required to complete a route. Roman numerals I–VI reflect these elements. Upon reaching grades IV–VI it becomes difficult for any but the most proficient climbers to complete the route in a single day.

On some of the more committing climbs, an "R" or an "X" might be indicated. Here, R suggests that there are some long run-outs and that a climber could be seriously injured or killed in the event of a fall. X indicates a likelihood of death should a climber fall while leading; less so when a second falls while seconding. Once again, these notations will only be listed if the first ascensionist has indicated them in his or her communication with us.

One last word of warning: there are a number of ice climbers out there who are just getting into the sport. As Washington is not often thought of as an ice climber's dream state, many first ascents have been done by climbers who are new to the sport. Be aware that some of the more recent routes have not seen many ascents to confirm their grades. There are routes in this book that may have ratings that are plain wrong. Always assess the route conditions and grade before committing to something over your head.

Alpine Ice and Water Ice

Many ice-climbing guidebooks differentiate between the traditional Water Ice Grade (WI) system and the Alpine Ice Grade (AI) system. Generally routes that receive an AI rating include sections of steep snow or unconsolidated ice. Though this book includes a selection of notable alpine routes, and in many books these routes would be given an AI rating, we do not use the AI system. The primary reason for this is simply to cut down on confusion in the grading system. You should still expect to find AI ground on any alpine ice route described; steep snow climbing is also a normal phenomenon on this type of route. Lack of AI ratings does not mean that alpine ice will not be encountered. In the Cascades, expect it.

AVALANCHE DANGER

People have been killed approaching some of the routes that are listed in this guidebook. Avalanche danger within this book is broken into three categories. They are:

Minimal: There is little to no avalanche danger on the approach or above these climbs.

Moderate: There is avalanche danger on either the approach or above these routes. Be wary and take the appropriate precautions.

Serious: Don't do this climb unless local avalanche conditions are low. Turn back at the first sign of avalanche danger.

Always assess avalanche conditions before approaching a climb on potentially dangerous slopes or climbing a route that may have avalanche terrain above it. Knowledge about how to assess avalanche conditions is considered an integral part of an ice climber's education. Proper training should be acquired from qualified individuals.

For recorded information concerning current avalanche conditions in Washington state, climbers may call the Northwest Avalanche Hotline at 206-526-6677.

FLOTATION AND APPROACH MEANS

Approaches are often endeavors in and of themselves. It is not uncommon to cross many miles of deep snow to access the base of an ice route. It is very important for climbers to bring some sort of flotation when there is a significant amount of snow to cross.

As a rule of thumb, if the approach requires maneuvering through heavily forested backcountry, snowshoes are the best floatation. If the approach requires negotiating many miles of logging roads or the crossing of large open cirques or snowfields, backcountry skis are an excellent means of travel. The best thing about skis is that when the climbing is finished, the descent back to the car is often quick and enjoyable.

Any climb in this book can be accessed with snowshoes. Not every climb described can be easily accessed with skis, but skis are the approach means of choice for many of the alpine routes listed.

Some of the routes listed were first discovered and then later accessed for climbing through the use of a snowmobile. These machines are very useful in covering large amounts of ground on snow-covered logging roads, the North

Casades Highway, or the Mountain Loop Highway. Some areas have specific guidelines that climbers should be aware of when operating these vehicles. And most importantly, those who choose to ride snowmobiles should be respectful of those who choose not to.

Everyday motor vehicles can be problematic in the winter. It is common for four-wheel-drive trucks to get caught in the snow in the vicinity of some Washington routes. As the Boy Scouts say, it's best to be prepared. A shovel is essential to winter backcountry travel. Other items that should be included in the vehicle are chains, a saw (preferably a chainsaw), a static heavy-duty nonclimbing rope, and a come-along.

CLIMBING ETHICS

BACKCOUNTRY WASTE

Access to climbs is a very large issue throughout North America. In particular, the access to climbs on private property has become an issue. Throughout the country private areas are being closed to climbers. This is a trend that does not have to continue. It is within our control to stop this, but there has to be a change in the way people think about certain issues.

Human waste in the backcountry is a problem. It is a problem throughout Washington state. It is a problem throughout North America. And waste disposal is a tremendous problem on private property. In all seriousness, how many can honestly say that they would keep their property open to visitors if those same visitors left human waste everywhere? Even worse, if they flagged it with used toilet paper?

Many people believe that when they are in the backcountry they have the prerogative to go to the bathroom wherever they want. They apparently don't believe that Leave No Trace or pack it in/pack it out ethics apply to them. Often they believe that they are the only ones using an area because they haven't seen others. All of these ideas are ignorant and dangerous to the climbing community at large.

Leave No Trace means leave no trace. If you go to the bathroom in the backcountry, the next visitor should find no evidence of your visit. There should be no toilet paper and no visible feces. Climbers who are unwilling to dispose of their waste in the proper fashion are a major problem. It is best for us to police this problem within our own community instead of allowing land managers and private property owners to do it for us. Following are three prescribed methods for dealing with human waste in the backcountry:

WAG Bags: The WAG bag is the best method of dealing with human waste. This method is quite similar to the long-standing Blue Bag method employed on Mount Rainier. In this method, bags specifically designed to carry human waste out of the backcountry are used. These bags have a small amount of kitty litter in the base to keep the smell down and include three bags so that there is no seepage into a backpack. The idea is that all waste is carried out. WAG Bags are available at most ranger stations and they can also be ordered on the Internet at *www.thepett.com*.

In western Washington or in the backcountry where there is a lot of snow, this is the best possible method of dealing with human waste in the winter. It is the only method that should be used on private property.

Smear Method: The idea behind the Smear Method is that fecal materials smeared on rocks will decay more rapidly due to exposure. Toilet paper is packed out. The human waste then bakes in the sun and eventually blows away. This method may be effective in some desert environments or in high-alpine environments, but should not be employed on private property. Ideally the Smear Method is never used in high-use areas such as on Mount Baker or Mount Rainier.

Cat Hole: The Cat Hole Method is the old stand-by. In this method, a hole at least 6 inches deep is dug in the soil. The human waste is placed in the hole and then buried. Once again, toilet paper is packed out. This is only effective in areas with no snow, below treeline. It may be useful in some of the eastern Washington ice-climbing locales. This method should never be used on private property.

PRIVATE PROPERTY

Because a climb is listed in the book does not mean it is automatically open to all climbers. Access is contingent on landowner permission. This guidebook does not encourage or condone trespassing on private property.

Throughout the state and throughout this guide, there are routes that require permission to approach or to climb. Don't shirk this responsibility. It is very important for us as a community to make sure that we have permission to cross private property or to climb routes that exist on anything other than public land.

If refused access to a climb, be polite, say thank you, and climb somewhere else. We cannot build a positive relationship with landowners by being rude.

Likewise, if granted permission to climb on private property, abstain from anything that might mar a landowner's view of climbers. Avoid loud profanity, littering, the consumption of alcohol, or the use of recreational drugs on private property. Hopefully this attitude will keep the door open for climbers to visit in the future.

One common concern of landowners is liability in the event of injury. Some climbers have been able to allay such worries by offering landowners signed liability release forms. You can contact the Access Fund for assistance in drafting such a release form.

Concerned landowners may also be interested to learn about the "recreational use statute" in the Revised Code of Washington (RCW). RCW 4.24.200 and 4.24.210 cover "Liability of owners or others in possession of land and water areas for injuries to recreation users"; the exact wording of the statute can be found on the website of the Washington state legislature, *www.leg.wa.gov/rcw*. A recently enacted amendment to the statute, signed into law by Governor Gary Locke on April 16, 2003, specifically addresses rock-climbing issues; it can be found by searching for Substitute House Bill 1195. Learning more about this statute may also help you draft a better liability release form, one that reflects the specific limitations of RCW 4.24.210.

Included in this book is information on some climbs that were closed to ice climbing at the time this book went to press. Such climbs are clearly marked CLOSED TO ICE CLIMBING. They are included in this book because they are an important part of Washington's ice-climbing history and may be reopened in the future. Climbers are strongly urged to respect these closures. Please do not climb the routes listed as CLOSED TO ICE CLIMBING until they are reopened.

If you have a significant problem concerning access to a climb listed in this book, please let us know by emailing us at *wastateice@yahoo.com*. Up-to-date information on climbing access issues will be available on the Washington state ice-climbing website, at *www.wastateice.net*.

A NOTE ABOUT SAFETY

Safety is an important concern in all outdoor activities. No guidebook can alert you to every hazard or anticipate the limitations of every reader. Therefore, the descriptions of roads, trails, routes, and natural features in this book are not representations that a particular place or excursion will be safe for your party. When you follow any of the routes described in this book, you assume responsibility for your own safety. Under normal conditions, such excursions require the usual attention to traffic, road and trail conditions, weather, terrain, the capabilities of your party, and other factors. Because many of the lands in this book are subject to development and/or change of ownership, conditions may have changed since this book was written that make your use of some of these routes unwise. Always check for current conditions, obey posted private property signs, and avoid confrontations with property owners or managers. Keeping informed on current conditions and exercising common sense are the keys to a safe, enjoyable outing.

The Mountaineers Books

MOUNT BAKER AND THE NORTH CASCADES

MOUNT BAKER

Bellingham has long been the town of choice for many aspirant alpinists. Its climbing community has included well-known, respected climbers ranging from the likes of Steve House to Alan Kearney, from Mark Houston to Kitty Calhoun. Dozens of strong climbers who have gone on to become names in the climbing world have spent time living in Bellingham. The combination of a university that supports climbing endeavors, a well-known climbing guide service, and an active branch of the Mountaineers Club continue to make Bellingham popular with climbers. As a result, it is not surprising that nearby Mount Baker is one of the better documented areas in Washington state.

The Mount Baker region includes some of the best-known ice climbing areas in this guide. Certainly Pan Dome Falls, inside Mount Baker Ski Area, has long been a staple of the Northwest ice climber's diet. So too has the glacier ice on the flanks of Mount Baker itself. The area also harbors one of the few developing drytool areas in the state. Indeed, Mount Baker is an area that should not be missed by any climber on the lookout for adventure.

USGS maps: Shuksan Arm, Twin Sisters Mountain, Mount Baker

MOUNT BAKER SKI AREA

There is a great deal of false security in climbing near a ski area. Though it would be easier to get an injured person out because the area is more accessible, don't take unnecessary risks. There have been more accidents on Pan Dome Falls than any other ice route in Washington.

To approach the ski area, drive the Mount Baker Highway (State Route 542) from Bellingham east to the ski area. From Bellingham, the drive will take about an hour and a half.

PAN DOME FALLS   WI 3+/4

A long pitch of variable ice, *Pan Dome* is a usually a good climb that comes in every season. Because it is easily visible from the ski area parking lot, its

Pan Dome Falls (photo by Scott Bingen)

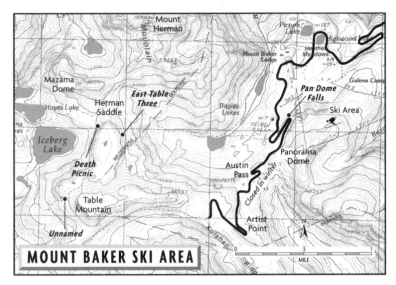

condition is generally well known and it gets climbed many times a season.

First ascent: Unknown

Length: One long pitch

Avalanche danger: Moderate. This area is not maintained by the ski patrol.

Approach: Park in the ski area's upper parking lot. Follow the Austin Pass Road until able to cut across slopes toward the climb. The approach takes about 10 minutes. Snowshoes may be required for the last part of the approach. *Coordinates*: 48°51.420' N, 121°40.710' W

Route: Follow the low-angled ice in the center of the falls up to the steep pillar above. Be aware that this upper portion is steep and sustained at about 80 degrees. Often the upper section is in solid WI 4 conditions. To set up a top-rope, walk around to the climber's right up the road. Be careful approaching the top of the falls, as the way is steep, slippery, and avalanche prone. Generally speaking a top-rope requires a rappel to the tree with many slings. Most parties top-rope the route with two ropes tied together.

Descent: Rappel the route.

TABASCO KID   WI 4

Tabasco Kid is the short, steep pillar found to the right of Pan Dome Falls, at the left end of the hairpin turn in the service road.

First ascent: Unknown

Length: One pitch

Avalanche danger: Moderate. This area is not maintained by the ski patrol.

Approach: Approach as for Pan Dome Falls and traverse to the right.

Route: Climb the short pillar to a steep snow top-out above.

Descent: Rappel the route or walk off to the right.

THE TOOL SHED

The Tool Shed is not truly a different area than Mount Baker Ski Area. In fact, it is found in the midst of the previously mentioned climbs, near Pan Dome Falls. But this new area is one of the few drytooling areas currently being developed in the Northwest, and so deserves its own section. Though there have been many proposals for other drytooling destinations throughout the state, few have actually resulted to date.

UNNAMED BOLT ANCHOR   M?

First ascent: Unknown
Length: Unknown
Avalanche danger: Moderate
Approach: This top-rope problem can be found just to the left of *Tabasco Kid*. Climb *Tabasco Kid* and set up the rope on the two-bolt anchor immediately to the left.
Route: Many options exist on this line.
Descent: Rappel the route from the double-bolt anchor.

GORILLA BAR   M8

It has been stated that this route is an excellent warm-up for trips to the Canadian Rockies.

First ascent: Roger Strong, probably 2001
Length: Unknown
Avalanche danger: Moderate
Approach: This route can be found just to the left of *Unnamed Bolt Anchor*.
Route: Climb past 6 bolts to the anchor. Periodically there is ice on this route.
Descent: Rappel the route.

ANNIHILATOR   WI 6, M7+

First ascent: Dale Remsberg, probably 2001
Length: Unknown
Avalanche danger: Moderate
Approach: This route can be found immediately to the left of *Gorilla Bar*.
Route: Climb past bolts through extremely steep rock and ice to an anchor.
Descent: Rappel the route.

Rumors of Ice

To the right of *Pan Dome* there are some interesting climbs. Besides *Tabasco Kid*, there can be two other lower-angled routes, often covered by snow under the hairpin, that go at WI 2.

MOUNT SHUKSAN

Rumors of Ice

There are reports of four to five multipitch ice routes on the Mount Shuksan arm near Lake Ann. These can be found on the opposite side of the Hemispheres ski run in the Mount Baker Ski Area. Approach via Austin Pass and drop down into the valley. The routes can be seen on the left after approximately an hour of skiing or snowshoeing.

The Hourglass on Mount Shuksan (the ice slope between the upper Curtis and Sulphide Glaciers) is a good early-spring alpine ice route.

TABLE MOUNTAIN

There are quite a few interesting routes that have been done on Table Mountain. Perhaps the most famous is *Death Picnic* because its existence was formally published, but there are other equally interesting lines that can form both here on Table Mountain proper and also north of Table Mountain, above and east of Herman Saddle. If Pan Dome Falls is in, these routes are probably in as well.

All routes on Table Mountain are accessed via the Mount Baker Ski Area, and if conditions allow there is a well-maintained parking lot for backcountry users (part of the ski area parking).

EAST TABLE THREE   WI 3

Routes on the east face of Table Mountain are typically mixed affairs with some small trees and such. This is the most obvious flow.

Ice on the Mount Shuksan arm (photo by Mike Layton)

First recorded ascent: Mark Houston and Kathy Cosley, February 1993

Length: One to two pitches

Avalanche danger: Serious

Approach: Drive as far as the road and ski-area conditions allow. From the car, continue up the road (usually closed) to the end. Ski or snowshoe westward the east face of Table Mountain. This route is the largest and most obvious waterfall on the east face.

Route: Ascend the most obvious falls in approximately one and a half pitches.

Descent: Descending off Table Mountain can be arduous, especially without skis. Rappel the route using trees as anchors.

DEATH PICNIC   WI 5

Death Picnic is a serious route with one full pitch of vertical ice, and then another lower-angled but no less terrifying pitch of snow or crappy steep ice. It is an obvious route found just west of Herman Saddle, at the north end of Table Mountain's large west face.

First ascent: Mark Houston and Alan Kearney, December 1986

Length: Two pitches

Avalanche danger: Serious

Approach: Approach Herman Saddle, which is the obvious col between Mount Herman to the north and Table Mountain to the south, as avalanche conditions allow. This area is well traveled by backcountry skiers, and in times of acceptable hazard there is a beaten ski track up the east flanks of Table Mountain. Traverse under the east face and continue around the mountain to the north side and Herman Saddle. The climb is just out of view from the saddle. Descend along the base of the mountain towards Iceberg Lake until the climb comes into view in a few hundred feet. The climb is the most prominent ice formation on the northwest face of the peak.

Route: Ascend the obvious flow up vertical and often hollow ice.

Descent: Descending off Table Mountain can be arduous without skis. Rappel the route.

Rumors of Ice

There is other route potential on the east face of Table Mountain. Many of these routes have been climbed, but information pertaining to them has been lost.

MOUNT BAKER

In 1979 the first ice-climbing festival in Washington state was held on the Coleman Glacier on the flanks of Mount Baker. This festival was organized by a group of young men that loosely called themselves "White Punks on Dope." The name was taken from a song by a punk band called "The Tubes." Alpine climbing prodigies in this group included Northwest climbers Rob Newsom, Doug Klewin, and the brothers Dan and Pat McNerthney.

This group of loose-knit climbing friends were responsible for naming Punk Rock in Leavenworth as well as for establishing numerous first ascents on the formation. Members of this group of high-achieving climbers were also responsible for the first serious attempt on the Moonflower Buttress of Alaska's infamous Mount Hunter.

COLEMAN GLACIER   GLACIER ICE, VARIOUS

The fall and summer ice-climbing practice area on Mount Baker has become increasingly popular over the last few years. It is not uncommon to see a number of parties out on the glacier throughout the summer and in early fall sending steep ice.

Lengths: Various

Avalanche danger: There is little danger of avalanches in the summer and fall. However ice fall is a constant hazard. Be aware of your surroundings.

Approach: From the town of Glacier on Mount Baker Highway (SR 542), drive up Glacier Creek Road to the Heliotrope Trailhead. Hike this trail to its eventual end below Survey Rock. There are a series of small camps at an elevation of about 5000 feet on the ridgeline overlooking the glacier. This area is referred to as the Harrison Camp by the climbing rangers and is called Mirkwood by the local guide services. Just below the lowest camp overlooking the glacier on the ridgeline, a small steep trail descends to the glacier proper. A second approach may be made from directly below Survey Rock.

Routes: There are routes of all grades on the glacier, from steep leads up seracs to top-ropes on overhung crevasses. This is truly an ice climber's playground. From below the main icefall, the right-hand side (southwest) tends to be the most stable.

Rumors of Ice

Glacier Creek Road just beyond the town of Glacier has had reports of ice.

On the Heliotrope Ridge Trail—the trail used to access the Mount Baker ice-climbing area—there is a short but interesting falls high on the trail. The approach, however, would be very difficult because the approach road (Glacier Creek Road found just beyond the town of Glacier) is unplowed. Once up the road, park at the trailhead at 3700 feet. With the difficulties of snow travel, the 40-foot route can be found 2 hours up the trail. If there is an early freeze with little snow, it may be possible to access this route in a short 40-minute hike on a dry trail.

TWIN SISTERS RANGE

There is quite a bit of potential throughout the Twin Sisters Range, but access can often be an issue. Unfortunately, roads in the area are closed and changed on a regular basis due to different logging operations. Most of the peaks beyond the North and South Twins have been ignored in winter conditions due to approach difficulties. One can only imagine that there is quite a bit of ice in this region.

DREAMIN' OF DRY CRAGS   WI 4/4+

First recorded ascent: Jon Otto and Ben Stanton, February 2000
Length: 120 feet
Avalanche danger: Serious
Approach: The Twin Sisters Range would be a Bellingham climber's dream if the approach roads were not so difficult. Many people resort to mountain bikes and skis to ascend parts of the roads that are closed to vehicles. Be wary of having gates closed while a vehicle is inside a logging area boundary. An updated road map or a climber friend who has recently been to the area is a rather important piece of the puzzle to cut down on approach time. Following is an extensive description of the approach; there may be errors, so pay attention to your surroundings.

Drive Mount Baker Highway (SR 542) to the town of Deming. Immediately after the town, take a right onto Mosquito Lake Road. Drive Mosquito Lake Road for 4.9 miles to Forest Service Road 38. A gravel road will appear on the left shortly after crossing a small bridge in the road. The FR 38 sign will not be visible from Mosquito Lake Road, but it will appear after making the left turn. Drive the gravel road for a few miles (3–5). After a distance the road will take a downward and right-trending curve. It is possible to go straight, but the road ahead is in poor condition. Take the downhill branch and park at the gate over the river. The gate is not visible from the main road.

Walk, ski, or mountain bike the main road for 45 minutes to 1.5 hours. If there is active logging going on, watch for log trucks. After walking for a bit, a trail (an old logging road) will come into view on the right next to a pile of gravel. The trail will be marked with bits of flagging tape here and there. Take this trail. If in doubt, continue up the main road toward the crest of the hill and another logging road branching off to the right. The North Twin can be seen from here. Then turn around and take a left at the last trail/road you passed. Walk for approximately 2 miles on this logging road, crossing several overgrown patches and washouts. Keep walking until an obvious branch in the road. Take the left (uphill) branch. Continue walking until a second branch appears in the road. Again, take the left (uphill) branch. Continue walking up the gravel logging road until it crests on a small hill, which is the terminus of the west ridge. Look for a small clearing with some logs and flagging tape. A faint trail heads up toward the ridge. The climbing route will be in view from here. Ascend through trees and snowfields to the left of the west ridge until the base of the route is reached. *Coordinates:* 48°43.458' N, 122°00.000' W

Route: This is the obvious route found on the northwest face of the North Twin Sister. The route does not push to the top, but there is potential for it to do so with a bit of mixed climbing and perhaps some snow slogging to make the summit.

Descent: Rappel the route with double ropes or continue climbing mixed terrain to the top. From the top, descend the north slope and then traverse beneath the northwest face back to the trail and logging roads.

Rumors of Ice

Two low-angle one- to two-pitch routes have been spotted on the approach to the north slope of the North Twin Sister. Each of these drop from the north slope into the western drainage.

A steep one- to three-pitch route has been spotted on the eastern side of the lower north slope of the North Twin Sister.

Mosquito Lake Road—the road used to access the north end of the Twin Sisters Range—supposedly has a number of areas on and above it where ice periodically forms.

NOTABLE ALPINE CLIMBS IN THE MOUNT BAKER AREA

COLFAX PEAK, NORTHWEST FACE: COSLEY-HOUSTON ROUTE
GRADE III, WI 4

During the 1990s, this route saw a bit of action. It is rumored that Steve House actually guided the climb in the late '90s.

First ascent: Mark Houston and Kathy Cosley, April 1982

Avalanche danger: Moderate

Approach: Ascend the Heliotrope Ridge Trail (see Mount Baker's Coleman Glacier description, above) and continue up to the Hogsback via the climbers trail. At approximately 7000 feet on Heliotrope Ridge, you can scout the route. This climb can be found to the right of the seracs hanging off Colfax Peak. It ascends a gully system that faces the glacier on the Northwest Face.

Route: This 600-foot route following an obvious gully system is mostly moderate in nature. The most difficult aspect is low on the peak. Climb 30 feet of vertical ice to a snow slope. Ascend this slope to the next ice step. Following the second ice step, climb steep snow to the summit. *Special gear:* An assortment of pins.

Descent: Descend toward the saddle between Mount Baker and Colfax Peak. Beware: This descent is steep and may require a rappel or two. From the saddle, descend the Coleman Glacier northwest back down to the approach trail. It may also be possible to rappel and downclimb the route.

COLFAX PEAK, NORTHWEST FACE:
THE POLISH ROUTE   GRADE III+, WI 5/5+

In May of 1987, Kathy Cosley and Mark Houston made an attempt on a steep route to the left of their 1982 line. They sent the first step to the snow band between major rock bands, but were unable to climb the second step. Between that time and the mid-'90s, little information was known about the climb, though there is a strong possibility that the route saw an ascent or two. Robert Rogoz and partner, both strong climbers from Poland, did the first recorded ascent.

First recorded ascent: Robert Rogoz and partner, October 1990s

Avalanche danger: Moderate

Approach: Approach as for the Cosley-Houston Route. The Polish Route can be found to the left of Cosley-Houston.

Route: Ascend the steep series of gullies to the summit. *Special gear:* An assortment of pins.

Descent: Same as for Cosley-Houston.

---

① The Polish Route

② Cosley-Houston Route

Colfax Peak (photo by Justin Thibault)

CASCADE PASS

Cascade Pass has long been a popular spring and summer destination for climbers. However, there is a small contingent of Cascades hardmen that believe this area has been seriously overlooked as a winter climbing destination. Many of the peaks and roadside waterfalls freeze up with a great deal of consistency every year.

A word of warning is due: though this may some day become a true winter climbing destination for people throughout the state, climbers should always be aware and concerned about the potential for avalanches in this region. It is not uncommon to see massive slides with enough snow to cover the entire river. All climbs in this area are either in avalanche chutes or in areas that must be accessed by crossing an avalanche chute. Be vigilant and aware of snow conditions at all times.

Lastly, access up the Cascade River Road may sometimes be problematic. It is not a bad idea to have chains, a four-wheel-drive vehicle with high clearance, a saw, and a shovel. Often trees fall across the road. Be prepared for an adventurous approach.

USGS map: Cascade Pass

LES CHAINES ONT EXIGÉS   WI 3

The approach difficulties are emphasized in this route name, which is French for "Chains Required."

First recorded ascent: Dan Smith and Nick Strait, December 2001

Length: Four pitches

Avalanche danger: Serious

Approach: From Marblemount, take the Cascade River Road up to where it is gated at approximately milepost 20. Some years, snow or trees on the road may force a shorter driving distance and a longer approach. Be sure to factor this into potential approach time. From the gate, ski or snowshoe to approximately mile 21.5. The route is in a very wide avalanche chute above the road. It is the last major avalanche chute before the mile 22 marker. *Coordinates:* 48°28.454' N, 121°05.000' W

Route: Ascend the route with one of many variations. This waterfall cascades over hanging slabs forming a number of different types of climbing. There are vertical-to-overhanging pillars, curtains, and 60-degree ice slabs. The route can be done as a stiff WI 3, or at a much harder grade depending on the variation.

Descent: Rappel from trees.

NORTHEAST PILLAR   WI 3/4 (ESTIMATE)

This interesting climb could be used to access the northeast rib of Johannesburg Mountain, a route first climbed in the winter by Bill Piling and Steve Mascioli. It is not known if this pillar was the original access to that extreme winter climb or if Piling and Mascioli used a more traditional approach.

Johannesburg Mountain, Northeast Pillar (photo by Jason D. Martin)

First ascent: Unknown

Length: Three to four pitches

Avalanche danger: Serious

Approach: Approach as for *Les Chaines Ont Exigés*. Continue up the road until able to traverse the bowl beneath Johannesburg Mountain. Beware: Avalanche danger here is extreme. The route can be found just below and to the right of the northeast rib.

Route: Ascend the obvious line. Beware of the major avalanche potential above the route.

Descent: Rappel the route.

NOTABLE ALPINE CLIMBS IN THE CASCADE PASS AREA

JOHANNESBURG MOUNTAIN, NORTHEAST FACE: BEBIE-STODDARD ROUTE   GRADE IV, WI 3–4, MIXED

In addition to the route described here, there is a great deal of potential for new lines above the hanging glacier on Johannesburg's northwest face. Many of these lines would be similar in character to the ephemeral lines found on Dragontail Peak (see the Leavenworth chapter).

First ascent: Mark Bebie and John Stoddard, December 1985

Avalanche danger: Serious

Approach: Ski or snowshoe up Cascade River Road until just across from Johannesburg Mountain. Drop down into the valley and ascend the Cascade-Johannesburg couloir to the hanging glacier. A safe tent site can be found just left of the bergshrund beneath the Fault Couloir.

Route: Begin in the deep chimney known as the Fault Couloir. Approximately a third of the way up the couloir begin a rightward traverse following gullies and slopes toward the summit. The vast majority of the route lies behind the leftmost buttress on the Northeast Face and so cannot be seen from the road. Expect sections of alpine ice and névé from WI 3 to 4, interspersed with 60-degree snow slopes and a few moves over thin névé-covered rock. Attain the ridge just left of the summit. Ascend easy snow and rock to the true summit. *Variation:* The Fault Couloir was completed in February 1986 by Josh Lieberman and Peter Keleman. Primary difficulties on this route include chockstones that create vertical steps. The first ascentionists bivied once on route.

Descent: It may be possible to descend the route via downclimbing with some rappels. Alternately, you may be able to descend the ridgeline to the Cascade-Johannesburg couloir and then downclimb the couloir.

Rumors of Ice

There are at least two other interesting waterfalls up the same drainage as *Les Chaines Ont Exigés* that would make a trip into the area well worthwhile.

Johannesburg Mountain has a number of short (one- to two-pitch) ice climbs around its flanks and some long multipitch routes.

NORTH CASCADES HIGHWAY

The North Cascades Highway (SR 20) is the gateway to some of the most spectacular alpine routes in the state. However, there has been little exploration of the ice-climbing potential in the area. During the coldest years ample amounts of ice exist relatively close to the highway, well before the highway's winter closure. And beyond the road closure . . . ? More exploration of this area is a must.

USGS maps: Diablo Dam, Washington Pass

ROSS LAKE

JOHN PIERCE WATERFALL   WI 3/4

First ascent: Unknown

Length: Two to three pitches

Avalanche danger: Moderate

Approach: This route can be found just before Ross Dam and the winter end of SR 20. The climb is on the right side of the highway about 3.5 miles beyond Colonial Creek Campground. Park unobtrusively, as snow plows come by frequently. A small, unmaintained trail provides access to the base of the falls in a short 10-minute hike. Be aware that the drainage beneath the road drops down approximately 400 feet into Diablo Lake, and traversing along the primitive trail while it is snowed up could be dangerous. *Coordinates:* 48°43.116' N, 121°04.115' W

Route: Little is known about this route, though its easy access suggests that it has seen many ascents throughout the years.

Descent: Rappel from trees.

RAINY LAKE

The routes found at Rainy Lake are approximately a mile off the highway and involve a considerably difficult approach. Unfortunately, these routes are seldom still in when the highway is plowed. However, with a snowmobile, these routes are doable in a day from Mazama, and the reward to climbers willing to venture so far back is great.

RAINY LAKE RIGHT   WI 5+

First ascent: Steve House and Sean McCabe, 2001

Length: Three pitches

Avalanche danger: Serious

Approach: This route is best approached from the east side of the mountains via SR 20 through Mazama. (See the introduction to the Mazama chapter for driving directions.) Drive SR 20 to the end of the plowed road at milepost 171. Silver Star Creek crosses the highway at this point. From here the only access in the winter will be via snowmobile, as it is at least 20 miles to the trailhead. Snowmobile SR 20 to the Pacific Crest Trail. Rainy Lake can be found up the next major drainage after the departure from the highway of the southbound Pacific Crest Trail. The lake is approximately a mile in. The climbs can be seen at the southwest end of the lake. Cross the frozen lake to access the climbs. Be sure to assess the conditions of the ice before crossing. *Coordinates:* 48°29.895' N, 120°44.099' W

Route: Climb a WI 3 pitch to a snow ramp. Continue up the second tier and right to an ice pencil with an ice cave behind it. Climb behind the pencil or out on the ice face to the start of pitch three; in either case this second pitch will be WI 5 to WI 5+. The third pitch is a full 200-foot pitch—a 60-meter rope is essential here. *Special gear:* 60-meter rope.

Descent: Rappel the route.

RAINY LAKE LEFT   WI 4

First ascent: Geof Childs and Sean McCabe, November 2000

Length: Three pitches

Avalanche danger: Serious

Approach: Approach as for *Rainy Lake Right.*

Route: This is the left-hand side of the 100-foot-wide curtain of ice that makes up Rainy Lake Falls. Ascend the WI 3–3+ first pitch through a steep section, some steep snow, and the second tier. Climb left on the second pitch (WI 4) up to a rock alcove. For the third pitch ascend an ice ramp to the right that climbs along a rock cliff. This third pitch is a genuinely unique WI 3 pitch and is a lot of fun.

Descent: Rappel the route.

POUR LES ENFANTS AVEC AUTOS   WI 3–5+ R

The name of this route is French for "For Children with Cars." Coined by Steve Amish, the catalog designer at Feathered Friends, the route is featured in a photo in the 1999/2000 catalog. Many people over many years have climbed on the various lines around this route, but if the other lines ever had names they have been lost.

First ascent: Unknown

Length: 70 feet

Avalanche danger: Serious

Approach: This route can be found on the road cut just east of Washington Pass. It can be seen just off the road, heading up toward the Liberty Bell massif.

Route: Ascend the obvious flows above the highway. There are at least four lines here with many variations and different difficulties. Parts of this area could be considered for ice bouldering. Be aware that the rock around these climbs is quite bad.

Descent: Either walk off or rappel the route.

WILLOW CREEK

WILLOW CREEK DRAINAGE   WI 2

First recorded ascent: Mazama locals, 2000

Length: One pitch (estimate)

Avalanche danger: Serious

Approach: This route is best approached from the east side of the mountains via SR 20 through Mazama. (See the introduction to the Mazama chapter for driving directions.) Drive SR 20 to the end of the plowed road at milepost 171. Silver Star Creek crosses the highway at this point. From here ski or snowmobile up the road for a few miles to a wide spot in the road. This is the parking area for the Wine Spires. The Willow Creek drainage drops down between

Steve House on the third pitch of Rainy Lake Right (photo by Sean McCabe)

Snagtooth Ridge and Kangaroo Ridge and is to the right of the Wine Spires. A good map and previous knowledge of the area will help with navigating to the climb. Descend from the road to the flows low in the drainage. *Coordinates:* 48°32.583' N, 120°37.127' W

Routes: This drainage is best done early in the season before there is a lot of snow covering it. Sometimes when there is a cold spell before snow, it may be possible to climb these routes before the road is closed. This is a good beginner area and considered to be a nice place to ice-boulder by locals.

Descent: Walk off or rappel. If walking off, beware of cliffs that may not be immediately obvious on the descent.

WILLOW CREEK RIGHT   WI 4+

First ascent: Mazama locals, 2000
Length: 100 feet
Avalanche danger: Serious
Approach: Approach as for the Willow Creek drainage. *Willow Creek Right* can be found in an area left of the drainage in a 150-foot-wide amphitheater. The route is one of three main lines and is the primary line to the right.

Route: Ascend 75- to 80-degree ice for about 50 feet. The route kicks back at this point and becomes dead vertical for the remaining 50 feet. The second half of the route usually ascends beautiful blue ice.

Descent: Rappel off a tree.

WILLOW CREEK CENTER   WI 3+

First ascent: Mazama locals, 2000
Length: 100 feet
Avalanche danger: Serious
Approach: Approach as for Willow Creek drainage. This line is the next major line to the left of *Willow Creek Right.*

Route: Ascend the path of least resistance to the top of the amphitheater.
Descent: Rappel off trees or walk off to the left.

WILLOW CREEK LEFT   WI 4

First ascent: Sean McCabe, Steve House, and Scott Johnson, 2000
Length: 100 feet
Avalanche danger: Serious
Approach: Approach as for Willow Creek drainage. This is the leftmost major route in the amphitheater.

Route: Ascend the vertical ice column for 50 feet. At this point there are two options. Either climb WI 3 easily to the right, or drytool up some interesting rock for 30 feet to the left.

Descent: Walk off to the left.

Rumors of Ice

Immediately after the North Cascades Highway has been plowed and opened, there tends to be a large amount of ice just off the road along a good portion of the highway. The plowing usually takes place in April or May.

There are three potential routes near mile marker 115 on SR 20. The rumor is that they are each three pitches and can be climbed at approximately WI 3–4.

There are at least two routes near Gorge Dam, east of Newhalem. Access may be a problem due to dam security concerns.

There is potentially a four-pitch route on the west side of Diablo Lake. The route is visible from mile marker 131 and would probably require a boat approach.

Approximately 300 feet to the left of the main flow at Rainy Lake, there is a very interesting 150-foot ice pencil that as of yet has not seen an ascent. Beware of avalanche danger on the approach.

NOTABLE ALPINE CLIMBS IN THE NORTH CASCADES HIGHWAY AREA

PYRAMID PEAK, NORTH FACE: RUCH-COTTER ROUTE — GRADE III–IV, WI 3+/4, MIXED

The first-ascent party climbed five pitches of beautiful ice. The route included at least one vertical section and a great deal of 80-degree ice.

First ascent: James Ruch and Robert Cotter, March 1988

Avalanche danger: Serious

Approach: From Interstate 5, drive SR 20 for approximately 67 miles. Park at the Pyramid Lake Trailhead and ascend the Pyramid Lake Trail for approximately 2 miles to the lake proper. From the east end of Pyramid Lake, climb the talus/snow slope up to the northeast arm of the peak. Ascend this arm to the northeast face cirque. Work from here to the north face, crossing past the north buttress to the west.

Route: Ascend the chimney, which accesses the lower face. Continue up a snow gully, which leads to an ice ribbon. Climb the ice ribbon to the upper snowfield. This leads to a final section of mixed climbing. *Special gear:* Be sure to include both knifeblades and angles on your rack.

Descent: Descend to the saddle between Pinnacle and Pyramid Peaks. Continue to descend to the east and down to the Colonial Glacier. Traverse back to the north and down to the lake.

PYRAMID PEAK, NORTH FACE: IT AIN'T OVER YET MOTHERFUCKERS! — GRADE IV, WI 3, M4

At the crux of this route, Robert Rogoz (also known as Polish Bob) was camming the shafts of his ice tools into a vertical crack and scratching his crampons up quarter-inch ice. Rogoz calls it "one of the best pitches I've climbed in the mountains, period." The route involves seven pitches plus some simul-climbing.

First ascent: Robert Rogoz, Coley Gentzel, and Kris Koziarz, February 2003

Avalanche danger: Serious

Approach: Approach as for the Ruch-Cotter Route.

Route: This route reportedly starts on the left side of the North Face in a large snow gully. The route proper begins approximately 400 feet (halfway) up the gully. Following is a pitch-by-pitch breakdown as it was climbed in 2003. **Pitch one:** A shallow groove of ice/névé is the start of the route. Ascend the groove (80-degree start) to a ledge under an overhanging wall. (About 50 meters). **Pitch two:** Ascend to the right, up a snow/névé ramp. (55 meters). **Pitch three:** Simul-climb for about 100 meters on snow to the 50-degree iced-up slab on the left edge of the snowfield. Beware, the pro here is not good. **Pitch four:** Ascend the 75-degree steep groove. Traverse slightly left. Pull into a small left-facing corner (90 degrees), then onto some ice and a 20-meter snowfield (angle left). (55 meters). **Pitches five and six:** Follow the ramp right. **Pitch seven:** Angle up and left to the final groove and the summit. *Special gear:* 4 knife blades, medium Lost Arrow, cams to 3.5 inches, 2 warthogs, 1 Spectra double shoulder-length sling, set of stoppers, 2 ice screws (10 and 13 centimeters).

Descent: Descend as for the Ruch-Cotter Route.

Rumors of Ice

There is a large potential for ice climbs on Pyramid Peak to the right of the North Face route.

Paul Bunyan's Stump has a very large ice climb on it that has been compared to the Pilsner Pillar on Mount Dennis.

MAZAMA

Mazama and the Methow Valley are excellent places to visit during a cold spell. But visiting climbers must be aware that most routes in the area only come in for between 5 and 20 days a season. Not only that, Mazama can be a difficult and remote place to get to in the winter. The North Cascades Highway (SR 20) usually closes in late November. As a result, the drive from the west side of the mountains becomes significant. Mazama is over 200 miles from Seattle via Leavenworth.

There are about a dozen climbs that come in throughout the Mazama area each season. However, only a few of these routes are climbed on a regular basis. This is all changing as the new-wave mixed scene has its effect on the small

Steve House on the first pitch of Scottish Gully, Chockstone Right (photo by Sean McCabe)

community of local climbers. Mazama residents Steve House, Sean McCabe, and Geof Childs are currently putting up a slew of new routes throughout the area. In many ways Mazama is the only area in Washington that currently harbors a group of active locals who are area-specific. This type of scene has existed in the past in areas such as Leavenworth and Banks Lake, areas now faded on the local scene. Mazama locals are protective of their ice and visitors should respect this. The locals are not interested in receiving numerous phone calls every week about whether or not things are in.

Watch the weather carefully, as many of the climbs are west and southwest facing. There must be a bit of a cold spell before anything comes in. Due to the orientation of these routes, make the approaches and the climbs early in the day. Avalanches and icefall are prominent hazards on many of the routes.

To approach Mazama after the North Cascades Highway is closed, drive U.S. Highway 2 to Leavenworth. It is 129 miles from Leavenworth to Mazama. From Leavenworth follow US 2 for 19.4 miles. Turn left onto US 97 and follow this highway for 53 miles, through Entiat and Chelan. Turn left (north) onto State Route 153. At 30.8 miles SR 153 will join with SR 20. Drive SR 20 through Winthrop to Lost River Road, 13.3 miles west of the town. Turn right to access the climbs listed in this area.

The most difficult aspect of the climbing scene in Mazama is parking. The road beneath Goat Wall (Lost River Road) is plowed, however it is important not to obstruct traffic. There are periodic pullouts, but they may not be close to a specific climb's approach. Expect to hike the road for short distances. Climbers may also choose to OBTAIN PERMISSION to park on private property.

To avoid cold camping after a good hard day on the ice, there are a number of hotels and motels in the Winthrop area. As winter tends to be the off-season, climbers may be able to haggle for better deals on rooms.

USGS maps: Mazama, McLeod Mountain

MAZAMA STORE

THE CHILDS ROUTE   WI 3–5-

First ascent: Geof Childs and Sean McCabe, probably 2000
Length: 125 feet
Avalanche danger: Moderate
Approach: The epicenter of the town of Mazama is the Mazama Store. This route can be found about 900 feet above the store on the hillside.
Route: The main route goes to the right and can be climbed at WI 3. If one wishes to up the stakes, a thin mixed climb that involves a bit of drytooling goes up to the left. This can be climbed at approximately WI 5-. Be aware that both options are south-facing.
Descent: Walk off to the left.

GOAT WALL AND LOST RIVER ROAD

Goat Wall is approximately 2.5 miles upvalley from the Mazama Store on Lost River Road, or about 2.5 miles past the rock climbing area Fun Rock. Routes on the wall are described left to right, which is how they are encountered when coming from the Mazama Store. Park unobtrusively.

GOAT ROPER (A.K.A. THE AMPHITHEATRE)   WI 5-

This is an excellent route that tends to come in just about every year. Watch the approach conditions closely.

First ascent: Tom Kimbrell, 1994

Length: Three to four pitches

Avalanche danger: Serious

Approach: Ascend an extremely dangerous avalanche funnel to the base of Inspiration Buttress on the right side of Goat Wall. The route is directly right of the buttress. Do not go anywhere near this approach on a big-snow day.

Route: Ascend the obvious route in three to four pitches.

Descent: Descend with two ropes on fixed anchors.

DESPERATION GULLY   WI 4

One local climber has found 5 ice screws on different occasions at the base of this route after people have bailed. Make sure the route is in solid condition and that you are capable of climbing it before committing to the route.

First ascent: Unknown

Length: Two pitches

Avalanche danger: Serious

Approach: This route can be found just to the left of the Inspiration Buttress. It is in a gully between Goat Wall proper and the buttress. Approach as for *Goat Roper*.

Route: Ascend the first thin pitch of WI 2/3. Expect to use rock gear to establish hard-to-find belays on this route. Ascend the second WI 4 pitch. Once at the top of this, ascend a snow gully for another hundred yards. *Special gear:* Bring a rock rack that includes knifeblades, small nuts, a few cams to 2 inches, and a second rope for double-rope rappels.

Descent: From the snow gully, go climber's right and down a ramp to a ponderosa pine tree. There are a few slings around this tree for the first double-rope rappel. The second rappel is off fixed pins and should allow a climber to attain the ground.

BIPOLAR DISORDER   WI 5, 5.7

This is another nice climb, but it only tends to come in once every three or four years.

First ascent: Tom Kimbrell and Geof Childs, 1995

Length: Three to four pitches

Avalanche danger: Serious

Approach: Approach as for *Goat Roper*. *Bipolar Disorder* can be found approximately 100 yards to the left of *Desperation Gully*.

Route: One should be a solid WI 5 climber to ascend this first steep curtain of ice. Climb directly up the curtain. Ascend a short section of 5.7 mixed terrain until the climbing eases to third class. Climb the third-class step into a snow chimney and then to the top. *Special gear:* Rock protection and a second rope for double-rope rappels.

Descent: Descend the route with double-rope rappels.

GOAT'S BEARD   GRADE V, WI 5/5+, 5.9, A2

This is the big boy of Mazama climbing—indeed this may be one of the hardest routes that currently exists in the state. To date it has only seen one complete ascent. A good section of the climb was linked together with stretches of free and aid climbing on horrendous rock. In the winter of 2000, climbers watched as over 300 feet of the route toppled to the ground. No doubt this is a

Goat Wall, Goat's Beard— thin as usual (photo by Jason D. Martin)

dangerous but spectacular climb, but be aware that this route only comes into good condition once or twice a decade. During a thin year, Steve House attempted to rock climb up to well-formed ice on the route. Unfortunately, it didn't work out; the rock is just too bad. Obviously, the *Goat's Beard* is an extremely elusive and difficult route.

First ascent: Tom Kimbrell and Jack Lewis, early 1990s

Length: Five long pitches

Avalanche danger: Serious

Approach: Approach as for *Goat Roper*. This is the next major route to the left of *Bipolar Disorder*. Directly to the left of this, Bryan Burdo bolted a nice, long sport climb. Don't even bother making the approach unless it is a very cold and shady day.

Route: Ascend steep, discontinuous ice for approximately five pitches. It is not uncommon for large parts of this route to sheer off in the early afternoon. Any team attempting this route must start early and move very fast. *Special gear:* Rock gear, aid gear, and a second rope for double-rope rappels.

Descent: The original party rappelled the route. Some of their gear may still be there. The quality of the rock on Goat Wall is very bad and most gear is shaky. Climbers should be ready to surrender gear on this descent.

CLAYMORE (A.K.A. THE CZECH GULLY)   WI 4-, 5.8 (OR HARDER)

First ascent: Eli Holmes and Karel Zikan, January 1987

Length: Five to eight pitches

Avalanche danger: Minimal to moderate

Approach: This route can be found in the Czech Gully (named for the Czechs that first climbed this route). This is the obvious gully left of the *Beard*. The most distinguishing feature of this route is the bus-sized chockstone lodged in the gully.

Route: This is a west-facing route that is shaded by the right side of the gully it climbs. This keeps the route in a rather stable condition. The first pitch can be climbed via an easy WI 2 tunnel in early season or by a bouldery M6+ later on (M5+ with aid). Climb the many ice steps connected by steep snow. Bypass two caves on the right by ascending short 5.8–5.9 rock steps. Upon reaching a third cave, traverse left 80 meters and climb up to a large pine tree and the forested plateau.

The second-ascent party (Steve House and Shawn McCabe) found two options at this point, a WI 3 face climb or climbing behind the curtain in the ice cave. The second-ascent party also found three more pitches of ice in the WI 3–4 range.

There are many variations in this gully and it is likely that different parties have taken different lines. One thing is for sure: the first pitch can be the crux in certain conditions. One party reported the difficulties to be as hard as WI 6 on a thin ribbon of ice in the first few feet of the climb.

Special gear: Rock gear and a second rope for double-rope rappels.

Descent: Continue to traverse left until it is possible to drop down into the Goat Wall Creek drainage. Descend the creek, rappelling when necessary. The second-ascent party rappelled the route.

SCIMITAR   WI 3, 5.9

First ascent: Eli Holmes and Karel Zikan, January–February 1987
Length: Five to eight pitches
Avalanche danger: Minimal to moderate
Approach: This route can be found in the second gully left of the *Beard* and is visible from the road. It ascends the wall to a tree ledge about two-thirds of the way up.
Route: This route ascends a series of easy ice cascades to an impassable cave. The wall just below the cave provides the key. Traverse left on a slabby ledge past a bolt and then head up a depression. Following is the crux pitch, sustained 5.9: a combination of stemming and drytooling works well to climb the crack and ascend past a moderate overhang and the impassable cave. Climb an easy snow gully to the tree ledge. Or continue up the wall via *Rapier*. *Special gear:* Rock gear.
Descent: Traverse left and descend a gully at the left end of the tree ledge.

RAPIER   WI 4, 5.7

This route ascends the remainder of the wall beyond *Scimitar*.
First ascent: Eli Holmes and Karel Zikan, January–February 1987
Length: Five to eight pitches
Avalanche danger: Minimal to moderate
Approach: Ascend *Scimitar* to the tree ledge two-thirds of the way up the wall.
Route: From the right side of the tree ledge follow an obvious gully/corner over thin ice to a ledge under the mildly overhanging headwall. This ledge can be followed right until the outside edge of the wall is reached. A spectacular pitch and a half in an awesome position attains the upper plateau.
Descent: Rappelling this route is an unappealing prospect. Traverse left until able to drop down into the Goat Wall Creek drainage. Descend the creek, rappelling when necessary.

THE STANDARD   WI 4-

This route is a wonderful introduction to Mazama ice climbing. It tends to come in every year and is climbed many times each season.
First ascent: Unknown
Length: Two to three pitches
Avalanche danger: Minimal
Approach: The drainage to the left of Goat Wall is called Goat Wall Creek.

This creek can be found approximately 3.1 miles upvalley on Lost River Road from the Mazama store. Find a pullout near the drainage and park. Hike straight up the hill and into the drainage. Eventually the drainage bottlenecks and gets brushy. *The Standard* is the first climb on the right. The approach should take 30 to 40 minutes. *Coordinates:* 48°37.630' N, 120°27.012' W

Route: The first pitch is generally climbed at WI 3. The second pitch is a bit harder and is generally climbed at WI 4-. It finishes at a large ponderosa pine. Most parties descend from here, however there is one more pitch of WI 2 that starts another 300 feet up the drainage.

Descent: Rappel the route.

MR. COFFEE   WI 4+

First ascent: Steve House and Sean McCabe, probably 2001
Length: 40 to 50 feet
Avalanche danger: Minimal
Approach: Continue up the drainage above *The Standard* for another 200 yards into the Lynx Gully area. *Mr. Coffee* is the route farthest to the right. It tends to come in every year and sports fat blue ice.

Route: Climb the obvious classic route. There is a WI 2 variation to the right of the route that is easily climbed to top-rope the main route.

Descent: Rappel the route.

PERCOLATOR   WI 5

First ascent: Steve House and Sean McCabe, 2001
Length: 200 feet
Avalanche danger: Minimal
Approach: This route can be found to the left of *Mr. Coffee*.
Route: For the first 40 feet, this route climbs a thin ribbon of ice that includes a bit of mixed climbing. At the top of this there is a steep pencil column. Ascending the pencil for 30 to 40 feet is the crux of the climb. The route eases in its last 50 feet and ends at a large ponderosa pine.

Descent: Rappel the route.

THE BEAR   WI 5/6

First ascent: Unknown (possibly Tom Kimbrell)
Length: Two pitches
Avalanche danger: Moderate
Approach: From the base of the Goat Wall Creek drainage (see *The Standard,* above), walk down the road about 100 yards. The next major climb—about 500 yards to the left of *The Standard*—is *The Bear*. Usually it is possible to tell if the climb is in from the road.

Route: The first pitch climbs 80 feet of WI 2. At the top of this, set a belay in the ice cave. The second pitch launches up 70 feet of sustained WI 5/6. At the top of the ice, veer left to a belay tree. *Special gear:* 60-meter rope.

Descent: Rappel from the tree with a 60-meter rope.

GATE CREEK FALLS   WI 3

First ascent: Unknown

Length: Three pitches

Avalanche danger: Moderate to serious

Approach: Drive the Lost River Road upvalley for 3.9 miles from the Mazama Store. Gate Creek is the second creek crossing, the first being Goat Wall Creek. Park unobtrusively. Climb steeply up through the forest following the creek to the major cleft. This approach takes approximately 30 to 40 minutes on snowshoes. *Coordinates:* 48°38.231' N, 120°27.630' W

Route: This route, created by a high-flow waterfall, comes in approximately every other year. Ascend the WI 2 ramp, followed by a short ice scramble. The third pitch finishes on a steep curtain.

Descent: Rappel the route. It may be possible to walk off.

Rumors of Ice

Steve House did a WI 4 climb to the left of Gate Creek Falls. The route can be climbed in three pitches.

Ice smears often form on Fun Rock, a popular rock-climbing destination approximately 1.4 miles upvalley from the Mazama store on Lost River Road. These are easy to top-rope via the anchors used for the rock climbs. It may also be possible to lead these smears by clipping bolts.

Between Winthrop and Mazama on SR 20 and on Goat Creek Road, there are a number of small potential climbs.

Falls Creek Falls above Falls Creek Campground near Winthrop is a nice WI 3 that climbs three short tiers.

STEHEKIN

There is never an easy approach to the town of Stehekin, at the northwest head of Lake Chelan, deep in the North Cascades. During the summer it is possible to hike from the north over Cascade Pass. Unfortunately, during the winter, that option is not as appealing. Climbers must take either a boat or a plane to reach this secluded town. And with only a single reported ice route, it may not be worth the cash. In any case, you can book a ride on one of the Lady of the Lake boats by calling 509-682-2224.

USGS map: Stehekin

RAINBOW FALLS   WI 5, ESTIMATE (AID POSSIBLE)

It's hard to look at these falls in the summer and not wonder what happens to them in the winter. As it turns out, the massive flow of water over Rainbow Falls seldom freezes solid. That and its secluded position combine to make it one of the hardest waterfall ice climbs in the Cascades to tick.

First ascent: Unknown

Length: Two to three pitches

Avalanche danger: Moderate

Approach: Take a ferry or float plane to Stehekin. It is possible to ski over Cascade Pass to make this approach, adding spice and adventure to this winter outing! This route can be found just outside of the main townsite. A snowshoe trail accesses the base of the falls. *Coordinates:* 48°20.612' N, 120°41.856' W

Route: The actual falls sees a seldom-freeze cycle. However, spray on the sides of the falls often freezes, creating a thin, somewhat discontinuous, sketchy climb. Points of aid here and there may be required to climb through. *Special gear:* Possibly aid or rock gear.

Descent: Rappel the route.

NORTH CENTRAL CASCADES

MOUNTAIN LOOP HIGHWAY

Due to its low elevation, there has been little exploration of the ice-climbing potential on the Mountain Loop Highway (SR 530). There is a great deal of alpine terrain and a number of waterfalls in this area of the Cascades, so it can be assumed that in the colder seasons, serious potential does exist.

Mountain Loop Highway can be approached from two directions, via Granite Falls or via Darrington. In the winter, the snowplow stops at Deer Creek Road, about 23 miles beyond Granite Falls, which means that reasonable access to the climbs listed is via Granite Falls.

All of the climbs that are currently in this area have an alpine flavor and should be considered alpine climbs.

USGS map: Silverton

HALL PEAK

HALL PEAK, NORTH FACE GULLY:
SILVERTON'S SICKLE   GRADE III, WI 3

The party that first completed this long rambling route considers it to be one of the best winter ice climbs in the state. It tends to be in best condition after a cold spell early in the season. The first-ascent team did not expect to find a climb of such quality; they never dreamed they would find so much ice. As a result they were not prepared with ice screws and technical tools. However they were able to find quite a bit of protection and adequate belays by using trees on the route.

First ascent: Scott Bingen, Lance Campbell, and Matt Cooper, November 2000

Length: Approximately eight pitches

Avalanche danger: Serious

Approach: Drive to Silverton via the Mountain Loop Highway from Granite Falls. Park on the south side of the road just before the bridge that crosses the South Fork Stillaquamish River. Walk across the one-lane bridge leading into the township. Please be respectful of the local residences.

Matt Cooper climbing Silverton Sickle (photo by Scott Bingen)

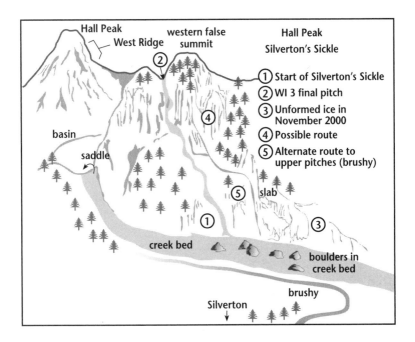

Follow the road for 0.2 mile to the Silver Gulch Trail. There is no sign posted. Follow this trail, faint at times, through dense forest. The trail meanders through slide alder and flanks the east side of the Rocky Creek bed. Depending on the amount of snowfall it may be easier to walk in the creek bed west of the trail. Eventually the creek must be crossed. Look for a slight drainage gully between the false summit and the west ridge of Hall Peak. This drainage will appear before the snow-filled creek bed reaches a saddle upstream. Be aware that this is a hard climb to spot, as it is tucked between cliffs and boulders.

Route: Begin the climb directly out of the creek basin. If the ice here is not solid, ascend brushy slopes to where the canyon walls keep the sun from the route. The lower pitches tend to include a lot of WI 2 and a little fourth-class scrambling. As altitude is gained on the route, the climbing gets more difficult. The crux of the climb is the final pitch before topping out on the West Ridge: Climb a thin smear of near vertical ice through a gully full of loose boulders. Expect to tie off screws here. Rock protection and knifeblades may be useful. At the top of this pitch it is possible to climb the remainder of the West Ridge to the true summit. *Special gear:* Rock gear and pins.

Descent: Either rappel and downclimb the route or ascend to the true summit where there are other descent options. Be aware that the first-ascent team surrendered a bit of gear for rappels. They were also able to rappel from trees.

Rumors of Ice

There are several large ice curtains on the slabs just prior to *Silverton's Sickle*. It is unlikely that any of these have seen an ascent.

BIG FOUR MOUNTAIN

The North Face of Big Four Mountain has a hard history to follow. There have been numerous ascents, however the exact location of these ascents is often difficult to nail down due to the simple problems involved in describing this vast face of the mountain.

In the early to mid-80s, many climbers were ascending winter lines on the North Face of Big Four. However, during that time period, most were not thinking of their specific line as a first ascent. Instead, they would approach the mountain and climb whatever seemed feasible at the time. The result is that many climbers came away from the mountain knowing the general vicinity of their climb, but perhaps not the exact line.

Even the first winter ascent by Rich Carlstad and Cal Folsom in 1974 is somewhat in dispute. There is no question that these two gentlemen completed their route, but as to its exact location, memories have faded and research can only supply the equivalent of educated guesses. The route is definitely somewhere to the right of the Kearney-Cronn line. Indeed, it is likely that the Carlstad-Folsom line was far enough to the west to have been the Spindrift Couloir line discussed below.

Perhaps the most well-known route on the North Face is the Spindrift Couloir. Once again, the exact history of the route is somewhat in question. Pat Timson and partners played on steep ice in the early 70s below the route, but for the most part they only went up a few pitches and never topped out. Steve Swenson and Greg Child made an ascent of the route that would become known as the Spindrift Couloir in 1984. Unfortunately, the two climbers never wrote up their ascent. Dan Cauthorn and Steve Mascioli also made an ascent in this vicinity in 1985, however memories have faded on the specifics. A pair of climbing prodigies did the first heavily recorded ascent of the line described here.

Bart Paull and Doug Littauer, at the tender age of sixteen, climbed the Spindrift Couloir and reported said ascent to the *American Alpine Journal* and *Climbing* magazine. Since these reports were made, the route—or at least the general vicinity of the route—has seen quite a bit of action.

BIG FOUR MOUNTAIN, NORTH FACE: SPINDRIFT COULOIR GRADE IV–IV+, WI 4–4+, (POTENTIALLY MIXED)

This is considered one of the most exciting and beautiful routes in the area. There is no place to bivy on the route, so parties must move fast. When looking for belays, try to identify areas that will be out of the line of fire of falling snow and ice. Every party that has sent this route has had complications due to the constant sloughing of spindrift (hence the route's name). Also note that avalanche danger on the North Face of this mountain is phenomenal. Pay very close attention to conditions before attempting any routes on Big Four.

Possible first ascent: Rich Carlstad and Cal Folsom, 1974

Avalanche danger: Serious

Approach: Drive to the end of the Mountain Loop Highway (SR 530), or at least as far as it is plowed, usually to within 3 miles of the Ice Caves on Big Four. Park in the Sno-Park facility on the north side of the highway.

Hike, snowshoe, or ski the remaining 2 miles up the road alongside the Stillaguamish River to the Big Four Picnic Area and continue for another mile on the Big Four Ice Caves trail to the base of the mountain. Usually this trail is well tracked by snowshoers. The route ascends the rightmost couloir, just left of the North Face bowl.

Route: From the base, three steps can be seen to the summit. Many parties solo or simul-climb large chunks of this route in order to move fast.

Step one: There are a few ways to bypass the lowest cliff band. Paull and Littauer found a steep (75-degree) ice runnel that led them into the couloir. Other parties have bypassed this step by climbing across avalanche debris and

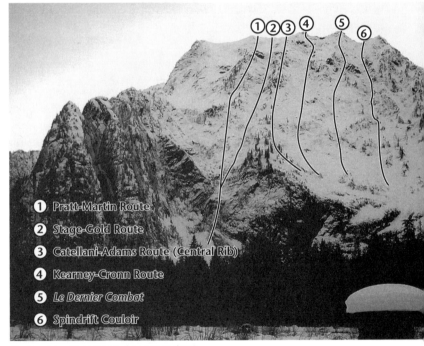

1. Pratt-Martin Route
2. Stage-Gold Route
3. Catellani-Adams Route (Central Rib)
4. Kearney-Cronn Route
5. Le Dernier Combat
6. Spindrift Couloir

Big Four Mountain (photo by Matt Perkins)

traversing to the base of the route. Climb easy snowfields to the base of the couloir proper.

Step two: Ascend 50-degree snow for another two pitches to the base of a steep, potentially mixed section. This area varies; bulges that exceed 70 degrees may exist here. Paull and Littauer found small sections of mixed climbing throughout this portion. The next two pitches should be in the WI 3 range and put a climber on top of the second step. Following this there will be approximately three pitches of steep snow. After ascending the snow, things start to get difficult. There may be many gullies and variations here, not all of which have been explored.

Step three: This third step at about 5000 feet is the crux. Paull and Littauer found severe difficulties at this point: WI 5, 5.9 ground, the top of which purportedly exceeded 95 degrees. Other parties have found a steep 120-foot pitch of rotten ice that can be climbed at WI 4–4+. It may be possible to circumvent this part of the climbing to the left, though it may or may not be just as difficult terrain. From the top of the third step, climb 70-degree ice and 65-degree mixed ground to the summit cornices. The only way to reach the summit ridge may be by tunneling through a cornice. The first-ascent party descended from here. To attain the true summit, ascend the ridgeline to climber's left across dangerous cornices.

Special gear: Rock gear and pitons.

Descent: Descend the northwest ridge to a col above the North Face bowl. Rappel off trees until able to downclimb.

Rumors of Ice

Many exciting and long lines have been climbed on the North Face of Big Four throughout the years. The exact history and locations of all the routes are often in question. The mountain is complex and as a result many climbers have had difficulty identifying their lines without a picture of the peak in front of them. Others have had difficulty remembering exactly where their given line was on the vast North Face. One thing is for sure, there is quite a bit of steep climbing on the face; in the right conditions, the entire North Face is climbable. Many lines exist and have the potential to provide a tremendous amount of enjoyable climbing. Other notable climbs on the face aside from the Spindrift Couloir follow:

Bruce Pratt and Debbie Martin climbed the next rib to the east of the Central Rib in 1984. This route reportedly finishes on the true summit of the mountain.

Dan Stage and Warren Gold made the first complete ascent of the couloir immediately left (east) of the Central Rib in 1979. The route probably saw a partial ascent prior to the Stage and Gold ascent. However, this pair was the first to ascend the route directly from the top of the conical avalanche debris field that creates the Big Four Ice Caves. The party encountered several pitches of 70- and 80-degree water ice and at least one pitch of 90-degree hard snow. The route passes through a difficult chimney and then ascends the gully to the east of the Catellani-Adams route directly. From the top of the Stage-Gold route, the summit may be easily accessed. Note: This party was able to bivy comfortably under an overhanging rock approximately halfway up the face.

Joseph Catellani and Gordon Adams climbed the Central Rib of the North Face in 1982. To attain the rib, traverse the large bowl below the North Face proper. From the base of the rib, climb 45-degree snow to the first large rock band. This was surpassed by Catellani and Adams with two 80-foot pitches on ice-covered slabs that required some thin ice climbing and mixed work up to WI 3+. Belays in this technical section were from small trees. Beyond this, 45- to 50-degree slopes lead to a second rock band and a 75-foot pitch of WI 3. Ascend snow and ice to lower-angle slopes and the summit ridge. Attain the true summit by ascending to the east. Catellani and Adams descended the same route they climbed via downclimbing and a few rappels. Note: Catellani and Adams were forced to bivy in a snow cave they carved in the steep North Face slope just above the first set of ice-covered slabs.

It is possible that Jack Lewis climbed a line directly to the right of the Central Rib sometime in the mid-80s. It was unclear at press time whether or not this line shared some features with the Kearney-Cronn line.

Alan Kearney and Greg Cronn climbed what appears to be the most obvious line on the mountain in 1992, a large couloir just to the right of the Central Rib. The vast majority of this route is approximately 50 degrees. Kearney and Cronn discovered one near-vertical WI 3/4 unprotected pitch near the top of the route.

In 1988, Robert Cordery-Cotter soloed a line to the east of the Spindrift Couloir that he calls *Le Dernier Combat* or "The Last Battle." The route climbs out of the North Face bowl directly toward the second summit in line from the west. This route ascends through three cliff bands, the third being the most difficult. Though mostly WI 3, the crux—a waterfall that splits the third cliff band directly below the "secondary" summit—is a solid 85-degree WI 4. The most amazing aspect of this solo is not only the fact that this climber sent a new route, but he apparently also descended a new route. Cordery-Cotter downclimbed and rappelled the couloir to the east, the same couloir that Kearney and Cronn would climb just a few years later.

Dan Cauthorn and Steve Mascioli climbed a route near the Spindrift Couloir; it is even possible that they climbed the couloir. The pair never roped up for their ascent. The crux of their climb was approximately 300 feet of 70-degree ice climbing. Note: Cauthorn and Mascioli were forced to bivy on the summit after finishing their ascent.

The Big Four Ice Caves are a popular place to practice ice techniques, though caution should be practiced while climbing here. There have been many injuries and a few fatalities in this area. Be wary of areas where ice may fall. The actual caves are quite dangerous and should be avoided. The ice caves are directly under the tremendously active avalanche slopes of Big Four Mountain, so pay close attention to avalanche conditions.

The West Face of Mount Sloan has a tremendous amount of ice on it. There are multiple lines on the face and some are reportedly very long. It may be possible to approach this area via Bedal Creek.

The slabs on the North Face of Vesper Peak apparently have a couple of long, moderate lines that run from Vesper Glacier to the summit. From a distance, these lines look very similar to those found on the North Face of Pyramid Peak.

INDEX

The town of Index is 37 miles east of Everett on U.S. Highway 2. In extremely cold years, a number of potential routes form up on steep granite in the Index area, both before reaching the town and shortly after it. Most of these routes would require a long approach, but might well be worth it.

The most commonly climbed route in the Index area is Bridal Veil Falls. Unfortunately, this route only comes in once every two or three years. Tick it when possible!

USGS map: Index

BRIDAL VEIL FALLS   WI 3+

This particular flow seldom forms, but is an incredible route below the towering walls of Mount Index. It tends to be very thin when it does come in. More often than not there is a tremendous amount of water still running when this waterfall freezes.

First ascent: Unknown

Length: Two to three pitches

Avalanche danger: Minimal

Approach: From Everett, drive US 2 to Mount Index Road, on the right just before the Skykomish River Bridge and about 0.5 mile before the exit for the town of Index. Drive the Mount Index Road for 0.3 mile. Take the first right and drive as far as possible. The road ends after approximately 1.5 miles. From here, hike or snowshoe the Lake Serene Trail to the base of Bridal Veil Falls. *Coordinates*: 47°47.397' N, 121°34.000' W

Route: There are two interesting sections down low on the falls that are right beside one another. Each of these sections ascends steep ice for approximately a pitch and a half. After the steep ice, many climbers choose to descend. However, it is possible to climb a few more pitches at WI 2.

Descent: Rappel from trees.

Bridal Veil Falls (photo by Eric Simonson)

CRYSTAL BLUE   WI 4+

This route tends to be one of the most reliable in the Index area.

    First ascent: Carl Deidrich and Jim Ruch, 1991

    Length: Two pitches

    Avalanche danger: Serious

    Approach: See approach directions for Bridal Veil Falls. Climb to the top of the Lake Serene Trail. The route can be found at the head of the lake, beneath the eastern slopes of the main peak of Mount Index.

Route: *Crystal Blue* is the fattest, most obvious line. *Special gear:* Bring rock gear and pins; depending on the conditions they may not be needed.

Descent: Rappel the route.

BLUE MOON   WI 4+

First ascent: Jim Ruch and Florian, 1991

Length: Two pitches

Avalanche danger: Serious

Approach: See approach for *Crystal Blue*. *Blue Moon* is approximately 200 feet to the right of *Crystal Blue*.

Route: Climb the obvious line. *Special gear:* Rock gear and pins may be required.

Descent: Rappel the route.

THE DIAMOND GULLY   WI ?

First ascent: Dave Anderson, Bruce Carson, Ed Gibson, and John Teasdale, early 1970s

Length: 400 feet of lower-angle climbing leads to steeper tiers above.

Avalanche danger: Minimal

Approach: This route can be found between the Diamond and the Cheeks on the Upper Town Walls of the popular Index rock-climbing area. Drive US 2 to Index. Cross the bridge and park in town. Walk the railroad tracks to the trail just past the Bush House. Ascend this trail past two boulder fields. Eventually the trail will split. Take the right trail. It will split once more, take the right trail a second time. Follow the trail past the base of the Cheeks to the gully between the Cheeks and the Diamond.

Route: This route tends to be the most stable of the Diamond gullies. The first-ascent party said that the route definitely had a thin Scottish feel to it. Climbers can expect to find a great deal of low-angle ice with a single steep section. *Special gear:* Rock protection is helpful.

Descent: There are two descent options. The first is simply to rappel the route; this is the easiest option. The second is to walk off above the Cheeks and *Town Crier* to the left. This is a long route above steep cliffs that eventually bisects a trail that cuts downward. Take this trail down and to the left. Once down below the cliffs, take another trail that cuts off to the left and walk back to the base of the climb. If unfamiliar with this walk-off descent or if there is a lot of snow, rappel the route.

Rumors of Ice

In addition to the routes described, several routes of varying difficulty have been completed in the Lake Serene basin above Bridal Veil Falls. It has been reported that to the left of the primary pillars and buttresses of Mount Index, at least three routes come in on occasion that climb all the way to the ridge crest. The avalanche danger in this area is serious.

In the mid-1980s, climbers found a bit of ice in the gullies to the right of *The Diamond Gully*. As these gullies receive sun throughout the day, they remain unstable at best.

From up on the Index Town Wall, a small slab is visible to the east of town near the railroad tracks. The route can be reached by walking along the tracks and can be top-roped. Walk off or rappel.

There is a monstrous ice flow that often runs up the north face of Mount Persis. It is unlikely that this route has been climbed. At least one longstanding Northwest climber has suggested climbing Mount Persis from the backside and rappelling to the route's start. The alternative—ascending the entire north face—seems an unreasonable approach for two pitches of ice.

The North Norwegian Buttress on Mount Index may have an extremely long and dangerous ice climb on it. Good luck.

An ice route has been climbed in the Mount Baring–Dolomite Tower gully by a Bellingham climber.

It is possible to see two large ice routes on Gunn Peak from milepost 40 on US 2. There is no information on these routes at this time.

NOTABLE ALPINE CLIMBS IN THE INDEX AREA

Just as the ice in the Index area doesn't come into shape very often, neither do the big alpine routes in the area. A number of things must be going the right way for these routes to be pleasant and climbable.

First, it must be cold. Really cold. It has to be really cold for a couple of weeks before these low-elevation routes come into shape. If Index ice is in and fat, these routes are probably in as well.

The second thing is that avalanche conditions must be in your favor. Lake Serene is notorious for its avalanche activity and a number of people have been killed in the Lake Serene basin by avalanches. It would behoove any climbers who enter this basin to make sure that the avalanche danger is low when attempting these routes.

And the third thing that must be on your side is speed. Speed is safety. Safety is speed. The objective dangers on these routes (and on many routes in this book) require fast parties who work well together. Because the routes are long, the parties must also be fit and constantly moving.

When all of these things come together, climbers tend to have a good experience. When they don't come together, sometimes climbers experience tragedy.

MOUNT INDEX, NORTH FACE OF MIDDLE PEAK GRADE IV–V, WI 3, 5.6

First ascent: Dan McNerthney and Doug Klewin, December 1978
Avalanche danger: Serious

Approach: See the approach for Bridal Veil Falls. Ascend the steep Lake Serene Trail to the lake in approximately 1 mile.

Route: From Lake Serene, ascend to the deep gully between the Middle and North Peaks of Mount Index. Break off to the left and up the gully that ascends the center of the Middle Peak. This will eventually become the north face of the peak. The first-ascent party bivouacked twice: once at Lake Serene, and once in the woods trying to find the way back to Lake Serene. *Special gear:* Rock gear and two 60-meter ropes for long pitches and rappels.

Descent: Traverse to the Main Peak. This begins with an easy descent into the Middle-Main Peak notch. Climb a short 5.6 pitch to the crest of a wedge gendarme. This tends to be most difficult at its base. Once up, bear left to the crest. Follow the sharp wedge's crest to its top. Then make a one-pitch descent into a minor notch behind it. Work west on fourth-class terrain and across a steep gully that comes from the upper face. Continue up an obvious ledge system to the west and under another upper wall. Traverse it around the northwest corner. Scramble up and right, southeast, to the summit of the Main Peak. From here the descent is down the east route of the Main Peak. Descend the obvious gully to the northeast. Continue down toward the saddle that can be found southeast of Source Lake. Stay just above and to the left of the saddle, dropping down snow or rockslides to the northwest.

MOUNT INDEX, MIDDLE-MAIN PEAK GULLY   GRADE IV–V, WI 5, 5.6

The first-ascent party left the town of Index at 6:00 in the morning and reached the summit at 11:30 at night. This is a long and serious route.

First ascent: William Sumner and Fred Dunham, January 1985

Avalanche danger: Serious

Approach: See approach for the North Face of Middle Peak.

Route: This is the deep gully that can be found just south of the South Norwegian Buttress. The climb consists of a number of steep steps, separated by lower-angled snow and ice slopes. The fantastic crux of the route is a 70-foot vertical-to-overhung waterfall. From the notch between the Middle and Main Peaks, continue up to the summit of the Main Peak (see the descent for the North Face of Middle Peak). *Special gear:* Rock gear and two 60-meter ropes for long rappels.

Descent: See the descent for the North Face of Middle Peak.

LENNOX MOUNTAIN

This is an area that local climbers Dave Burdick and Phil Fortier first discovered while looking for new backcountry skiing terrain during the winter of 2000–2001. Avalanche conditions were bad on their first foray into the area, but they returned a year later to climb the first route in the area, *Sno Sense*. Goat Basin is a low-elevation cirque on the north side of Lennox Mountain, just off U.S. Highway 2. Only five routes have been climbed in the basin (as of March 2003), but not for lack of trying, and there is still much new route potential. Like many west-side climbs, the climbs around Lennox Mountain are created through a combination of snowfall and freeze-thaw cycles.

While the approach does not require a snowmobile, it does take a fair amount of time. When there is no snow down low, ugly bushwhacking through the valley bottom leads to a large treacherous boulder field. When there is enough snow to cover some of the brush and boulders, the approach takes on a different, but no less committing flavor with skis or snowshoes and significant avalanche hazard. Take adequate flotation regardless of how much snow you encounter on the first, low-elevation section of the approach.

To approach Goat Basin and Lennox Mountain, take the Money Creek

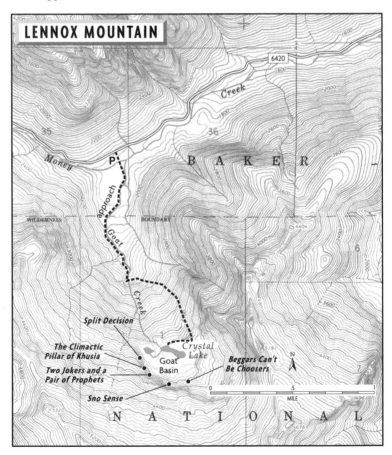

Campground exit, which is past the town of Index but before the small hamlet of Skykomish as you head east on US 2. Cross the railroad tracks and follow the pavement until you can turn right onto Miller Road. Take an immediate right onto gravel Money Creek Road (Forest Service Road 6420). Follow the road to a bridge at about 0.5 mile. In midwinter the plowing stops here, but later in the season the road can be driven a bit farther.

Continue up the road almost 4 miles, steadily gaining elevation, until an obvious small clearing at 2000 feet affords a good view up Goat Basin. You can see some of the climbs from here, so bring binoculars. You can also park here, if you made it this far with a car. Approach the climbs from the north along the creek, at first bushwhacking through heavy trees. At the base of a large avalanche slope (boulder field in early season), assess the avalanche danger. If the danger is high, make a steep rightward traverse through trees up the headwall of the valley just left of a slabby waterfall. Climb up forested terrain until you reach the basin. If avalanche danger is low, it is possible to climb directly up the avalanche slope.

All of these climbs and the approaches in Goat Basin are extremely avalanche threatened. Do not climb here unless avalanche danger is low.

USGS maps: Grotto

BEGGARS CAN'T BE CHOOSERS WI 3+

The leftmost major ice route in Goat Basin was climbed in terrible conditions, one week after the ascent of *Two Jokers* and *Split Decision*.

First ascent: Dave Burdick, Loren Campbell, Jens Klubberud, February 23, 2003

Length: Three pitches

Avalanche danger: Serious

Approach: See the approach described in the introduction above. *Beggars* is a wide curtain of ice, the left-hand most major ice route of the Goat Basin headwall.

Route: The route starts near the center of the flow, just right of some blocky ice steps. Climb two full pitches of WI 3, trending slowly leftward across the curtain. The final pitch takes you to trees at the top left-hand edge of the climb.

Descent: Rappel the route from trees on its left-hand side.

SNO SENSE WI 4

A lower-angled pitch leads to a long steep section of mixed snow and ice.

First ascent: Dave Burdick and Phil Fortier, February 2002

Length: Two pitches

Avalanche danger: Serious

Approach: See the general approach given for this area, above. *Sno Sense* is a wide flow, just right of a narrower pillar near the center of the main wall. *Coordinates:* 47°40.660' N, 121°28.053' W

Sno Sense (photo by David Burdick)

Route: Start from the lowest tongue of ice and climb 30 meters of WI 3, then traverse left up a ramp. Several steep steps and short pillars with intermittent ledges lead to the top.

Descent: Rappel the route.

TWO JOKERS AND A PAIR OF PROPHETS   WI 3

The longest ice route in Goat Basin ascends the center of the headwall for several pitches of lower-angled ice to a final pitch of WI 3 with interesting options.

First ascent: Alex Krawarik and Dave Burdick, February 15, 2003

Length: Three to four pitches

Avalanche danger: Serious

Approach: See the approach described in the introduction above. This climb is located at the center of Goat Basin, just to the left of *Khusia*.

Route: The route starts in the center of the headwall and ascends several pitches of rolling, gradually steepening terrain (buried in heavy snow years) to where it constricts at the base of the final pitch. There are two possible variations here, separated by a small rock outcropping: a steeper and mushroomed pillar forms on the left, and a nice curtain leads slightly off to the right.

Descent: Rappel and downclimb the route, or walk off to climber's right 15 minutes back to the base of the route.

THE CLIMACTIC PILLAR OF KHUSIA   WI 4

A lower-angled pitch leads to an obvious steep pillar.

First ascent: Dave Burdick and Loren Campbell, March 2002

Length: Two to three pitches

Avalanche danger: Serious

Approach: See the general approach given for this area. This pillar is located on the far right-hand side of Goat Basin. *Coordinates:* 47°40.722' N, 121°28.249' W

Khusia (photo by David Burdick)

Route: Climb thin ice (WI 2+) and low-angled rock until a 5-foot fracture wall is surmounted (or steep snow if the slope has not slid) for a full rope-length pitch. The second pitch climbs the main pillar for approximately 100 feet of steep and sustained ice, followed by another 60 feet up and right through snow to a tree belay. *Special gear:* Bring 60-meter ropes for long pitches.

Descent: Rappel the route or walk off to the right.

SPLIT DECISION   WI 3

This is a shorter and slightly more sustained climb than *Two Jokers,* but with less character.

First ascent: Alex Krawarik and Dave Burdick, February 15, 2003

Length: Two to three pitches

Avalanche danger: Serious

Approach: See the approach described in this area's introduction. This is the first major route located to the right of *Khusia.*

Route: A short and rambling WI 2 step leads to a pitch of WI 3. At the top of the pitch, two options to exit the climb exist. Climb either of the constrictions to the right or left, topping out through some brush.

Descent: Rappel the route or walk off to climber's right 15 minutes back to the base of the route.

STEVENS PASS

Because of the relatively high elevation (4056 feet), Stevens Pass and environs offer some good, reliable, and accessible ice climbing.

Though the ice along U.S. Highway 2 near the ski area looks great, it really isn't. Many climbers who have experimented on this extremely visible ice have received tickets from the highway patrol. One climber was even threatened with a night in jail for getting a little too cocky with the Man . . . . In any case, it is not advisable to climb ice on highly visible roadcuts.

The vast majority of the accessible and known ice climbing can be found on the highway east of the pass. There are access and private property issues in some of these areas, so be sure to OBTAIN PERMISSION before crossing private property. Be aware of and respect "No Trespassing" signs.

USGS maps: Mount Howard, Lake Wenatchee, Big Jim Mountain

WHITEPINE CREEK

WHITEPINE DROOL   WI 3

First ascent: Unknown

Length: 80 feet

Grey Beard at Lake Julius (photo by Jeff Street)

Avalanche danger: Minimal to moderate

Approach: This climb can be seen from US 2 just west of Rayrock Knifeworks. Approach via the Whitepine Creek Road, which is 13.1 miles east of Stevens Pass. Drive, ski, or snowshoe Whitepine Creek Road for 1 mile to the railroad trestle and a small parking area. Currently there is an access issue concerning crossing the railroad bridge; and because the train comes by every 15 minutes, it is quite dangerous to cross.

Instead, continue down Whitepine Creek Road under the trestle to a second bridge. Cross this bridge and follow the creek to the east beneath the cliff band. Upon reaching the railroad tracks, walk alongside them for a short distance to a road on the right. Hike the road approximately 200 yards, then climb up a timbered rib to the route.

Important: Walking on the railroad trestle is no joke. Yes, the apparent shortcut would cut off a significant amount of approach time, but the time saved is not worth the risk. Trains come careening by at an astounding rate, seemingly every few minutes. The last thing that anyone wants is to be stuck in the middle of this trestle above the river as a train approaches. Please use the recommended approach.

Route: Climb the obvious flow. It is somewhat stepped.

Descent: Walk off to climber's right or rappel using trees as anchors.

Rumors of Ice

There are climbs of various grades on Whitepine Wall, the cliff band that *Whitepine Drool* is found on. A number of interesting routes from WI 2 to 5 can be found on this wall above the boulder field. In a good year, this includes numerous two-pitch routes, a few steep pillars, and some thin mixed routes.

Directly (west) behind the Whitepine parking area and above the railroad tracks there is a cliff band called Arrowhead Wall that harbors a number of interesting routes. Many of these have been explored, but the names and grades have been lost.

MERRITT

GILL CREEK FALLS   WI 2–3

There is a high volume of water flowing here and this falls seldom forms. It is not a bad idea to scout the route from US 2 with binoculars before making the approach; this will make the approach obvious.

First ascent: Unknown

Length: One to two pitches

Avalanche danger: Minimal

Approach: This route can be found south of US 2 near Merritt. Follow the signs toward the Lake Ethel Trailhead. Park at Merritt and snowshoe up the Lake Ethel Trail along Gill Creek and cross-country to the falls. Walk under the powerlines for a bit before launching up the trail (probably snow covered) toward the falls.

Route: Ascend the obvious route.

Descent: Walk off through timber either right or left.

CHANDELIER FALLS   WI 3

This route is named for a defunct café just to the east, not for the nature of the climbing. Be aware that mountain goats use this area during the winter. Be sure to give them room.

First ascent: Unknown

Length: One pitch

Avalanche danger: Moderate to serious

Approach: This is the route that can be seen at milepost 80 to the north of US 2. Park near the east end of the chain-up area on the highway. *Important:* The approach crosses private property and climbers must OBTAIN PERMISSION to access this climb.

Hike or snowshoe up through recently logged clear-cuts. Continue up, angling left through timber and an avalanche zone to the base of the falls.

Route: Ascend the route. Be aware that there is possible avalanche danger from above.

Descent: Walk off to the left.

LAKE JULIUS

Lake Julius is an alpine lake located in the Scottish Lakes region east of Stevens Pass. This area is a haven for backcountry skiers, and many stay at the Scottish Lakes Huts, a private resort enterprise located several miles east of Lake Julius.

The approach to this area is via an 8-mile road owned and operated by High Country Adventures, which runs the Scottish Lakes Huts. This road is approximately 17 miles east of Stevens Pass, just west of milepost 82. The road is on the south side of the highway, directly across from the Nason Creek Rest Area. It is possible to ski up this road to access the lakes, however there are also frequent High Country Adventures snowmobile shuttles. In the 2002 season, a roundtrip ride to the Scottish Lakes High Camp cost $45, and lodging within the small resort there was approximately $55 per person per night. For more information, call High Country Adventures or check out their website (425-844-2000; *www.scottishlakes.com*). Access to this area is not recommended with a private snowmobile without the permission of High Country Adventures.

The routes in the area form in the drainage from Lake Donald to Lake Julius, at the west end of Lake Julius. The base elevation is above 5000 feet, and the routes are found on a north-facing slope.

LAKE JULIUS WEST   WI 3

This wide curtain is fed by a small drainage and cascades down a blocky wall of black rock.

   First ascent: Unknown, possibly George Sherrit and Jack Lewis, early 1980s
   Length: One pitch
   Avalanche danger: Moderate
   Approach: This is a long, but well-worn approach on a snowmobile, on

Lake Julius West (photo by Jeff Street)

skis, or on snowshoes (see the general Lake Julius approach directions, above). Whatever your approach means, the goal is to reach Lake Julius's east shore. Traverse around the lake via the north shore, and ascend steep slopes to the routes. *Coordinates:* 47°44.177' N, 120°53.021' W

Route: Ascend the curtain. Be aware that there is possible avalanche danger from above.

Descent: Rappel the route or walk off.

GREY BEARD   WI 4

This route forms just to the right of *Lake Julius West* on the right-hand side of an obvious rock buttress.

First recorded ascent: Jeff Street, March 10, 2002

Length: One pitch

Avalanche danger: Moderate

Approach: Approach as for *Lake Julius West. Coordinates:* 47°44.083' N, 120°52.866' W

Route: A steep, short, narrow curtain leads up to lower-angled slopes and then to trees. Be aware that there is possible avalanche danger from above.

Descent: Rappel the route or walk off.

ABOVE LEFT   WI 3+

This route forms to the left of *Lake Julius West,* at the south end of the lake.

First ascent: Unknown

Length: One short pitch

Avalanche danger: Moderate to serious

Approach: Approach as for *Lake Julius West,* but instead, climb the steep slope through trees to this smaller flow several hundred yards to the left.

Route: Ascend the route. Be aware that there is possible avalanche danger from above.

Descent: Rappel the route or walk off.

Rumors of Ice

There are other distinct lines found in the vicinity of *Grey Beard* and *Lake Julius West,* the two main Lake Julius flows. Route information is unknown, but the area clearly offers many opportunities for adventurous parties.

LAKE WENATCHEE

There is ice to be had in Washington and Lake Wenatchee's small contingent of routes proves it. It is only in recent years that the lake's solid ice season has been rediscovered.

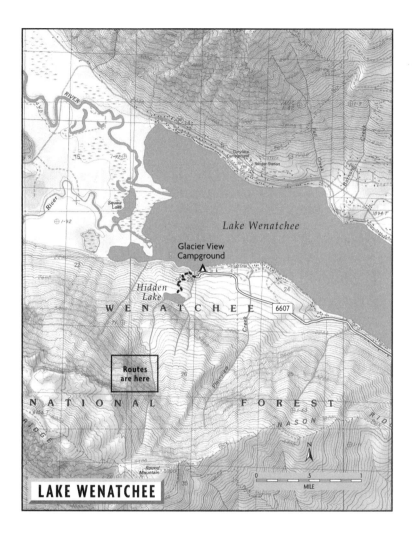

Still, the long approaches and serious avalanche danger should give climbers pause. Though the ice and the routes are excellent, the approach requires you to cover a good bit of ground in the winter backcountry. Fortitude and a sense of adventure are a must for any of these excellent routes.

To get to the Lake Wenatchee routes, turn off U.S. Highway 2 at Coles Corner, 19.2 miles east of Stevens Pass. Drive State Route 207 toward Lake Wenatchee for 3.2 miles to the south entrance of the state park. Turn left onto Cedar Brae Road and drive for 3.7 miles to the end of the plowed road at Forest Road 6607.

USGS map: Lake Wenatchee

THIS TOO SHALL PASS   WI 4

First recorded ascent: Rat, 1997

Length: One to two pitches

Avalanche danger: Serious

Approach: This route and those that follow can be found high above Hidden Lake on the north side of Round Mountain. Hike Forest Road 6607 for about 1.5 miles to the Hidden Lake Trailhead and the Glacier View Campground. Ski or snowshoe up the trail to the lake. From Hidden Lake, ascend the inlet stream to avalanche slopes below the cliff holding the route. Above the lake, snowshoes are probably more efficient. This approach is slightly over 3 miles.

To check for route conditions, this climb can be seen from the north shore of Lake Wenatchee prior to reaching the Forest Service office on SR 207. Views of the climb become better as the spring season rolls around.

Route: The route climbs up a left-facing corner on the far right side of the cliff.

Descent: Walk into the trees to the right and down a large avalanche path that forms the right side of the climbing area.

TIMEQUAKE   WI 3+

First recorded ascent: B. Gaines and Rat, November 2001

Length: Four to five pitches

Avalanche danger: Serious

Approach: This climb is the fourth line to the left of *This Too Shall Pass*.

Route: This climb ascends a number of pitches separated by short snow ramps. Ascend two to three pitches of WI 2–3, finishing on two WI 3+ pitches.

Descent: Either rappel, downclimb, or traverse left to *Last Rite* or *My Ten Years* and walk off or rappel as described below.

LAST RITE   WI 5

First recorded ascent: M. Gunlogson and Rat, March 2001

Length: One long pitch (150 feet)

Avalanche danger: Serious

Approach: Traverse left and down from the top of *Timequake*.

Route: Ascend the beautiful, steep WI 5 pillar in one long pitch.

Descent: Either rappel the routes to the ground or walk off to the left. The left descent will require rappelling off trees to get to the bottom of the first pitch. Continue descending through steep trees and hidden cliffs. An additional rappel may be required.

MY TEN YEARS ON AUTOMATIC PILOT   WI 4

First recorded ascent: Rat, January 2001

Length: One to two pitches

Avalanche danger: Serious

Approach: Climb *Timequake* to the first WI 3+ pitch.

Route: Traverse left to a long WI 2 pitch that leads to the snow slope below *Last Rite*. Continue up a beautiful WI 4 pillar to the left.

Descent: Either rappel the routes to the ground or walk off to the left. The left descent will require rappelling off trees to get to the bottom of the first pitch. Continue descending through steep trees and hidden cliffs. An additional rappel may be required.

Rumors of Ice

There are two brushy, potentially unclimbed lines between *This Too Shall Pass* and *Timequake*. There is also other route potential in the area.

LEAVENWORTH

Leavenworth is a picturesque little town on the east side of the Cascades. It is well known for its rock climbing and its access to large alpine climbs. However, it is also a popular destination for ice climbers.

In a good season it is possible to find many lines throughout the Leavenworth area. Usually there are a few beautiful, short pillars along Icicle Creek and a number of interesting top-ropeable smears and mixed climbs. Listed here are a number of routes that come in on a relatively regular basis. Remember, there is a lot more available in this area for those willing to venture well above the road or far into the canyons.

Owners of the local climbing shop, Leavenworth Mountain Sports, have granted permission to contact them regarding information concerning ice conditions. Call 509-548-7864 or visit them in the heart of the pseudo-Bavarian town at 940 U.S. Highway 2, #B.

The hamlet of Leavenworth is approximately 87 miles east of Everett on US 2. Tumwater Canyon is approximately 80 miles east of Everett.

USGS maps: Winton, Leavenworth, Enchantment Lakes, Cashmere Mountain, Mount Stuart

TUMWATER CANYON

DRURY FALLS   GRADE IV, WI 4

One of the crown jewels of Washington state ice climbing, Drury Falls offers many pitches of moderate but sustained climbing. The length, exposure, and position of the route, combined with possible approach difficulties, serious avalanche hazard, and a lengthy descent make this a serious adventure for climbers of all abilities. Drury Falls has been the scene of many epics, attempts, and ascents, and has witnessed numerous climbers falling into Jolanda Lake and

the Wenatchee River attempting the crossing. Some climbers have even fallen through fragile parts of the climb itself. Do not underestimate any part of the approach, climb, or descent.

First ascent: Steve Pollack and Bob McDougall, February 1978

Length: Five to seven pitches

Avalanche danger: Serious

Approach: Drury Falls is a significant flow located in Tumwater Canyon several miles west of Leavenworth. It is easily visible from US 2, above mile marker 94 in the Fall Creek drainage. To access the route, the Wenatchee River must somehow be crossed. It is possible to cross the Wenatchee near the Fall Creek drainage during periods of low water. Scout the river carefully and locate a spot where there are eddies on both sides. That will make it easy to start, and easy to coast into the opposite side. Most climbers choose to cross with a small boat at Jolanda Lake near the Candy Shop, several miles downstream. During cold periods, an ice dam forms across the river that may be creatively crossed. One report indicates an excellent crossing above Lake Jolanda, just after US 2 crosses a small creek. Theoretically it is possible to place a canoe in the river here and paddle from one eddy to the next, providing an easy crossing. In any case, care must be taken when crossing; this is a wide and wild river.

Once on the other side, hike into the Fall Creek drainage at approximately 1500 feet. Hike directly up the drainage to the base of the falls. Beware of avalanche conditions on this approach: There is serious avalanche hazard where the drainage constricts and steepens, but this is not easily seen from below. There are good bivouac sites available below the upper falls and above the first few pitches on the right in trees. *Coordinates*: 47°38.210' N, 120°44.719' W

Route: The falls is broken into two distinct sections. The lower falls is climbed in two full-length, moderate pitches, separated by some low-angle snow. Once past the second pitch, more snow trudging leads through declining avalanche hazard to bivy sites and the base of the upper falls. With almost 500 feet of steep climbing, the upper tier is wide and offers many lines. It tends to be steeper on the right. *Special gear*: 60-meter ropes are recommended for long pitches and long rappels.

Descent: There are two descent options: either walk off to climber's right with a short rappel, or rappel and downclimb left of the falls.

The first option is easier and only involves a short rappel back to the long lower-angled ramp at the base of the upper tier. Walk off several hundred feet to the right, skirting the initial steep cliffs, to where your ropes will reach the ramp.

The second option is a lengthy descent best attempted in daylight (take headlamps when in doubt; 60-meter ropes are recommended). From the top of the route, hike to the east (left) and find an unobvious, but large, tree with slings

Drury Falls (photo by Matt Kerns)

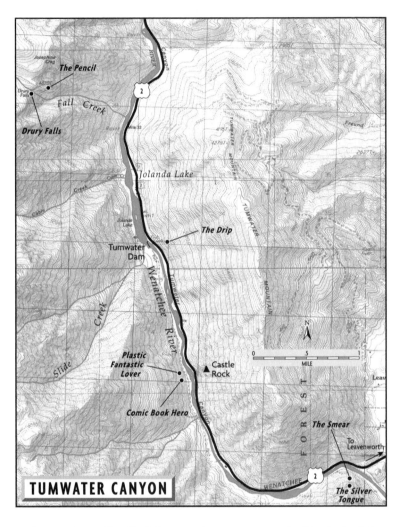

TUMWATER CANYON

at the top of a small gully. A free rappel past some mean-looking ice leads to a small bench with another tree anchor. Hike steeply 100 feet down and east to find another very long rappel. Downclimb a little and then hike down to the base of the upper tier. From here the descent options are more abundant. Rappel the lower pitches from natural anchors (boulders) and V-threads; there are no trees.

THE PENCIL   WI 5

In many ways this is an odd climb. In years where it seems like there is little ice in the state, this route appears to come in. On the other hand, during big ice years this route is often nowhere to be found.

Pat McNerthney climbing The Pencil (photo by Matt Kerns)

First ascent: Kjell Swedin and Bob McDougall, February 1983

Length: Three 60-meter pitches

Avalanche danger: Serious

Approach: This climb is also found in the Fall Creek drainage. See the approach for Drury Falls. *The Pencil* is several hundred yards west (right) of Drury Falls. *Coordinates:* 47°38.277' N, 120°44.113' W

Route: Ascend dead vertical ice to a belay. The second, often mixed, pitch blasts up and to the left. The third and easiest pitch ascends a large curtain at WI 4. *Special gear:* A 60-meter rope is recommended.

Descent: Bring a second rope for the rappels. Descend snow-covered slabs, climber's left. Continue down a ramp until the end. From here rappel into the gully below.

THE DRIP   WI 5/6

Though this route doesn't come in often, it is considered to be a spectacular test piece.

First ascent: Unknown

Length: 80 feet

Avalanche danger: Minimal

Approach: This route can be found approximately 200 yards south of the

The Drip (photo by Matt Kerns)

Plastic Fantastic Lover (photo by Mitch Merriman)

Tumwater Dam and approximately 10 minutes above and east of the highway. Park at the dam or at a small turnout directly below the cliff. Hike up the stream gully to access the climb.

Route: Climb the obvious steep line, usually in WI 6 conditions.

Descent: Walk off to the left.

PLASTIC FANTASTIC LOVER   WI 4

First recorded ascent: Mitch Merriman and Allan Helton, 2001

Length: Two pitches

Avalanche danger: Moderate. Pay attention to the rock slabs above on the approach.

Approach: This route comprises three short pillars which can be viewed directly across the Wenatchee River from Castle Rock. Park downstream at a small parking lot, near the old rusty bridge. Cross the bridge and follow the old pipeline road back upstream, past *Comic Book Hero,* to the base of the route. Snow-covered slabs with significant avalanche hazard may need to be negotiated near the route. Access via this bridge may also be an issue. If "No Trespassing" signs are present, find another way to access this route. *Coordinates:* 47°35.978' N, 120°42.959' W

Route: The first pitch climbs a WI 3 apron on the right side of the ice for 100 feet to the base of the largest, steepest pillar. The second pitch climbs this pillar for 50 feet, then up and right through a shorter step to a belay at a large, partially charred tree.

Descent: Walk off right and back to the base of the route.

COMIC BOOK HERO   WI 3

First recorded ascent: Mitch Merriman, Alec Gibbons, and Ben Stanton, January 1997

Length: Three short pitches

Avalanche danger: Minimal to moderate

Approach: Park east of Castle Rock at the small parking lot, as for *Plastic Fantastic Lover.* Cross the bridge and continue up the Wenatchee River until directly across from Castle Rock. The climb is the ice nearest the river toward the right edge of the bowl. *Plastic Fantastic Lover* is located uphill and right from here. If the bridge is closed or harbors "No Trespassing" signs, find alternate means to cross the river.

Route: Climb a short pillar to a long rambling section of WI 2. This WI 2 section could be up to 100 feet long. Above, short steps and slabs to WI 3 lead up for several pitches. *Special gear:* Pitons may be useful for belays.

Descent: Walk off to the left. Some tree rappels may be required.

THE SMEAR   WI 2

First ascent: Unknown

Length: Two pitches

Avalanche danger: Low to moderate

Approach: This is the obvious route on the west side of the river at the lower (southern) end of Tumwater Canyon. Access is across PRIVATE PROPERTY, creating serious issues for this climb as well as for *The Silver Tongue.* The easiest way to access this climb is to turn right onto Icicle Creek Road in Leavenworth, cross the bridge, and turn into the first driveway on the right. Be sure to park unobtrusively. Do not park here after a snowstorm, as it creates problems for the snowplow. Walk down to the end of the driveway. OBTAIN PERMISSION from the last house before continuing the approach across their property. (It is possible to avoid crossing private property by cutting up the steep hillside and walking around the house.) After gaining permission, continue past the last house and walk along the abandoned irrigation canal to the climb.

It may be possible to reach this climb by crossing the same bridge used by *Plastic Fantastic Lover,* though this approach also entails considerable difficulties. If this second approach is used, be aware that trail must be broken for approximately 1.5 miles to the climb. *Coordinates:* 47°35.072' N, 120°40.692' W

Route: Ascend the obvious, slabby route for two pitches.

Descent: Walk off to climber's right or continue on to *The Silver Tongue.*

THE SILVER TONGUE   WI 2/3

First recorded ascent: Mike Kane and Rolf Larson, 1997

Length: Two pitches

Avalanche danger: Moderate

Approach: Continue uphill for 15 minutes above *The Smear.* Note access issues above.

Route: Climb the route up to the ridge crest. The first pitch is somewhat hidden by trees from the base, though the second pitch can be seen from the road.

Descent: Either rappel and downclimb, or hike up to the top of the ridge crest and then descend directly to your car.

Rumors of Ice

Aside from *The Pencil* and *Drury Falls,* there are other short climbs high in the Fall Creek drainage. Some are as long as two pitches.

ICICLE CREEK CANYON

To access Icicle Creek Canyon, turn south onto Icicle Creek Road at the western edge of Leavenworth.

CARENO CRAGS AND RAINBOW GULLY

Careno Crags and Rainbow Gully are near the Snow Lakes Trailhead, about 4.2 miles along Icicle Creek Road.

CARENO FALLS RIGHT   WI 4

First ascent: Unknown

Length: 40 feet

Avalanche danger: Moderate. In the 1996–97 season an avalanche came down in this area and knocked a house off its foundation.

Approach: Park in the Snow Lakes parking area, approximately 4.2 miles from the start of Icicle Creek Road. The Careno Falls routes are visible on the right just before parking. Walk back down the road for a few minutes, then hike

Careno Falls Left (photo by Matt Kerns)

up to the base of the climbs. Avoid approaching these climbs across private property. *Special gear:* Rock protection.

Route: Climb the steep pillar to the top. Be careful topping out, as climbing onto the rock in order to finish the route is required.

Descent: Rappel from trees.

CARENO FALLS LEFT   WI 4

First ascent: Unknown
Length: 40 feet
Avalanche danger: Moderate. See note for *Careno Falls Right.*
Approach: Follow approach for *Careno Falls Right.* As the name implies, *Careno Falls Left* can be found just to the left.
Route: Climb up the double-stepped pillar. *Special gear:* Rock protection.
Descent: Rappel from trees.

RAINBOW FALLS RIGHT   WI 3

Rainbow Falls Right and *Rainbow Falls Left* have traditionally been referred to as a single climb. We separate them here because there is a lot of rock between the two routes and each part can be climbed in its own right.

Climbing Careno Falls Right (photo by Mitch Merriman)

Rainbow Falls Right (photo by Mark Shipman)

First ascent: Unknown

Length: One to two pitches

Avalanche danger: Moderate. In the 1996–97 season a huge slide came down over this route and out into the road. In the right conditions (wrong for climbing), this area can be very dangerous.

Approach: Park in the Snow Lakes parking lot approximately 4.2 miles from the start of Icicle Creek Road. Cross the road to the obvious steep falls in the gully (Rainbow Gully) left of Careno Crags.

Route: There are a number of lines that climb the falls. Those on the left side of the main flow may be a bit easier, but thinner. Those on the right tend to be a bit steeper.

Descent: Rappel the route or walk off to the left.

RAINBOW FALLS LEFT   WI 4+

First ascent: Unknown

Length: 40 feet

Avalanche danger: Moderate. See note for *Rainbow Falls Right.*

Approach: This route can be found in the left-hand corner of the same gully that *Rainbow Falls Right* sits in.

Route: This tends to be a very steep series of pillars. It may be possible to top-rope this climb by walking around the base of the gully to climber's left. However, good anchors at the top of the route are hard to come by.

Descent: Walk off to the left.

PIVOTAL MOMENT   WI 4

First recorded ascent: Mitch Merriman, date unknown

Length: One to two pitches

Avalanche danger: Moderate

Approach: This route is approximately 4.4 miles along Icicle Creek Road, above the right side of the road. It is in the canyon above the rock climb *Air Roof*. Park in the Snow Lake parking area, as for the Rainbow Falls routes.

Route: A series of narrow columns leads to some large trees near the top.

Descent: Rappel the route.

Rumors of Ice

There are a number of pure ice and mixed climbs that come in periodically between Careno Crags and Rainbow Gully. Most do not have names. There is one three-pitch mixed climb that comes in every now and then right above the road gate.

SNOW CREEK VALLEY

Millennium Walls

The three Millennium Walls can be found about an hour's hike up the Snow Lakes Trail (the parking area is 4.2 miles along Icicle Creek Road). The ice crags are at the turnoff for Snow Creek Wall, or at approximately 2800 feet. The routes found here are excellent short climbs with a lot of variety between the grades. They also tend to form early, which is a plus.

FIRST MILLENNIUM WALL   WI 2–3

First recorded ascent: Krista Eytchison and Jason Martin, January 2000

Length: 30 to 40 feet

Krista Eytchison climbing First Millennium Wall (photo by Jason D. Martin)

Avalanche danger: Moderate

Approach: See general approach directions for the Millennium Walls, above.

Routes: There are four to six easily top-roped routes here. Some are low angled and fat, while others are somewhat steeper and a little thinner.

Descent: Rappel the routes.

SECOND MILLENNIUM WALL   WI 4–5

First ascent: Unknown

Length: 30 to 40 feet

Avalanche danger: Moderate

Approach: Approximately 100 feet beyond the First Millennium Wall, right at the turnoff for Snow Creek Wall.

Routes: There are one to three thin routes here. All can easily be top-roped.

Descent: Rappel or walk off.

THIRD MILLENNIUM WALL   WI 3–4

First ascent: Unknown

Length: 30 to 40 feet.

Avalanche danger: Moderate

Approach: This ice crag is 100 feet beyond the Second Millennium Wall and slightly up the hillside. It is easily seen from the trail.

Routes: There are three to six easily top-roped climbs on this wall.

Descent: Rappel or walk off.

Snow Creek Wall

Snow Creek Wall is a popular rock-climbing destination, but it is also important to note that the wall has seen a number of winter ascents. The most popular rock routes on the wall—*Outer Space* and *Orbit*—are climbed under serious winter conditions almost every year. It is not uncommon for parties attempting these routes in winter to fix ropes and turn what would be a half-day trip in the summer into a very serious winter ascent. These are good routes for aspiring Alaskan alpinists to practice on.

It is as an ice-climbing destination that the wall will be discussed here. There are two established mixed ice routes on the wall and a number of possibilities for other climbs. Many other climbs may have been completed in this area, but currently information on them is lacking.

WHITE SLABS   WI 3+/4, MIXED

Calling this route by one name is a bit misleading, as it applies to three variations on the wall.

First ascent: Possibly Don Peterson

Length: Six pitches

Avalanche danger: Serious

Approach: Approach via the Snow Lakes Trail, as for the Second Millennium Wall. Turn off the main trail at about 2800 feet and cross the creek. Climb steeply through the trees to the base of Snow Creek Wall. The *White Slabs* routes can be found to the right of the popular rock route, *Outer Space*. Beware of avalanche potential on the approach.

Routes: There are three potential routes here that may vary greatly in difficulty and grade. Though they may all look like they are in from the trail, it is important to decide which of the routes is in the best shape while at the base of the wall. Take the time to look at each of them. All three options are extremely serious endeavors that require strong mixed climbing skills.

White Slabs Direct tends to be the route of choice. It ascends left of the ice that will be hanging in the center of the wall. Climb the low fifth-class start of *Outer Space* until it veers off to the left toward the tree ledge. Continue mixed climbing up the corner system to *Country Club Ramp*. It may be possible to escape via the ramp or continue up the corner system via *White Fright* (a rock route). Be aware that the entire route is thin and requires rock gear up to 3 inches. Do not pass up any opportunities for belays or for protection. Expect ice difficulties up to WI 3+ and rock difficulties up to 5.9.

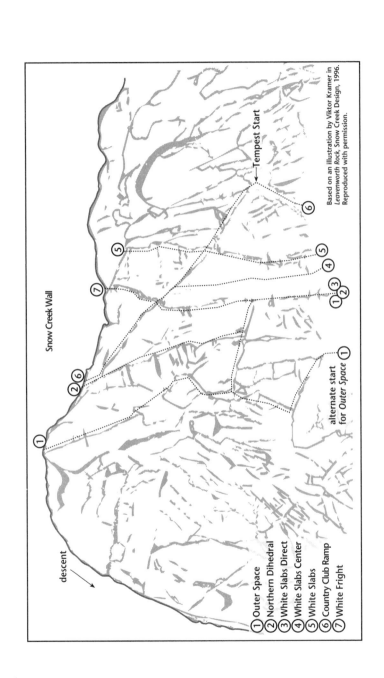

Snow Creek Wall

descent

Tempest Start

⑤

⑦

②⑥

①

⑤
④
①③
②

alternate start
for *Outer Space* ①

⑥

① Outer Space
② Northern Dihedral
③ White Slabs Direct
④ White Slabs Center
⑤ White Slabs
⑥ Country Club Ramp
⑦ White Fright

Based on an illustration by Viktor Kramer in
Leavenworth Rock, Snow Creek Design, 1996.
Reproduced with permission.

There is ice between *White Slabs Direct* and *White Slabs*. To keep these climbs straight, this route will be referred to as *White Slabs Center*. It has been climbed, but tends to be quite thin. An escape from this route is possible once it hits the *Country Club Ramp*. The other option would be to traverse left on *Country Club Ramp* and then to finish the wall via *White Fright*. Like the preceding route, this is a serious endeavor. Neither belays nor protection should be bypassed.

The *White Slabs* route is potentially the easiest option in this area of Snow Creek Wall. There is more potential protection on this route than on the above variations. However, once again, opportunities to place pro and to create bomb-proof belay stations should not be ignored when they present themselves. The summer route here is 5.7. Ice conditions are very thin and are often in the WI 4 range. Expect to link ice via rock climbing.

Special gear: All routes require rock gear.

Descent: Ascend to the top of the wall, climber's left. There is a large gully/drainage that often harbors a bit of ice. Descend the steep gully until able to traverse along the base of the wall. This descent is steep and avalanche prone.

COUNTRY CLUB RAMP   WI 5, ESTIMATE

The grade for this route seems slightly suspicious. As the other routes on the wall have seen recent ascents and have been graded at least a little below WI 5,

Snow Creek Wall (photo by Jason D. Martin)

① *White Slabs Center,* finishing on *White Fright*
② *Country Club Ramp*

we wonder whether or not this grade is a bit hard for the route. Only climbers with a sense of adventure will ever know.

First ascent: Climbers unknown, 1970s

Length: Six pitches

Avalanche danger: Serious

Approach: Approach as for *White Slabs*. The route can be found to the right and up a short gully.

Route: *Country Club Ramp* is the ramp that bisects Snow Creek Wall starting at the base of the *Tempest* (a rock route), crosses above *White Slabs*, beneath *White Fright,* and then finally finishes at the top of *Northern Dihedral*. This is a serious mixed route and protection may be scarce. It is important to build solid belays whenever the opportunity to do so arises.

Descent: Descend as for *White Slabs*.

Snow Lakes

NADA FALLS   WI 3

First ascent: Freeman Keller, Dave Jaeks, and Eric Jaeks, 1979

Length: Two pitches

Avalanche danger: Moderate

Approach: Nada Lake is the first of the Snow Lakes encountered on the Snow Lakes Trail. Continue past the Snow Creek Wall turnoff to attain the lake approximately 5.5 miles from the Snow Lakes parking area. The first-ascent team, perhaps the only team to have ever climbed this route, took 5 plus hours to reach the lake in deep snow.

Route: Ascend the falls in two pitches. The first pitch is approximately 80 feet and the second is approximately 60 feet.

Descent: Rappel the route.

Rumors of Ice

Northern Dihedral on Snow Creek Wall has a bit of ice on it and has probably seen an ascent at some point. Expect hard mixed climbing up to 5.9.

At least one other line has been climbed in the Nada Lake region by forward thinking alpinists.

ICICLE BUTTRESS

ICICLE BUTTRESS   WI 4–5, MIXED

First ascent: Unknown

Length: Two to four pitches

Avalanche danger: Minimal

Approach: Icicle Buttress is the next major piece of rock upvalley from the crag that *Pivotal Moment* climbs (see Careno Crags and Rainbow Gully, above). The buttress appears on the right-hand side of the road, approximately 6.4 miles down Icicle Creek Road. Park as close as possible to the buttress. During inclement weather, snowplows come down the road on a regular basis.

Routes: At least three routes have been done on Icicle Buttress. One climber reported that he ascended directly up the center of the slabs at WI 4. He then continued up the right side at WI 3. Another ascent was done up the far right side. The third known route appears to climb the *Cocaine Connection* and the *R&D Route* (rock climbs). Expect up to 5.6 rock climbing for this variation. Whichever way this formation is climbed, expect two things: first, a need for

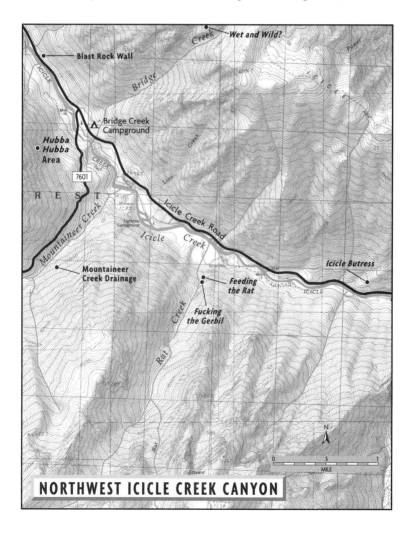

NORTHWEST ICICLE CREEK CANYON

rock gear, and second, thin sketchy ice. *Special gear:* Rock protection.

Descent: If the top is attained, walk off to the left. If not, rappel the route and be prepared to surrender gear.

RAT CREEK VALLEY

The Rat Creek drainage is the next drainage on the opposite side of Icicle Creek beyond Icicle Buttress. Access to this area is extremely difficult. At the current time it is NOT PERMITTED to use the private road nearby to cross the Icicle Creek in order to access these climbs. The only way to get to the following routes is to find alternate means across Icicle Creek. Unfortunately, in the height of winter this is not easy to do. And the consequences of falling off of a log while crossing above the icy torrents of the river may be too much for most climbers to risk.

FEEDING THE RAT   WI 3

   First recorded ascent: Rat, February 2000

   Length: Two to three pitches

   Avalanche danger: Serious

   Approach: See the approach given for Rat Creek Valley, above. After crossing Icicle Creek, ascend the first large snowfield on the left. *Feeding the Rat* can be found on the first left-facing corner encountered as the approach gully is climbed. This route can be seen from Icicle Creek Road and becomes more prominent in the spring.

   Route: Climb the obvious flow.

   Descent: Walk off to climber's left and down a gully.

FUCKING THE GERBIL   WI 3/4

   First recorded ascent: Rat, February 2000

   Length: Two pitches

   Avalanche danger: Serious

   Approach: This route can be found approximately 200 yards farther up Rat Creek from *Feeding the Rat.*

   Route: Climb the obvious flow.

   Descent: Walk off to climber's right.

Rumors of Ice

Slightly down Icicle Creek (toward Leavenworth) from the Rat Creek drainage, there is a possibility that the rock climb *Dog Nasty Dike* on the far left side of Dog Dome harbors a small amount of interesting climbing.

HUBBA HUBBA AREA

From Bridge Creek Campground, approximately 8.4 miles from US 2 on Icicle Creek Road, it is possible to see three large falls on the hillside across the

Icicle. There are actually four routes up there in the WI 2–3 range. The fourth route is to the left of the largest falls *(Hubba Hubba)* and is only visible when you are close to the base of the routes.

HUBBA HUBBA (A.K.A. THE FUNNEL) WI 3

This is a beautiful classic climb that tends to come in early in the season and stay in for a good portion of the year. However, "in" is a tricky word. People climb this route when a good portion of the ice is a mere 2 inches thick.

First ascent: Unknown

Length: One to three pitches

Avalanche danger: Serious. The locals still call this route *The Funnel* for a reason. There have been numerous incidents in which either people or gear have been swept away. So far there have not been any reported fatalities, but this doesn't mean that there won't be any in the future.

Approach: Park at Bridge Creek Campground. Cross the bridge and turn right onto a small gated roadway. Follow this road for about 100 feet. Turn left and make a beeline straight up the hillside toward the falls. Beware of avalanche danger in the gully. *Hubba Hubba* and adjacent routes are at approximately 3300 feet. It should take about an hour to make the approach. *Coordinates*: 47°33.625' N, 120°47.286' W

Route: There are a number of variations here. Most people start on the right side of the falls and stay to the right. Be aware that depending on snow cover and ice conditions, this route varies in length. *Special gear*: Rock protection or pitons may be needed to protect the route.

Descent: Either rappel the route or walk off to climber's right.

LEFT OF HUBBA HUBBA WI 3 R

First ascent: Unknown

Length: Two short pitches

Avalanche danger: Moderate to serious

Approach: See approach for *Hubba Hubba*. This line is the thin route in the gully to the left of *Hubba Hubba*.

Route: Climb the first short but slightly run-out pitch to a good belay on a ledge. Many people elect to call it quits here, for the second pitch is a thin smear running up a slab to the top. The pro on this second pitch is nearly nonexistent. *Special gear:* Rock protection and pitons.

Descent: Either rappel the route or walk off to climber's right.

RIGHT OF HUBBA HUBBA WI 2+/3 R

Though a little less appealing than *Hubba Hubba* and routes to the left of the falls, there are two routes to the right. Often these two potential routes form into one thin sheet of ice.

Length: One pitch
Avalanche danger: Moderate to serious
First ascent: Unknown
Approach: See approach for *Hubba Hubba.*
Routes: These two routes are both thin. *Special gear:* Rock protection would be very helpful.
Descent: Either rappel the route or walk off to climber's right.

MOUNTAINEER CREEK DRAINAGE

As the modern mixed scene makes its mark on Washington, a few areas are being developed at the top of the mixed range and a few areas are being developed at the bottom. The relatively short routes that are slowly being put up along Mountaineer Creek fill the gap. Many of these routes are moderate in grade and as a result are good places for those with a little mixed talent to hone their skills.

It should be noted that this particular area is perhaps one of the longest areas to remain "in" throughout the state. Climbs have been completed in this area well into March, and routes have been visible from the road as late as April.

To approach these routes, park at Bridge Creek Campground, about 8.4 miles from US 2 on Icicle Creek Road. Hike up Mountaineer Creek Road (Forest Service Road 7601). After about 45 minutes to an hour, a wall on the left side of the road comes into view—this is what you're heading for. Drop down into the valley and cross Mountaineer Creek. Depending on the depth of the creek, this crossing can be very dangerous; take appropriate precautions here. The bottom routes are found on the wall's first (lower) tier above the creek, a small climb sits alone above this, and then the last three established climbs are found on the second (upper) tier. The approach to the lower tier takes approximately 2 hours.

SCOTTISH MIST   WI 2+, M4

First ascent: Bruce White, Travis Hammond, and Mike Toigo, 1999
Length: 100 feet
Avalanche danger: Moderate
Approach: See the general approach directions along Mountaineer Creek Road, above. This route can be found on the extreme left side of the lower tier.
Route: Ascend an ice gully to a cave where a bird has nested. Drytool around a large chockstone and ascend thin ice on slabs to the top. Be aware that, depending on conditions, this route may require rock climbing on a slab with crampons up to 5.9. *Special gear:* Rock gear may be necessary.
Descent: Rappel the route or walk off.

Mark Shipman on Scottish Mist (photo by Bruce White)

MR. SEATTLE   WI 4

First ascent: Bruce White, Travis Hammond, and Mike Toigo, 1999

Length: One to two short pitches

Avalanche danger: Moderate

Approach: This tends to be the fattest route on the lower tier. It can be found to the right of *Scottish Mist*.

Route: Climb the obvious fat route. A belay may be established approximately halfway up to eliminate rope drag. Climb to the top and set a belay in the trees on the left.

Laurel White climbing Mr. Seattle (photo by Bruce White)

Descent: Walk off or rappel the route.

PAULIE'S TEMPER TANTRUM   WI 3, MIXED

Apparently this route was in thin conditions when it was first sent. Paulie Detrick, a sixteen-year-old climber, had just returned from climbing fat ice in Canada with his father, a well-known local climber. During the attempt to send this thin route Paulie could not help but complain about the conditions, and thus the name.

First ascent: Bruce White, Laurel White, Paul Detrick, Paulie Detrick, and Randy Bracht, 2001

Length: 50 feet

Avalanche danger: Moderate

Approach: Approach as for *Scottish Mist*. The route can be found on the far right side of the lower tier.

Route: Ascend the obvious mixed route. Some of the mixed climbing may involve tool placements in frozen dirt. *Special gear:* Rock gear may be necessary.

Descent: Walk off or rappel.

THE MIDDLE ROUTE   WI 3

First ascent: Mark Shipman and Bruce White, 1999

Length: 40 feet

Avalanche danger: Moderate

Approach: Approach as for *Scottish Mist*. This little route can be found between the lower and upper tiers.

Route: Ascend 75- to 80-degree ice for approximately 40 feet.

Descent: Walk off.

SHIPMAN'S SLIPPERY TONGUE   WI 3, MIXED

First ascent: Bruce White and Mark Shipman, 1999

Length: 45 feet

Avalanche danger: Moderate

Approach: Approach as for *Scottish Mist*. The upper tier can be found slightly above and to the right of the lower tier. This route is the first route in the left-hand corner of the second tier. You can easily walk around *The Middle Route* to attain this and the other upper routes if so desired.

Route: Ascend approximately 20 feet of free-hanging ice to a small ledge system. Climb through mixed ground to attain the top. *Special gear:* Rock gear may be necessary.

Descent: Walk off or rappel.

TWO DOPES ON A ROPE   WI 3/4

First ascent: Bruce White and Mike Toigo, 1999

Length: 50 feet

Mark Shipman heading for Emerald City (photo by Bruce White)

Avalanche danger: Moderate

Approach: This route can be found to the right of *Shipman's Slippery Tongue* in a right-hand corner.

Route: This route is a straightforward pillar. Ascend near-vertical ice to the top.

Descent: Walk off or rappel.

EMERALD CITY   WI 4

First ascent: Bruce White and Mark Shipman, 1999

Length: 60 feet

Avalanche danger: Moderate

Approach: This is the next major route to the right of *Two Dopes on a Rope*.
Route: Ascend the classic pillar.
Descent: Walk off or rappel.

Rumors of Ice

To date, not all of the routes have been climbed in the Mountaineer Creek area. Following is a short breakdown of the current history of these routes.

To the left of *Mr. Seattle* there is a route that has been repeatedly top-roped, however it has not yet been led. The route requires steep ice climbing and drytooling.

There are a few free-standing pillars on the lower tier that have not yet seen any ascents.

There is a beautiful free-hanging pillar approximately 20 feet to the right of *Emerald City* that has not yet been completed.

There is quite a bit of other mixed potential in the valley. Explorations need to be made for further information.

BRIDGE CREEK DRAINAGE

This particular drainage has always held some mystery for climbers. Every rock guidebook published that has included routes in this area has indicated that little information was available. It is not only ironic, but fitting, that this is also the case with information about ice climbing in the area.

Approach from the Bridge Creek Campground, approximately 8.4 miles upvalley from US 2 along Icicle Creek Road.

WET AND WILD   WI 4, ESTIMATE

First ascent: Tom Hall-Hargis and Matt Kerns, December 1983
Length: Four to five pitches
Avalanche danger: Serious
Approach: The Bridge Creek Wall is the huge wall that can be seen high above the Bridge Creek Campground. To approach climbs on this wall, ascend steep slopes from the campground for approximately 2500 feet.
Route: The climb can be found in the gully system to the left of the Bridge Creek Wall. The first pitch ascends 60-degree ice for 100 feet. Ascend a short section of snow to reach the next real pitch. Climb 20 steep feet up vertical icicles until reaching an ice ramp. Continue up this ramp to the base of a 300-foot granite wall. Ascend the thin ice strip on this wall for two more pitches. Be aware: This route gets a lot of sun and tends to be wet even when the temperature is below freezing. *Special gear:* An assortment of pitons that includes knifeblades.
Descent: The first-ascent party descended the east side of their route with a double-rope rappel. They then continued to downclimb to the west of their lower pitches.

Rumors of Ice

There is new route potential on this wall. Other thin icefalls tend to form every year for those who are truly twisted.

BLAST ROCK WALL

The Blast Rock Wall, just beyond the Bridge Creek Campground and about 9.7 miles from US 2 on Icicle Creek Road, sports a number of short, interesting top-rope problems. Many of these climbs require a bit of drytooling here and there. Though not as spectacular as many other climbs in the Icicle Creek area, they tend to be a lot of fun. This is a good area for beginners to top-rope.

BLAST ROCK WALL   WI 4, MIXED

First ascent: Unknown

Length: 30 to 40 feet

Avalanche danger: Minimal

Approach: Usually the road is closed at Bridge Creek Campground, 1.2 miles before the wall. If this is the case, snowshoe, ski, or hitchhike a ride on a snowmobile to the wall alongside the road.

Routes: There are a number of variations and drips on the wall. Most are short and in the WI 4 range. Be aware that when there is a lot of snow, these routes can be extremely short. All of the routes here may be top-roped.

Descent: Walk off or rappel.

NOTABLE ALPINE CLIMBS IN THE LEAVENWORTH AREA

DRAGONTAIL PEAK, NORTHWEST FACE: WASSON-WILSON ROUTE   GRADE IV, WI 3, MIXED

First ascent: John Wasson and Tim Wilson, 1984

Avalanche danger: Serious

Approach: Mountaineer Creek Road is approximately 9 miles along Icicle Creek Road from US 2. Drive as far as possible on Mountaineer Creek Road and park when it is impossible to go any farther; the road is approximately 3 miles long. Park at Bridge Creek Campground if Mountaineer Creek Road is closed.

From the end of Mountaineer Creek Road, follow the trail for 3 miles to a fork. Take the left fork and ascend snow slopes for another 2 miles to the north shore of Colchuck Lake. (A working knowledge of this approach in the summer and a topographic map are essential when the trails are buried in snow.) Skirt the lake to the southwest side and ascend the Colchuck Glacier to the Serpentine Arête.

Route: The route can be found to the right of Serpentine Arête. The first-

Tom Hargis in front of Wet and Wild (photo by Matt Kerns)

① Triple Couloirs

② Cotter-Bebie Route

③ Wasson-Wilson Route

Aasgard Pass

Dragontail Peak (photo by Joseph Puryear)

ascent party climbed a thin ice smear in their first pitch. The next four pitches ascended solid ice into a snowfield. At the top of the snowfield, they climbed a hard mixed pitch. From there, they moved up and left to join the Serpentine Arête, which they ascended for two more mixed pitches to attain the summit.

Descent: Walk off the backside of the peak, traversing to climber's left. Eventually Aasgard Pass will come into view. Descend from the pass to the lake.

DRAGONTAIL PEAK, NORTHWEST
FACE VARIANT: COTTER-BEBIE ROUTE   GRADE IV, WI 3, MIXED

There are a few discrepancies between descriptions of this Dragontail route and the previous route. It appears that two routes on Dragontail Peak have been named "Northwest Face." The first is the previous line, climbed by Wasson and Wilson. The second is the route that is described in Fred Beckey's *Cascade Alpine Guide: Columbia River to Stevens Pass.* The particular variation we describe here is a continuation of the route described by Beckey.

First ascent: Robert Cotter and Mark Bebie, 1988

Avalanche danger: Serious

Approach: See approach for the Wasson-Wilson Route. This variation can be found between the Backbone and the Serpentine Arête.

Route: Ascend ice between the two popular routes, following Beckey's Northwest Face route. Toward the top of the route, finish in the corner to the right of the slab known as the Fin.

Descent: See descent for the Wasson-Wilson Route.

MOUNT STUART, NORTHWEST FACE COULOIR: THE '80S TEST PIECE   GRADE IV/V, WI 3+, MIXED

In the mid-1980s, this route was considered a standard test piece for aspiring alpine ice climbers. Dan Cauthorn, a well-respected climber from that era, calls it a "superb ice-runnel climb that seems to have disappeared into obscurity." Indeed, perhaps once again the route may become a Northwest test piece.

First ascent: Unknown

Avalanche danger: Serious

Approach: From US 2 in Leavenworth, drive Icicle Creek Road for approximately 9 miles to Mountaineer Creek Road. Drive as far as possible on Mountaineer Creek Road and park when it is impossible to go any farther. The road is approximately 3 miles long. If the road is closed, park at Bridge Creek Campground.

From the end of Mountaineer Creek Road, follow the trail for 3 miles to a fork. Take the left fork and continue to follow the trail for an additional mile. As the primary trail begins to switchback toward Stuart Lake, cross the creek and drop down. Follow the creek to where it forks. Continue right at the stream fork

Dragontail Peak (photo by Alex Krawarik)

and climb steeply through a forest to flatter terrain beneath the Sherpa Glacier at 5400 feet. Camping is possible at this location. Traverse beneath the north ridge and onto the Stuart Glacier. From here, climb toward the access gully used to attain the upper north ridge of Mount Stuart. It should be noted that this is a somewhat complex and time-consuming approach when covered by snow. Previous knowledge of the area will cut down on approach time significantly.

Alternate approach: It is possible to approach Stuart from the south. From State Route 970 east of Cle Elum, drive Teanaway River Road to its end (the road becomes Forest Road 9737 as it follows the North Fork Teanaway River). From the very end of the road, follow the Longs Pass Trail for 1.5 miles to a fork. Take the left fork and continue up to Ingalls Lake. From the lake, traverse toward the left-hand (west) side of Mount Stuart and Goat Pass at 7650 feet. From the pass, drop down and traverse below the northwest buttress, the Razorback Ridge route, and the Stuart Glacier Couloir to the base of the route. Be aware that this second approach will probably be quite difficult without a snowmobile in winter conditions.

Route: The base of this route can be found a short distance to the right of the upper north ridge entrance gully. The first pitch of the route is the most severe. It is usually climbed on thin, potentially mixed ice and rock at WI 3+. This section is

Mount Stuart, Northwest Face Couloir (photo by Jim Nelson)

the technical crux of the line. The remainder of the route generally follows steep intermittent ice gullies and snow patches, eventually gaining the north ridge just below the base of the Great Gendarme. From the gendarme, make a 75-foot rappel on the west side of the north ridge. Alternatively, you might find easier climbing below the ridge and never attain the North Ridge proper. Regardless of the route traveled, the base of the Gendarme route will eventually be gained. From here, follow the path of least resistance to the summit. Parties should expect to find steep snow and ice climbing on this route, along with a spattering of rock climbing up to 5.6.

Descent: There are a number of options available. Previous knowledge of these descent routes will make the experience safer and more fun. Descent options are as follows.

Cascadian Couloir: This is perhaps the safest of the descent routes, as it is the least complex and exposed of the descents. But if you approached via Mountaineer Creek, this is also one of the longest descents. It is important to be wary: If the wrong gully is picked for the descent, a rappel or two may be required.

The Cascadian Couloir terminates to the east just below Stuart's false summit. Traverse the ridge to the false summit and drop down the Cascadian Couloir on the southeast side of the mountain. Descend to Ingalls Creek. If the original approach was made from Mountaineer Creek, ascend toward Stuart Pass, then over Goat Pass to reattain the Stuart Glacier. If the original approach was made from Teanaway River Road, ascend the opposite side of the valley and drop down over Longs Pass.

Sherpa Glacier Couloir: This descent is a bit more complex and slightly more prone to rock and ice fall especially after the spring melt begins in earnest; but it is very direct if you approached from Mountaineer Creek.

Descend the east ridge to the false summit. Skirting below the edge of the ridge on both the north and south sides may be required for this descent. Descend past the top of the Ice Cliff Glacier Couloir to the top of the Sherpa Glacier Couloir at 8700 feet. Descend this steep gully to the top of the Sherpa Glacier. Be wary of ice fall. A few rappels may be required.

Northwest Buttress: Some parties elect to descend via the 1958 Northwest Buttress Variation. This fourth-class descent terminates at Goat Pass. It may be very steep and dangerous in winter conditions.

Rumors of Ice

Dragontail Peak, Folsom-Heller Route: In approximately 1975, Cal Folsom and Don Heller climbed a line on the North Face of Dragontail Peak which may have been one of the first winter excursions on the mountain. Their route climbed snow and ice starting in the hidden couloir of the popular Triple Couloirs route on the mountain. The route reportedly climbs out of this couloir onto the face, later rejoining the Triple Couloirs route at the third couloir. Tragically, Heller slipped below Aasgard Pass on the descent and was killed.

Cashmere Mountain, Northwest Side: Reportedly, there is a gully route here that includes intermittent ice connected by steep snow. Some sections of steep ice and snow exceed 500 feet.

In addition to the gully route, a small waterfall climb has been reported as well.

Reportedly, a small peak across the valley from Cashmere Mountain is known to the locals as J Peak. This particular peak apparently has at least three gullies that are very similar in nature to the north-facing gullies on Mount Stuart. However, unlike Mount Stuart, at least two of these routes can easily be completed in a day.

McClellan Peak: This peak near Dragontail and Prusik Peaks reportedly has at least one long, alpine, water-ice route on it.

WENATCHEE

Wenatchee is about 20 miles east of Leavenworth along U.S. Highways 2 and 97. Because the area's one ice route stands alone and because it is within short driving distance of Leavenworth, we have included it in the Leavenworth chapter of this guide.

REQUIEM FOR THE POST-MODERN WORLD   WI 5+ R/X

First ascent: Mitch Merriman, Alec Gibbons, January 27, 1997

Length: One full pitch

Avalanche danger: Minimal

Approach: Drive north from Wenatchee on U.S. Highway 97 Alternate (US 97A) and park 1 mile south of the Rocky Reach Dam. The route is about 200 feet off the highway.

Route: This route only forms in good years. It involves 150 feet of steep and thin climbing, and is difficult to protect. On the first ascent, substantial portions of the climb were mushrooms and cauliflower ice plastered to rotten rock. *Special gear:* 60-meter ropes are recommended.

Descent: Walk off to climber's right.

ENTIAT RIVER VALLEY

This is an extraordinary little valley with a climbing history that remains nearly unrecorded. Most of the routes throughout the region have been climbed, but the exact details of who did what first have been lost.

Though the routes in the Entiat River valley appear interesting and very accessible there are some private property issues. Many of these approaches cross PRIVATE PROPERTY. Residents and property owners have a pervasive fear of hunters in this valley and as a result there are "No Trespassing" signs everywhere. Some of the signs promise criminal prosecution for crossing property

What Do Ardenvoirs Eat? (Photo by Matt Kerns)

without permission. It is therefore very important to OBTAIN PERMISSION to cross private property whenever possible. It is truly unfortunate that these types of access issues in this valley may prevent the area from seeing the modern ice-climbing development it might deserve. For current access information, log onto *www.wastateice.net.*

As a side note, it has been stated that if one climbs in the Entiat River valley, a visit to the Ardenvoir Café (Coopers Café) for burgers and the local favorite, Buckhorn Beer, is a must.

To reach the Entiat River valley from Leavenworth, drive U.S. Highway 2 for 19.2 miles to US 97. Follow US 97 for 0.7 mile until reaching US 97A. Drive it north toward the town of Entiat for 14.1 miles. Just before reaching Entiat, turn left onto the Entiat River Road. This is the road used to access the following routes.

USGS maps: Tyee Mountain, Brief

TYEE FALLS   WI 4

First ascent: Jim Yoder, mid-1970s

Length: Two to three pitches

Avalanche danger: Minimal to moderate

Approach: The route is on the property of the Tyee Ranch. The route is a pillar on the west (across the river) side of the valley at approximately milepost

20. It is on the lower flank of Tyee Mountain/Ridge, north of the Tyee Creek drainage. The large ice pillar on a light-colored cliff high above the river is *not* Tyee Falls. Information on this large pillar is currently nonexistent. Tyee Falls is located 0.5 mile north of this large pillar near the mouth of the next drainage. It is much closer to the valley floor than the unclimbed large pillar.

The approach to Tyee Falls is a rather touchy issue. To access it climbers must cross a private bridge and then cross land owned by the Tyee Ranch. You must OBTAIN PERMISSION before crossing any private property.

Route: Ascend the beautiful route in two to three pitches.

Descent: Rappel the route.

PRESTON FALLS   WI 2–3

First ascent: Unknown

Length: 100 feet

Avalanche danger: Minimal

Approach: Drive Entiat River Road for 20.8 miles. Preston Falls can be seen on the right at the Tyee Drive turnout. After OBTAINING PERMISSION (there is a house near the turnout), walk to the obvious falls minutes off the road.

Route: Climb the obvious line in two easy steps. Be aware that this route has a high water volume.

Descent: Walk off to the west.

MCCREA CREEK FALLS   WI 3–4

First ascent: Unknown

Length: One to two pitches

Avalanche danger: Minimal

Approach: This route is approximately 22.8 miles along the Entiat River Road. It is directly up a small drainage behind a house. It may be possible to skirt around this person's property, but there is nowhere to park except in their driveway. Therefore, you must OBTAIN PERMISSION to park and climb on these falls.

Route: Ascend the obvious falls in one long pitch or two shorter ones.

Descent: Either rappel the route or walk off to climber's left.

WHAT DO ARDENVOIRS EAT? (A.K.A. THE FANG)   WI 5

This is an incredibly striking freestanding ice pillar that finishes as a hollow tube. The climb is easily seen across the Entiat River between mile markers 23 and 24 on the Entiat River Road.

First ascent: Unknown

Length: One pitch

Avalanche danger: Minimal

Approach: This route is approximately 23.5 miles along the Entiat River Road. Parking might be an issue, and access is a problem. Be sure to OBTAIN

PERMISSION before crossing private property. Cross the river on ice (hopefully).

Route: Ascend the fanglike pillar. A second pitch of lower-angled ice has been climbed a short way above the initial pitch. There may be more climbing farther up the drainage.

Descent: Rappel the route.

Rumors of Ice

Near milepost 20, there is a large rambling climb on the right side of the river basin, 700–1000 feet above the road.

A number of other routes have been completed farther up the valley on the west walls. Information on these climbs is nearly nonexistent. However, there are a number of steep, interesting fangs to be climbed. It is possible to see interesting routes across the river at 21.5 miles, 22.8 miles, and 23.3 miles.

There is a history of climbing farther along the road on Entiat and Silver Falls, but as the plowing ends at milepost 25, a snowmobile or skis are required to make the approach.

COLUMBIA BASIN

It may seem a little strange, at first, that some of the finer ice climbing in Washington can be found not in the mountains, but in the drier eastern high desert regions of the Palisades, Moses Coulee, Banks Lake, Soap Lake and Lake Lenore, the Quincy Wildlife Area, and Vantage. It seemed strange to climbers who explored the area early on as well. It appears that some time in the early to mid-1970s Bruce White's parents brought home photos of their ice fishing trips in the region. What struck White was not the ice fishing, but what was pictured in the background. White, a new convert to the sport of ice climbing, joined forces with the likes of Mark Shipman and Glen Frese to explore the area. These climbers ultimately became perhaps three of the most prolific first ascentionists on waterfall ice in Washington state.

The Columbia Basin is geologically and geographically diverse, with large basins that drain over numerous cliff bands, and with cold winter days and easy access. All these features combine to make the coulees and cliffs of the eastern Washington desert ideal for the reliable formation of an interesting assortment of routes, among them some of the longest and most classic routes in the state.

While some of these routes are fed by large drainages and snowmelt, many are fed by springs, by perennial streams, or by other groundwater flows. This is especially true at Banks Lake, where spectacular ice climbs sometimes form from small seeps halfway up prominent cliff bands.

Avalanche danger is just about nonexistent in the Washington desert, but other objective hazards, not the least of which are falling ice, poor-quality rock, and difficult top-outs, make these routes just as serious as any climbs in the Cascades.

THE PALISADES

There are a number of enjoyable shorter climbs in the Palisades Canyon. This is a 25-mile-long canyon with a river, Douglas Creek, at its base that empties into the Columbia River. The geology of the rock that the ice forms on is similar to that in Frenchman Coulee. Most of the routes fall from basalt cliffs and columns.

There are a few climbs that form reliably, such as *February Falls*, *Falling Falls*, and the *Byram* routes, but most of these climbs, like *Yerba Buena* and *White's Delight* only form in fortunate years. *Falling Falls* in particular tends to come in early and lasts until late in the season.

Unlike most other climbing areas in this book, the climbs in Palisades Canyon

White's Delight (photo by Mark Shipman)

are all either on or accessed across private property. While some of the land in this area is Washington state land or public lands administered by the BLM, most is private land held by a few landowners who use it for commercial agriculture. These landowners have been generally friendly and receptive to discussions about access issues, and are familiar with ice climbing and its history in the canyon; when told about this guide, one enthusiastically suggested we get an X-Games–style ice-climbing structure in Leavenworth.

Historically, the climbs in the Palisades have not formed often, and when they have formed only a small band of local climbers have visited the area. Obtaining permission to climb was easier in the past, and landowners tolerated the presence of climbers. However, as of the writing of this book, the local landowners have asked that we inform our readers that these climbs and the lands they are located on are CLOSED TO ICE CLIMBING. We are fortunate that the landowners we have spoken with remain open to continued discussions about access for the future, and are interested in the legislative protections to landowners that have been introduced recently. Among the concerns that landowners have cited is the potential for lawsuits in the event of injury to a climber. Landowners have also mentioned having bad experiences with climbers, and have therefore requested that we notify our readers of the closure of these climbs.

All climbs in the Palisades, including *Falling Falls*, are CLOSED TO ICE CLIMBING. Land is clearly posted. Do not cross private property or climb these routes. Though there are historic ascents in this area and climbers have been granted permission in the past, we encourage you to respect the wishes of the landowners in this area. If you are interested in learning more about the area, you can obtain the Moses Lake Surface Management Status map from the Bureau of Land Management for detailed information about public and private property lines.

We also look forward to the day when we can resolve these access issues and announce that the Palisades climbs are open. For current access information, please check our website *www.wastateice.net*.

To get to the town of Palisades, from the junction of State Routes 285 and 28 in East Wenatchee drive SR 28 south for 14.2 miles. Turn left onto Palisades Road Southwest and follow it for 11.5 miles into town. Three miles beyond the town Palisades Canyon turns and upper Douglas Creek flows into the main creek from the left.

USGS map: Palisades

AEROBIC SEX   WI 4–5

First ascent: Bruce White and Mark Shipman, 1979
Length: Three pitches
Avalanche danger: Minimal

Approach: The route is 2.7 miles up Palisades Canyon, just before the alluvial fan. It is the left falls of the two. CLOSED TO ICE CLIMBING.

Route: The first pitch of this route is the crux; it is steep, tricky, and often thin. The subsequent two pitches are both easy, with short vertical sections.

Descent: Walk off to climber's left.

WHITE'S DELIGHT   WI 4

First ascent: Bruce White and Mark Shipman, January 1979

Length: 50 feet

Avalanche danger: Minimal

Approach: This route is 50 feet to the right of *Aerobic Sex*. CLOSED TO ICE CLIMBING.

Route: Though not quite as steep as *Aerobic Sex, White's Delight* is still a good short outing.

Descent: Walk off to climber's left.

THE BEST ICE I EVER CLIMBED IN THE PALISADES   WI 5

This is a stiff route found in the lower canyon.

First ascent: Mitch Merriman, Dennis Harmon, Ben Stanton, and Chris Reed, February 1997

Bruce White making the first ascent of White's Delight (photo by Mark Shipman)

Length: Two to three pitches.

Avalanche danger: Minimal

Approach: This route can be found on the right (east) side of the main canyon, across the valley from *Anaerobic Sex*. CLOSED TO ICE CLIMBING.

Route: Climb a full pitch of surprisingly difficult cauliflower ice to the right of a freestanding column. The second pitch climbs the column (which widens near the top) to a slightly overhanging crux, before easing to WI 3. *Special gear:* A 60-meter rope may or may not reach the top of the route. A shorter rope will certainly require an additional short pitch to the top, beyond what is described.

Descent: Walk off.

NEITHER PERMITTED NOR FORBIDDEN   WI 3

First ascent: Mitch Merriman and Ben Stanton, February 1997

Length: One pitch

Avalanche danger: Minimal

Approach: This climb can be found on the right (east) side of the main canyon after *White's Delight* and *Anaerobic Sex* but before the *Byram* climbs. CLOSED TO ICE CLIMBING.

Route: Climb a good pitch of WI 3 to the top.

Descent: Walk off to climber's left.

Byram Left and Right (photo by Mark Shipman)

BYRAM LEFT AND RIGHT   WI 5

First ascent: Mark Sheek and Mark Shipman, January 1984
Length: Two short pitches
Avalanche danger: Minimal
Approach: Immediately after Douglas Creek, on Palisades Road, there is a driveway on the right. The route can be found approximately 300 yards behind the house and can easily be seen from the road. Enter the driveway and OBTAIN PERMISSION before attempting the falls or trespassing. Once permission is obtained, continue up the driveway toward the falls.
Route: Climb the first pitch to a small stance about halfway up. Belay here, then climb the second pitch.
Descent: Walk off.

ANAEROBIC SEX   WI 5

First ascent: Bruce White and Mark Shipman, 1979
Length: 40 feet
Avalanche danger: Minimal
Approach: The route is 600 feet off the main road to the left, near the Douglas Creek Bridge. CLOSED TO ICE CLIMBING.
Route: Though short, this route is steep and difficult. Unfortunately it's often wet, but still fun.
Descent: Walk off.

SKOOKUMCHUCK   WI 5

First ascent: Glen Frese and Bruce White, December 1985
Length: Two pitches
Avalanche danger: Minimal
Approach: This route is 0.5 mile from town on the left. It is on private property, so be sure to OBTAIN PERMISSION. The family that owns this property has had difficulty with trespassers, so tread lightly and DO NOT climb without permission.
Route: Unfortunately, this climb seldom forms. When it is in condition, the best line is on the left side of the falls. There is a good belay stance about halfway up. Usually the second pitch involves climbing on or beside a water tube of ice. Note that because of this tube, it is impossible to hear your partner.
Descent: Walk off.

YERBA BUENA   WI 3

First ascent: Bruce White and Mark Shipman, 1980s
Length: 45 feet
Avalanche danger: Minimal
Approach: This route can be found between mile markers 17 and 18 on

Palisades Road, on the left across the valley. CLOSED TO ICE CLIMBING.

Route: The climb ascends a groove in the hillside, which tops out in a patch of mint. A fun climb.

Descent: Walk off.

THE BLUE COCOON   WI 5

First ascent: Bruce White and Mark Shipman, 1980s

Length: Two pitches

Avalanche danger: Minimal

Approach: Shortly after mile marker 18 on Palisades Road, make a hard right up a steep hill. From the top of the hill note the valley to the right. In the past, two climbs have formed on the left side of the valley. CLOSED TO ICE CLIMBING.

Route: Climb two thin pitches with short vertical steps.

Descent: Walk off.

TRACKS OF MY FEARS   WI 5

First ascent: Mark Shipman and Bruce Tracy, possibly 1980s

Length: One to two pitches

Avalanche danger: Minimal

Approach: The route can be found approximately 200 feet right of *The Blue Cocoon*. CLOSED TO ICE CLIMBING.

Route: Send the route in one to two pitches. Note that the bottom of the route will not come into view until you are close to it.

Descent: Walk off.

FALLING FALLS (INCLUDES JUNGLE LOVE)   WI 5

First ascent: Bruce White and Glen Frese, 1979

Apparently Brad Rogers took a fall at the top of the first pitch way back in 1979. Hence the name, *Falling Falls*! This is one of the most consistent climbs that forms in the Palisades.

Length: Three pitches

Avalanche danger: Minimal

Approach: This route can be found before mile marker 20 on Palisades Road, after a sharp left turn. It is possible to see the route on the right side of the road in a deep bowl. CLOSED TO ICE CLIMBING.

Route: The first pitch includes several short vertical steps, which can be climbed around. The second pitch is usually climbed on the more solid, somewhat vegetated left side, known as *Jungle Love*. Those looking for a real adventure may want to venture onto the relentlessly steep and often chandeliered right side. The third

Falling Falls (photo by Mitch Merriman)

pitch doesn't often form well, but when it does it creates a large freestanding column, which may or may not be attached well at the top. Many parties elect to rappel from the top of the second pitch, unwilling to risk the dangerous third pitch.

Descent: It is possible to descend easily from any of the three pitches. From on top of the first pitch, you can easily walk off to the right. From the top of the second pitch, walk along a large ledge to a bush that can be used as a rappel anchor. From the top of the third pitch, walk to the right until a hill is reached that may be easily walked down.

FEBRUARY FALLS   WI 5

First ascent: Fred Dunham, 1968
Length: 60 feet
Avalanche danger: Minimal
Approach: Continue past *Falling Falls* for a few miles. Park at the cattle guard above the valley. Walk north toward a large bushy tree. Pass the tree on the right. Cross a small fence and continue north toward cliffs. Climb down through a few short cliffs to a small group of trees with red bark. Here the creek can be found that feeds February Falls. Gear up and leave packs on top of the route. CLOSED TO ICE CLIMBING.
Route: Rappel down the beautiful freestanding 60-foot pillar or easily walk down and around to the base. Once at the base, ascend the route.
Descent: Once back on top of the route there should be no need to descend again.

MAYME AND ROSE   WI 4

First ascent: Pitch 1: Justin Busch and Dan Morales, February 21, 2001. Pitch 2: Bruce White and Mark Shipman, 1984
Length: Two distinct 70-foot pitches
Avalanche danger: Minimal
Approach: This route is 300 feet to the west of *February Falls*. When approaching, the lower pitch is not visible and only comes into view when walking downhill and looking over the next basalt cliff in the same drainage as the original (upper) pitch. CLOSED TO ICE CLIMBING.
Route: The lower pitch is a half-rope of WI 3. The original (upper) pitch climbs the beautiful steep ice in the center at WI 4 or harder.
Descent: Walk off.

MOSES COULEE

Twenty miles west of Coulee City, U.S. Highway 2 crosses the Moses Coulee. Rimrock Road (the local name for Moses Coulee Road) accesses the coulee to points south, while Jameson Lake Road accesses the coulee, as well as Jameson and Grimes Lakes, to the north.

Several prominent routes have seen ascents in this part of the Columbia Basin, but there are many other possible routes.

USGS: Jameson Lake SW

BUTCH CASSIDY   WI 5 R

First ascent: Glen Frese and Mark Shipman, January 1985
Length: Two pitches

Glen Frese on Butch Cassidy (photo by Mark Shipman)

Approach: Drive north of US 2 on Jameson Lake Road for 3.5 miles. Park on the road.

Route: This drip is a difficult route to protect. Some parties elect to climb behind the curtain of ice on the first pitch and some ways up, they punch through the ice and continue to climb—an adequate but scary way to protect the first pitch. At the top of pitch one, traverse left to the last 75-foot portion of the climb.

Descent: Walk up and left until on ledges, dropping down as soon as possible. Rappel 70 feet into the gully below.

THE SUNDANCE KID   WI 5

First ascent: Glen Frese and Mark Shipman, January 1986
Length: 125 feet
Approach: This route can be found approximately 4 miles north of US 2 on Jameson Lake Road. At 4 miles, the road splits. Take the left fork and drive to within a couple hundred feet of the route.
Route: Ascend the steep but wonderful ice in the center of the route.
Descent: Walk up and left, dropping as soon as possible.

DAMMIT BOB!   WI 4/5

First ascent: Mitch Merriman, Ben Stanton, and Dennis Harmon, January 1997
Length: Two pitches
Approach: Drive Rimrock Road 0.5 to 0.75 mile south of US 2. Park at a sign indicating a winding road, below the obvious two-tiered climb to the west.
Route: A short 50-foot pitch of WI 3 or 4 leads to the base of the second tier. Climb this for 90 feet to the top, over WI 4 or 5 ground.
Descent: Rappel from equalized sagebrush anchors.

BANKS LAKE

Banks Lake is a man-made lake created by the Columbia River's Dry Falls Dam, which is nothing like its spectacular peer, the Grand Coulee Dam, just up the ol' coulee. Banks Lake is a wildlife area, but is also home to a good concentration of reliable ice climbs. The combination of multitiered basaltic cliffs, springs, seeps, and cold winters makes this a worthwhile destination. In good years, like the winter of 2000–01, an enormous amount of climbable ice can be found here from Thanksgiving to March. In poor years, such as the winters of 1998–99, 1999–00, and 2001–02, very little may form except *Devil's Punch Bowl* and some of the other large lines.

Although it is close to large urban areas (Seattle and Everett are a little more than a 3-hour drive away, and Spokane is closer), Banks Lake ice has not been

More Banks Ice at Banks Lake (photo by Laura James)

visited often by outsiders until very recently. This is a surprise, since reliable ice and its unequalled ease of access makes the area easy to explore. These days, weekends at the *Devil's Punch Bowl* practice area can be crowded with many beginners and climbing classes run by local climbing organizations.

There are numerous one-pitch routes that are steep and sustained in the area, though they sometimes end in hideous top-outs through alders and shrubs. Paul Detrick only half-jokes when he says he is going to bring pruning shears with him on climbs in future seasons. Local climbers and visitors alike climb the looming multipitch classics on the East Shore many times every winter. The taunting weeps across the lake on the West Shore, so visible from the road, see far fewer ascents, both because access can be difficult and dangerous, and because the climbs themselves require a high standard.

Coulee City, at the southern end of Banks Lake, is the gateway to climbing in the area and can be reached a number of ways. From the Seattle area it is fastest to drive Interstate 90 to Ephrata and approach from the south via State

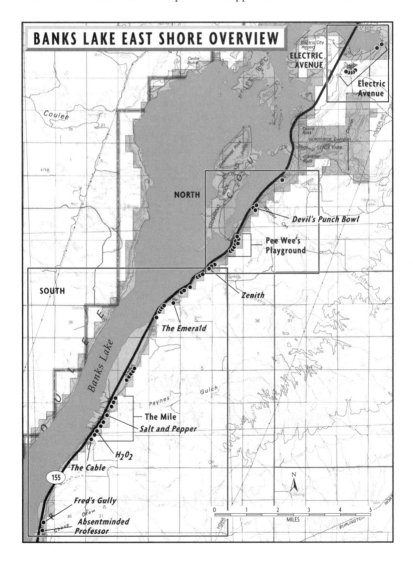

Routes 283, 28, and 17. From Everett and points north, the area is approximately 84 miles east of Leavenworth on U.S. Highway 2. From Spokane, either US 2 or I-90 are adequate. Coulee City has gas stations and small stores.

On the east end of Coulee City, turn left (north) onto SR 155, heading toward Grand Coulee Dam. All of the routes can be accessed from this highway.

Unlike the format that this guidebook generally follows, Banks Lake climbs are described from south to north.

USGS maps: Coulee City, Electric City, Mold, Steamboat Rock SW

BANKS LAKE: WEST SHORE

These large climbs form only after a significant period of cold.

The easiest but most dangerous way to approach these climbs is to walk across the ice on Banks Lake, which is sometimes not as frozen as most climbers would like. Alternately, roads on the west side of the lake might make access to some routes possible from the north and west, but there are currently no known approaches and crossing private property may be an issue.

If you choose to cross the lake, be extremely careful. The lake is a reservoir and the water level fluctuates. If the water recedes, the ice on the lake becomes very brittle and dangerous. Falling through the ice and drowning is a very real possibility. An earlier guidebook recommended carrying or dragging a small inflatable raft as an extra precaution. Another variation on that theme might be to take along a large truck inner tube.

TEA 'N' THE SAHARA   WI 5

First ascent: Bruce Anderson, Bill Crawford, and Mark Shipman, December 1983

Length: Three to four pitches

Approach: Drive 5 miles north on SR 155. This route can be found directly across the lake.

Route: It is possible to climb the curtain, the freestanding pillars, or the easier ramp on the right. The most exciting and exposed route climbs the pillars. The second and third pitches are each approximately 120–130 feet in length, ending in good belay stances. The fourth pitch ascends a short wall to the top.

Descent: Rappel the route.

DELUSIONS OF GRAND DO-ER   WI 6

First ascent: Glen Frese, Mark Shipman, and Curt Haire, January 1985

Length: Three pitches

Approach: Drive approximately 11.5 miles from Coulee City on SR 155. This route can be found across the lake, just south of the boat ramp. As with *Tea 'n' the Sahara*, the easiest approach is to walk directly across the frozen lake.

Route: Ascend the first pitch to an ice cave. Two extremely steep pitches

Glen Frese on the third pitch of Delusions of Grand Do-er (photo by Mark Shipman)

with short overhangs follow. Most climbers choose to ascend the right side for the first pitch and the left for the second two pitches.

Descent: Rappel the route.

Rumors of Ice

There are at least three other very prominent, unclimbed lines on the west side of Banks Lake.

BANKS LAKE: EAST SHORE

Banks Lake's East Shore, from mile 4 to mile 17 along SR 155, has one of the best concentrations of good and reliable ice in Washington. Many worthwhile classics form, while numerous one-pitch routes often fill in the empty spaces. Because many of these climbs form from slow, spring-fed drips, it only takes about two weeks of cold temperatures for even some of the larger routes to form.

While the larger routes have all been climbed, many of the routes listed here have not seen any ascents (sometimes for good reason); ascent information is scarce.

Unfortunately, because some of the shorter routes tend to form from small natural springs in the basaltic cliffs, there is often unpleasant vegetation to contend with. Sometimes it's a nuisance and sometimes it's downright danger-ous. By all means explore; there is enough here for everyone. But be wary that the shrubs are a lot more resilient when confronted with a slashing ice tool than many climbers anticipate from the base of the route. Of course, these same resilient shrubs can offer good anchors, too! For your own safety, when explor-ing new routes with obvious vegetation, pack along a small pruning shear or a pruning saw. You may need it.

THE ABSENTMINDED PROFESSOR (A.K.A. SATAN'S PANTIES)   WI 3/4

First ascent: Unknown

Length: Two pitches

Approach: This route can be found to the east of SR 155 near mile marker 4. A prominent lone tree at the side of the highway serves as a good landmark.

Route: This climb includes four short, vertical steps. Belay at the top of the second step.

Descent: Walk off to the south.

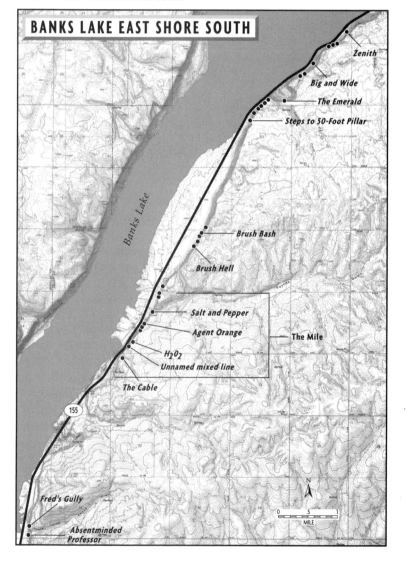

BANKS LAKE EAST SHORE SOUTH

FRED'S GULLY   WI 2

Named for Fred Stanley, this route is an interesting curiosity.

First ascent: Fred Stanley and friends, date unknown

Length: 15 feet

Approach: This route can be found just north of *Absentminded Professor* on SR 155 near mile marker 4, in a deep T-shaped fissure.

Route: Climb a short step to where the ice flattens out, and walk deep into the recesses of the fissure.

Descent: Downclimb or rappel the route.

THE MILE

The Million-Dollar Mile is an expensive road cut where several climbs are clustered, including *The Cable* and H_2O_2.

THE CABLE   WI 5

A striking line, this route's highlight is the very steep and demanding first pitch. In thin conditions or times when there is no ice, it's possible to see the cable for which the route is named. The first pitch can be easily top-roped with two full-length ropes.

First ascent: Jim Yoder, 1984

Length: Two pitches

Approach: This route appears suddenly in a small recess close to the side of SR 155 at milepost 8, directly across from a Banks Lake Reclamation District sign. Park in the large turnout opposite the climb.

Route: Ascend a very steep and sustained full-length pitch. The second, shorter pitch tends to be mixed and scary, and does not always form.

Descent: Walk off to the south.

H_2O_2 WI 5

A true "bumper belay" climb, this is a steep route in two distinct tiers.

First ascent: Mark Shipman and Tom Schibig, December 1984

Length: Two pitches

Approach: This is the first major flow past milepost 8, north of *The Cable* and close to the road. Park as for *The Cable* or directly below the route.

Route: Although the first pitch is much shorter than that of *The Cable* and may form in WI 4 shape, it is nonetheless quite steep and sustained. Ascend the first pitch for about 80 feet to a ledge. The second pitch continues up for another 50 feet or so.

Descent: Rappel the route.

UNNAMED/NORTH OF H_2O_2 WI 4–5

Just north of H_2O_2, slightly set back from the road, is a large one-pitch flow that does not always form. But even when the main column is not in, the lower-angled

The Cable (photo by Greg Mueller)

ice that forms below can make for some practice similar to what you find in the *Devil's Punch Bowl* area (farther up the highway), without the possible objective hazards.

First ascent: Unknown

Length: One to two pitches

Approach: Park below the obvious route just north of H_2O_2 and approach up the hill for a few minutes.

Route: This route may be just some low-angled practice flows, or, if the route is completely in, there is often a steep 80-foot column.

Descent: Rappel the route.

TWO SHORT FLOWS   WI 3

These are two shorter climbs, 40 feet apart, between H_2O_2 and *Agent Orange*.

First ascent: Unknown

Length: One short pitch

Approach: These climbs are found 300 feet right of *Agent Orange*. A short approach up a scree hill leads to the base of the longer flow. The second shorter flow is just uphill to the right.

Route: The shorter flow on the right is only a half-pitch long and ends in shrubs. The longer flow on the left begins with a low-angled ramp for 30 feet, and leads to a steeper 30-foot column.

Descent: Rappel the routes from bushes at the top.

AGENT ORANGE   WI 4+

This is a nice, very full pitch in two tiers. The initial curtain is steeper than it looks, and the final pillar can be desperate. Originally named "Determinator" for Dan Erickson's dogged efforts on lead, Laura James calls this "Agent Orange," and the name is apt: it's what you want for the shrubs at the top.

First recorded ascent: Dan Erickson and Alex Krawarik, 2001

Length: One or two pitches

Approach: This is the first major flow past milepost 8, north of *The Cable*, and close to the road. Park as for *The Cable* or directly below the route.

Route: Start up the vertical flow for 30 to 40 feet to where the climbing eases somewhat. Finish on a stunning 50-foot pillar. Unfortunately, the climb is marred by a difficult top-out through shrubs; exit to the extreme right to reach a tree belay.

Descent: Rappel the route.

SALT AND PEPPER   WI 4/5, MIXED

This is the massive, superlative multitiered climb that graces a minicirque several hundred yards east of the highway. While its second pitch formed very fat at the time of the first ascent, its first pitch has never touched down.

Agent Orange (photo by Laura James)

When it does, it will be a stiff and dangerous full-pitch lead. Until then, reach the start of the second pitch by climbing very loose rock on the left.

First recorded ascent: Paul Detrick and Bruce White, January 2001

Length: Two to four pitches

Approach: The climb is clearly visible from the road, 0.5 mile north of H_2O_2; it is quite unmistakable. A convenient pullout provides ample parking for several vehicles.

Route: This route begins with either a very demanding vertical full-pitch lead, similar in length to but wider than *The Cable*, or a very loose foray on rock to the left of the climb. If the first ice pitch has fallen off or is not quite formed, the ice may still be reached by climbing a treacherous mixed pitch along the left-hand side of the falls. This pitch has a few terribly exposed fourth class moves on horrible rock that is difficult to protect. From the top of the long first pitch, a second pitch ascends directly up in two long tiers, with a large cave and ledge about halfway up. *Special gear:* Ice screws, double ropes. For rock pitch, take knifeblades, Bugaboos, a no. 3 Camalot, and small to midsized nuts. Ice hooks can be pounded into frozen dirt.

Descent: Rappel the route or walk off left. Two ropes reach the top of the first pitch. From here it is possible to rappel the falls directly, though the ropes may end up short of the ground. Or traverse to the extreme left (the top of the

Bruce White and Paul Detrick on the first ascent of Salt and Pepper (photo by Alex Krawarik)

East Shore overview, Banks Lake (photo by Laura James)

rock pitch), V-thread from here, and reach a ledge system after a freehanging rappel over a rotten roof.

Rumors of Ice

Between *The Cable* and H_2O_2 is an obvious right-facing corner that sports an interesting mixed climb. Ascent information is not known.

MILEPOST 9 TO 10

MORE BANKS ICE   WI 5

At milepost 9, a distinctive double-columned flow can be found to the right of a rock buttress. There is a ledge at 20 feet, which offers good rests, but tackling either column to the top means technical and difficult climbing.

   First ascent: Unknown

   Length: One pitch

   Approach: Approach up a scree hill to the base of the route a few minutes from the road.

   Route: Ascend either column.

   Descent: Rappel from the numerous shrubs.

BRUSH HELL   WI 3+

   First ascent: David Burdick and Phil Fortier, February 2001

   Length: 100 feet

Approach: This route is several hundred yards right of *Brush Bash,* south of milepost 10.

Route: Fight up the brushy flow.

Descent: Rappel the route.

BRUSH BASH   WI 4

First ascent: David Burdick, Lenn Kannapell, and Silas Wild, January 2001

Length: 80 feet

Approach: This route can be found just south of milepost 10. There is a triangle of yellow grass beneath the route. Park on the roadside and hike up to the climb.

Route: From the belay under the roof to the right, ascend a short vertical step for 15 feet. Continue up brush-laden, low-angle ice to the final headwall. Ascend 85- to 90-degree ice for another 35 feet to the top.

Descent: Rappel the route using a tree anchor.

Rumors of Ice

Farther along the road, in a group to the left of *More Banks Ice* and another group near *Brush Bash* and *Brush Hell* at milepost 10, are numerous short, one-pitch routes from WI 3 to WI 5 that ascend various curtains, columns, and gullies. Many of these routes sport poor top-outs in alders and shrubs or end in blank roofs, but no one can say they don't offer exciting climbing.

MILEPOST 11 TO *ZENITH*

STEPS TO 50-FOOT PILLAR   WI 4–5

First ascent: Unknown

Length: One full pitch

Approach: This is the solitary, significant route between mileposts 11 and 12. It is on the east side of the highway, just past a short dirt access road and north of *Brush Bash* but before the pullout to *The Emerald.*

Route: Climb ice steps to a final 50-foot pillar.

Descent: Rappel the route.

THE EMERALD (A.K.A. PILLSBURY PILLAR)   WI 4–4+

This is a nice and aesthetic route hidden from the highway in a small valley. Locals have named it *Pillsbury Pillar* for the nonlocal doughboys who come to climb it. The route is usually found in 4+ conditions.

First ascent: Unknown

Length: One full pitch

Approach: There is a small pullout on the east side of the road near milepost 13. From it, a steep path climbs up and left to a small valley above,

Mitch Merriman climbing The Emerald (photo courtesy of the Mitch Merriman collection)

hidden from the road. This route is found at the back of this valley, after a short 10-minute hike.

Route: A short, 20-foot step leads to a shelf. A long, steep, 100-foot pitch of ice leads to a brush-free conclusion.

Descent: Rappel the route.

BIG AND WIDE   WI 4–4+

This is a solitary, wide curtain found almost exactly halfway between *The Emerald* and *Zenith*.

First ascent: Unknown

Length: One full pitch

Approach: Park about 1 mile north of *The Emerald* and approach the climb on the east side of the road.

Route: Climb the large curtain toward the best top-out.

Descent: Rappel the route.

ZENITH   WI 5

Zenith is a large multitiered route, obvious from the road. A superlative, rope-stretching first pitch leads to a shorter pitch and the top. Because it is fed by a fairly voluminous spring, the route comes in very early in a normal year, taking only about two weeks to form in cold temperatures. The bottom pitch typically snaps off several times a season.

First ascent: Unknown

Length: Two to three long pitches

Approach: This route can be found on SR 155 between mile markers 14 and 15, in a minicirque much like the one that shelters *Salt and Pepper*.

Route: Climb two pitches, with the first pitch running nearly 180 feet. It is difficult to set up a belay earlier than this, as the route is near vertical. Be aware that the first pitch of this climb can be tricky. Either use a 60-meter rope or be prepared for the second to simul-climb. In early season the first pitch will have a large solid cone, leading to very thin ice around midpitch, and fattening again at the top. The second pitch can be ascended to the right, up very steep ground for about 80 feet. It is also possible to climb an easier gully to the left.

Descent: Climb or scramble 600 feet up and right. Descend a slope for 300 feet to walk off.

PILLAR ONE   WI 4

This is the first pillar to the left of *Zenith*.

First ascent: Unknown

Length: One pitch

Approach: Approach as for *Zenith*. Hike up the hill to the left of *Zenith* to reach the base of the route.

Route: One steep pitch leads to the top.
Descent: Rappel the route.

PILLAR TWO   WI 3+

The second pillar to the left of *Zenith* is slightly shorter and easier than its immediate neighbor.
    First ascent: Unknown
    Length: One pitch

Zenith (photo by Matt Kerns)

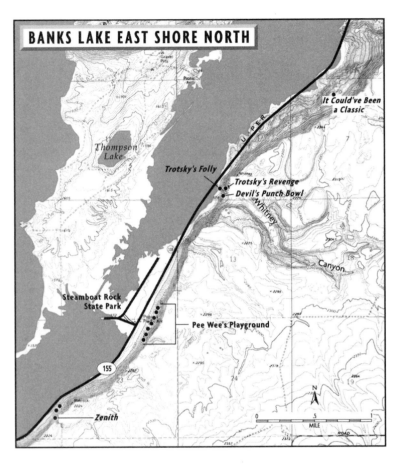

Approach: Approach as for *Zenith,* hiking to the left of it to reach the second pillar.

Route: One steep pitch leads to the top.

Descent: Rappel the route.

Rumors of Ice

Between *The Emerald* and *Zenith* there are up to six one-pitch routes from WI 3 to WI 5. Many of these routes sport poor top-outs in alders and shrubs or end in blank roofs; however, many offer exciting climbing. You can rappel or walk off from the routes.

PEE WEE'S PLAYGROUND

Pee Wee's Playground is a collection of eight or nine distinct lines found directly across from the entrance to Steamboat Rock State Park. Some of the more prominent lines have been climbed as of the winter of 2000–01, but more remain unclimbed.

The one-pitch routes ascend curtains, columns, and gullies and are between WI 3 and WI 5. Many sport poor top-outs in alders and shrubs or end in blank roofs. But look closely, because some of these flows offer high-quality climbing. You can rappel or walk off from the routes.

DEVIL'S PUNCH BOWL AREA

DEVIL'S PUNCH BOWL   WI 2+

Devil's Punch Bowl is perhaps one of the best and most frequented beginner ice climbs in the state. It is spring fed, comes in reliably every year, and is wide enough to support several parties at once. There is one real hazard however: the death-cicles. Typically, huge icicles can form on the roof high above the climbing area, and periodically they come crashing down, obliterating absolutely everything around (hence the name "Devil's Punch Bowl"). When the icicles are present, climbing this route is extremely dangerous.

First ascent: Unknown

Length: One pitch

Approach: This route can be found on SR 155, approximately 1.3 miles north of Steamboat Rock State Park. Note the location of the climb and park

Devil's Punchbowl (photo by Alex Krawarik)

in a turnout just after a guardrail. Cross some large boulders and hike up the scree hill to the base of the climb, about 10 minutes from the road.

Route: There is one short, vertical step that leads to easier ground above. This route makes for a great outing for a first-time ice leader. Again, beware of large icicles above the climb; these can sheer off onto the route at any time.

Descent: There is an old piton anchor at the top of the route on the right, but we recommend you walk off easily to the south.

TROTSKY'S REVENGE (A.K.A. PHASE TRANSITION)   WI 4

This is the steeper line that graces the cliff to the left of the lower-angled *Devil's Punch Bowl*. *Trotsky's* isn't nearly as threatened from above as *Devil's Punch Bowl* is, just to the right, but icicles can still form high above the route and pose a serious threat.

First ascent: Unknown
Length: 120 feet
Approach: This route can be found approximately 40 feet to the left of *Devil's Punch Bowl*.
Route: Ascend ice steps to a steep column.
Descent: Walk off across the top of *Devil's Punch Bowl* and continue south.

TROTSKY'S FOLLY   WI 3

A short practice route is found low and close to the road, on the left of the *Devil's Punch Bowl* area.

First ascent: Unknown
Length: 90 feet
Approach: On the approach to *Devil's Punch Bowl* and *Trotsky's Revenge*, note the small cove to the northeast.
Route: Climb the narrow flow to a fun exit. Continue up the streambed to get to *Trotsky's Revenge* and *Devil's Punch Bowl*.
Descent: Walk off.

IT COULD'VE BEEN A CLASSIC   WI 2

This is a short beginner route that looks more impressive from the road than from close up.

First ascent: Paul Detrick and Alex Krawarik, March 2001
Length: 40 feet
Approach: A little more than a mile north of the *Devil's Punch Bowl* area is a pleasant wooded and rocky glade. The route is visible above the center of a large stand of trees. Approach from the road for about 15 minutes, directly through the trees and avoiding an alder thicket.
Route: Climb the short flow.
Descent: Rappel from the clump of alder on the left.

ELECTRIC AVENUE

This area is variously called The Four Horsemen or Electric Avenue, and is found just south of Electric City and east of Osborn Bay in a recreation area. There is an access road that intersects SR 155 and runs along on the south side of Osborn Bay; this road is usually snowed-in during the winter, so park along SR 15 and hike in. The first five climbs (from which the initial name "Four Horsemen" was derived) are easily visible from the access road, high above a stubble field, south and east of the road. The next five climbs are 1.5 miles farther south on the access road. Only half the routes in this area have seen ascents, all during the winter of 2000–01; however, the routes come in fairly reliably.

Access is an issue; make sure to OBTAIN PERMISSION before crossing private property.

KILOWATT   WI 4+

From the access road, there are five pillars visible above the stubble field. This is the center route, or third pillar.

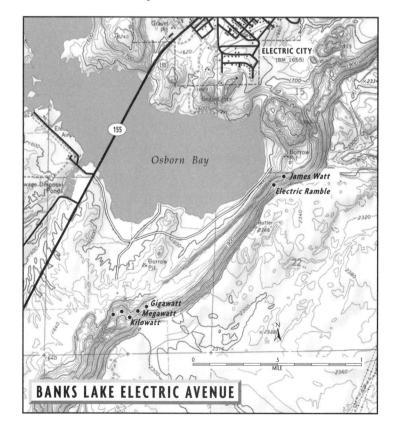

BANKS LAKE ELECTRIC AVENUE

First ascent: Paul Detrick and partner, February 2001

Length: One full pitch

Approach: From the access road, hike in around the private property and then up the scree field. OBTAIN PERMISSION before crossing private property.

Route: Climb a short step to a long steep finale.

Descent: Rappel from the top of the route or from the large ponderosa at the top of *Electric Avenue B* (see below), the unclimbed route one pillar to climber's right.

Mitch Merriman on the first ascent of Megawatt (photo courtesy of the Mitch Merriman collection)

Electric Avenue (photo courtesy of the Mitch Merriman collection)

MEGAWATT   WI 5

First ascent: Mitch Merriman and partner, February 2001

Length: One full pitch

Approach: Approach as for *Kilowatt. Megawatt* is on the second pillar from the left of the five pillars visible above the field. OBTAIN PERMISSION before crossing private property.

Route: This route is steeper and more sustained than *Kilowatt.* Short screws are required for the thin top-out. Belay from equalized sagebrush anchors set far back from the top of the climb. *Special gear:* Short screws.

Descent: Rappel from the top of the route or from the large ponderosa at the top of *Electric Avenue B,* two pillars to climber's right.

JAMES WATT   WI 4

A steep column is easily visible from the end of the access road, directly above it.

First ascent: Paul Detrick and Alex Krawarik, March 2001

Length: 90 feet

Approach: This is the steep column found above the northern end of the small pond, near the end of the access road. Climb the steep and strenuous hillside for 15 minutes to the base of the route.

Route: Climb a steep half pitch with one rest near the top.

Descent: Rappel the route from slings around some small trees, or walk off easily to the right.

ELECTRIC RAMBLE   WI 2

This is a low-angle gully with a dead tree in it, found several hundred feet right of *James Watt*. Paul Detrick and I agreed that while the grade was easy, it was still a pretty fun climb!

First ascent: Paul Detrick and Alex Krawarik, March 2001

Length: 90 feet

Approach: Approach to the base of *James Watt,* then follow the base of the cliff to the start of the route.

Route: This is an easy ramble with one steeper step.

Descent: Rappel the route from trees at the top.

Rumors of Ice

Of the five pillars first encountered and visible above the stubble field from the access road, ascent information is not known about three of them. The rightmost route is *Electric Avenue A*. It is a low-angled flow and may not reach the ground, but it can be approached from above after climbing a neighboring route, such as *Kilowatt* or *Megawatt*. *Electric Avenue B* is a 115-foot route on the next pillar to the left. *Gigawatt* is on the leftmost of the five pillars. The route is one full pitch of WI 5+ on a very steep—even overhanging—pillar. You can rappel all three routes from the large ponderosa on top of *Electric Avenue B*. Make sure to OBTAIN PERMISSION before crossing private property to reach any of these routes.

There are five routes visible from the north end of the access road, including *James Watt* and *Electric Ramble*. *Electric Avenue C* is the one several hundred yards left of *James Watt*. *Electric Avenue D* is the route second from the left of the five routes visible from the end of the road. *Electric Avenue E* is on the left end of the routes visible from the end of the road.

BLUE AND PARK LAKES

Blue Lake is located in Lower Grand Coulee, north of Lake Lenore along State Route 17. There are several prominent ice climbs in the area.

USGS map: Park Lake

Children of the Sun (photo by Mark Shipman)

CHILDREN OF THE SUN
(A.K.A. EVEN COWGIRLS GET THE BLUES)   WI 5

While most area climbers know this route as *Children of the Sun,* Mark Shipman calls this route *Even Cowgirls Get the Blues.* On the way out to bag yet another new route, Mark Shipman and friends encountered a female bartender that had run off the road. Being friendly climbers, they opted to give the woman a ride to a place where she could call for help. As they drove, the story unfolded that the night before, she had gone home with a few of the bar patrons and had enjoyed a "good time." In her rush to get back to her husband before he discovered her side of the bed was empty, she accidentally put her cowboy boots on the wrong feet. She ran her car off the road while trying to correct this unfortunate podiatry problem.

First recorded ascent: Mark Shipman, Freeman Keller, Glen Frese, and Bruce White, date unknown

Length: 130 feet

Approach: This route can be seen above the golf course at Sun Lakes State Park (on SR 17), at the north end of Park Lake. The route is located on a prominent rock wall below the highway as it climbs out of the Lower Grand Coulee from the lake. It is possible to approach from above (a handy telephone pole makes a good top-rope or rappel anchor) or from below, through the small golf course.

Route: Ascend the very steep and beautiful column.

Descent: Walk off.

CLOCKWORK ORANGE   WI 5

First ascent: Glen Frese and Tom Hargis, January 1985

Length: Three pitches

Approach: This route can be found directly across the road from *Children of the Sun* at the north end of Park Lake. Park at Sun Lakes State Park just off of SR 17 and hike up the drainage for approximately 20 minutes to reach the base of the route.

Route: Ascend the center of the climb in three pitches. The first-ascent party climbed the back of the pillar, where water ran over them throughout the climb. Eventually they were able to wrap around and come back out onto the main falls.

Descent: Walk off to climber's right.

SCOTCH ON THE ROCKS AND SCOTCH CAVE   WI 5

First ascent: Glen Frese and Mark Shipman, January 1985

Length: 120 feet

Approach: This route is toward the south end of Blue Lake, directly above the Blue Lake Rest Area and 1 mile north of *Champagne* (see below). Park at the rest area or approximately 900 feet south of it. Hike up the drainage for about 20 minutes to reach the base of the route.

Route: Climb the center of the beautiful route. Alternately, play around in the wonderful "cave" plastered with ice at the base of the first pitch.

Descent: Walk off.

CHAMPAGNE   WI 5

A step up from beer and an area classic! Easily visible from SR 17 at the south end of Blue Lake, the multitiered falls is imposing in its position above the highway.

First ascent: Glen Frese, Mark Sheek, and Mark Shipman, January 1985

Length: Two or three pitches

Approach: Park at the Blue Lake Fire Station and hike up the short but steep hill to the base of the climb.

Route: Climb the first steep section approximately 200 feet to an obvious belay. Walk up the creek a short distance to the second, easier 110-foot section. *Special gear:* A 60-meter rope may be very useful.

Descent: Walk off to climber's right and descend through cliff bands. A short rappel will return you to the ground.

Rumors of Ice

A potential route that seldom forms is found several hundred yards north of *Scotch on the Rocks*.

SOAP LAKE AND LAKE LENORE

Soap Lake and Lake Lenore are two long and narrow lakes that occupy the Lower Grand Coulee just north of the town of Soap Lake. Soap Lake and the larger town of Ephrata just to the south offer all amenities. Large drainage basins and springs feed the routes around the lakes. Like their more famous cousins on Mount Dennis in the Canadian Rockies, some of the routes around Lake Lenore are named after various types of beer. They are excellent stepping-stones for those moving from the WI 4 to the WI 5 climbing arena.

Driving north on State Route 17 out of Soap Lake, there are many places where dark water streaks mark seasonal drainages in the Lake Lenore and Blue and Park Lakes areas, but climbs other than those described below rarely form. Access to these climbs is through Ephrata and Soap Lake from the south, or via U.S. Highway 2 and State Route 17 from the north.

USGS maps: Soap Lake, Park Lake

SOAP LAKE

The west side of Soap Lake hosts three climbs on the lower cliff band, and one higher between the second and third. The leftmost climb on the lower band,

Miller Time, rarely forms, while the rightmost climb on the lower band is the most reliable. Little is known about the climbs other than *Miller Time.*

MILLER TIME   WI 5

First ascent: Mark Sheek and Mark Shipman, January 1985

Length: 75 feet

Approach: When it forms (rarely), this route can be found on the southwestern side of Soap Lake. Exit SR 17 onto Road 23, heading northwest. Drive approximately 1.8 miles before the route comes into view. Rappel the cliff.

Route: Rappel to the base of the climb. Ascend the very steep and challenging 75-foot route.

Descent: Retrace your approach.

SOAP LAKE A   WI ?

This route is the center route of the three located on the lowest cliff band on the west side of Soap Lake. It rarely forms. Walk off to descend.

SOAP LAKE B   WI ?

This route is the rightmost route of the three located on the lowest cliff band on the west side of Soap Lake. It forms the most reliably of the four routes around Soap Lake. Walk off to descend.

SOAP LAKE C   WI ?

This route is the higher route above the three located on the lowest cliff band on the west side of Soap Lake. It rarely forms. Walk off to descend.

LAKE LENORE

Lake Lenore is the next major lake north of Soap Lake along State Route 17. There are several reliable ice routes here that come into shape for some time almost every winter.

GUINNESS   WI 4/5

First ascent: John Barry, Bruce White, and Mark Shipman, January 1986

Length: 140 feet

Approach: Both *Guinness* and *Kickapoo Joy Juice* are obvious from the road at the top of a large shaded gully on the west side of Lake Lenore at mile marker 82. Walk across the frozen lake and up a large hill and gully several hundred vertical feet to the base of the route.

Route: Though it can be done in one rope length, the route has an obvious belay about halfway up. As a result, many parties elect to do *Guinness* in two pitches.

Descent: Rappel the route.

Dan Erickson climbing Rainier Light (photo by Alex Krawarik)

KICKAPOO JOY JUICE   WI 4/5

This route is somewhat shorter than its more prominent neighbor.

First ascent: Unknown
Length: 120 feet
Approach: This route is approximately 100 feet north of *Guinness*.
Route: Generally, climbers ascend the left side of the route, which starts in a gully. Expect to negotiate a few bushes near the top.
Descent: Walk off to climber's left.

LAKE LENORE A   WI ?

This route is found on the west side of Lake Lenore near mile marker 82 on SR 17, lower in the cliffs to the north of *Guinness* and *Kickapoo*. It almost never forms.

LAKE LENORE B   WI ?

This is a short and somewhat reliable pitch of ice.

First ascent: Unknown
Length: 50 feet
Approach: This route is easily seen from SR 17 at the very northern end of Lake Lenore, just past the "Public Fishing" and "Refuse Drop Box" signs.
Route: Ascend the 50-foot pitch.
Descent: Walk off.

LAKE LENORE C   WI 3

First ascent: Unknown
Length: 40 feet
Approach: This short pitch is just south of milepost 83 on SR 17, along the east side of Lake Lenore below the highway. Park at the pullout and hike to the base of the climb.
Route: Ascend the 40-foot pitch.
Descent: Walk off.

BAVARIAN DARK   WI 5

This is considered a landmark route. With its neighbors, it is prominent from SR 17, in the sheltering shade of a short north-facing cliff band east of the highway.

First ascent: Mark Sheek and Mark Shipman, January 1985
Length: One pitch
Approach: Turn south off SR 17, just past mile marker 81. Drive 0.25 mile and park at the gate. Continue another 0.25 mile south until the route comes into view. This is the route on the left.
Route: Ascend the route. Be aware that this route is often thin and difficult to protect.
Descent: Either rappel the route or walk off to climber's left. Alternately, it

is possible to walk about 75 yards right to a bush and make a 30-foot rappel.

SODY POP   WI 4

First ascent: Unknown
Length: 40 feet
Approach: This route is approximately 300 yards north of *Bavarian Dark*. Approach up a short, steep hill and continue 5 minutes to the base of the climb.
Route: Climb the center of the short route.
Descent: Rappel from bushes at the top of the climb or see the descent for *Bavarian Dark*.

RAINIER LIGHT   WI 3–4

First ascent: Mark Sheek and Mark Shipman, January 1985
Length: 70 feet
Approach: This route can be found a few hundred feet right of *Bavarian Dark* along the cliff band.
Route: Steep and short, this route is a little less intimidating than *Bavarian Dark*.
Descent: See the descent for *Bavarian Dark*.

HENRY'S   WI 2

First ascent: Unknown
Length: 70 feet
Approach: This route can be found in a right-facing corner to the right of *Bavarian Dark* and *Rainier Light*. It rarely forms.
Route: Ascend the center of the route.
Descent: See the descent for *Bavarian Dark*.

QUINCY WILDLIFE AREA

The Quincy Wildlife Area currently hosts several known routes. It is likely that these climbs have seen more than one ascent, but the information has been lost to the sagebrush of the Washington desert.

The wildlife area is just north of Interstate 90, south of the town of Quincy. There are several lakes here, with Evergreen Lake being the largest. The routes exist above and below the lakes in large coulees, very similar in character to the nearby popular rock-climbing destination of Frenchman Coulee. The resulting geography of this area is complex and difficult to navigate. A current map of the area and its access roads is essential to facilitate the approach.

Two options exist for approaching these routes:

Option one: The most realistic approach is to exit off I-90 at George. Follow State Route 281 north for 5.2 miles. Turn left (west) onto 5 NW and follow this road for 2.9 miles. As the road begins to curve to the right there will be a sign that says "Public Fishing/Hunting." Turn left onto a road here and follow it for 0.4 mile to a small parking lot and a gate. The gate may be open or shut, either way leave your car here. To park in this lot obtain a Stewardship Decal (available from Colonial Store in George or anywhere hunting and fishing licences are sold) or suffer a $66 ticket. If you find the cost of the decal prohibitive, park in the small lot at the start of the road near the "Public Fishing/Hunting" sign.

Option two: With a mountain bike or skis (depending on snow cover or lack

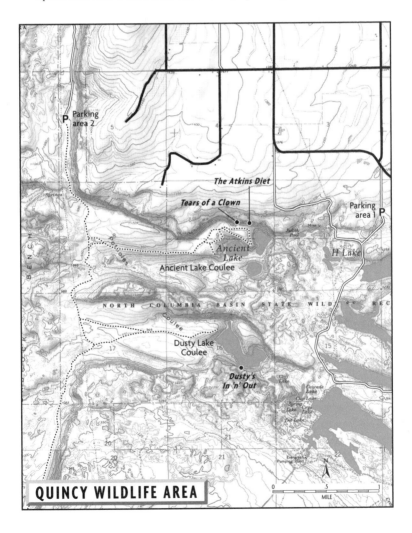

QUINCY WILDLIFE AREA

thereof) this option is perhaps better than the first. Continue on 5 NW past the "Public Fishing/Hunting" sign. The road eventually veers to the right (north) and becomes U NW. Follow this until you reach 9 NW and turn left here. Follow this road as it makes a hairpin turn, dropping down and veering back south. Follow this road until it ends. From the road end, a trail leaves the parking lot heading south. The first left turn into the first coulee provides access into the Ancient Lake Coulee and the second left provides access to the Dusty Lake Coulee.

USGS map: Babcock Ridge

TEARS OF A CLOWN   WI 5

First recorded ascent: Bill Robins and Paul Certa, 2000
Length: One pitch
Approach: This route can be found at the east end of Ancient Lake, a very small lake near the northwest corner of the wildlife area. From the option one parking area follow the road beyond the gate. A short way down the road, just past the first lake, a second road bisects the first. Turn right onto this road toward H Lake. Upon reaching this lake, skirt its left side and continue west cross-country toward the large coulee. After a short distance, another small lake will appear below. Find the trail down and past this lake on its north side. Continue down the coulee, eventually dropping down to Ancient Lake.

Route: Ascend the steep gully and pillar on the rim rock.
Descent: Rappel the route.

THE ATKINS DIET   WI 3+

First recorded ascent: Bill Robins and Paul Certa, 2000
Length: 50 feet
Approach: This route can be found approximately 100 yards east of *Tears of a Clown.*

Route: Ascend the thin pillar.
Descent: Rappel the route.

DUSTY'S IN 'N' OUT   WI 3

First recorded ascent: Rat, 2000
Length: 80 feet
Approach: Dusty Lake is just south of Ancient Lake. This route can be found just west of Dusty Lake on the north-facing side of the coulee. This is a difficult lake to access. From Ancient Lake, walk to the west end of the coulee, skirt around the cliff band, then hike, bike, or ski cross-country back into the next coulee.

Route: Ascend the obvious route.
Descent: Rappel the route.

Rumors of Ice

There is route potential for up to eight more routes in the Ancient Lake area.

There are potentially two to three more lines that come in on occasion, to the west of the route in Dusty Lake.

VANTAGE/FRENCHMAN COULEE

The Vantage/Frenchman Coulee area on the eastern side of the Columbia River has become an extremely popular destination for rock climbers. It is often teeming with climbers on spring weekends when it's wet on the west side of the

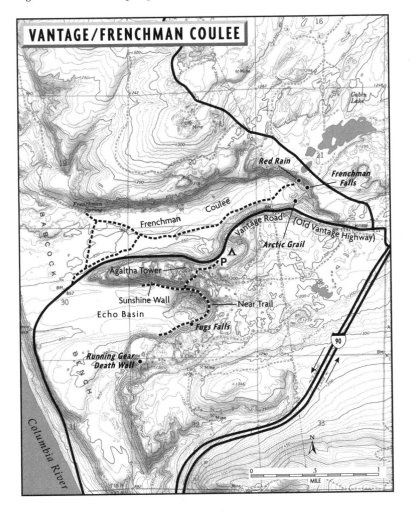

mountains. Vantage also merits discussion as an ice climbing destination, with an additional bonus being that avalanche danger is nonexistent on routes in this area.

Frenchman Coulee is located 2 miles north of Interstate 90. It is smack dab between the towns of George and Vantage. From I-90, take exit 143 and go northwest on Silica Road. After traveling approximately 0.7 mile, turn left (west) onto Vantage Road (Old Vantage Highway). This road continues down to the Columbia River. For our purposes, climbers will want to park at The Feathers parking lot. This can be found on the left 1.5 miles down the road at the base of Agaltha Tower. Park and look for ice!

USGS map: Evergreen Ridge

RED RAIN   WI 4

First ascent: Possibly Jim Oliver
Length: 75 feet
Approach: This route can be found approximately 600 feet to the left of *Frenchman Falls* (see below). Unfortunately, it only comes in every few years.
Route: Ascend the center of the thin and difficult-to-protect route.
Descent: Rappel the route.

FRENCHMAN FALLS   WI 4

First ascent: Unknown
Length: One to two pitches
Approach: This is the ice climb that can be seen while driving down Vantage Road to The Feathers. In the off-season it is the wet streak on the north side of Frenchman Coulee; it is the most obvious falls at the head of the coulee. It is possible to descend into the coulee from just beyond The Feathers parking area.
Route: Ascend the center of the route. There is a step that can be used to break the route into two pitches.
Descent: Rappel the route.

ARCTIC GRAIL   WI 4

First ascent: Possibly Jim Oliver
Length: 75 feet
Approach: This route can be found approximately 400 feet to the right of *Frenchman Falls*.
Route: Ascend the center of the steep ice.
Descent: Rappel the route.

FUGS FALLS   WI 3+

First ascent: Unknown
Length: Two pitches

Approach: This waterfall can be found between Rump Rider Wall and Fugs Wall at the head of Echo Basin. From the base of Agaltha Tower, take the Near Trail across the top of the mesa. Hike past the Tower to the Y in the trail. Follow the steeper trail west up switchbacks until on top of the basaltic plateau. Continue to follow the trail down the notch of the Near Chimney. Once at the base of the chimney, continue in a southerly direction to the base of the falls.

Route: Climb the center of the route and note the good belay stances on ledges. Pins and rock gear are very important for establishing belays. The ice tends

Jens Klubberud leading up Frenchman Falls (photo by Brett Bergeron)

to peter out a bit between the steps. *Special gear:* Pins and rock gear are required.

Descent: Either walk off to the south or rappel the route.

RUNNING GEAR DEATH WALL   WI 3+/4

First ascent: Unknown

Length: 60 feet

Approach: Drive down Vantage Road toward the river. Stop at a pullout just before the road begins to descend steeply. This route is in the next coulee south of *Fugs Falls*. From the pullout, go around a small fence and hike east for 15 minutes.

Route: Climb the obvious route. At the top, there is a nice large boulder to sling for an anchor.

Descent: Walk off to the south.

SPOKANE

Though Spokane is not an ice-climbing destination in and of itself, if you are in the area there are areas to explore. Spokane is easily accessed via Interstate 90.

USGS map: Spokane NW

INDIAN CANYON FALLS   WI 2

Historically, this falls was a favorite winter camp for the Spokane Indian Tribe. Much like Umptanum Falls in the Ellensburg area, this route is certainly not considered a destination climb, but it might be worth checking out if you are in Spokane. The falls and canyon area is popular with winter hikers and photographers; be sure to respect these people. One local climber mentioned that the area always feels less crowded and includes fewer gawkers when climbing in the evening by headlamp.

First ascent: Unknown

Length: 30 feet

Approach: From I-90 on the west edge of Spokane, take Government Road north to Greenwood Road. Follow Greenwood Road as it veers to the west. Take a left on Indian Canyon Drive and continue uphill until a dirt road comes into view on the right. Take this road and park unobtrusively. From here Indian Canyon will be on the right. Descend the trail on the east side of the canyon, enter the canyon, and hike easily to the falls.

Route: Climb the obvious line at the head of the canyon.

Descent: Rappel or downclimb the route.

Rumors of Ice

It should be mentioned that Chilcoe Falls and Copper Falls, both found in Idaho, are considered local climbs by Spokane climbers.

CENTRAL CASCADES

SNOQUALMIE PASS

The Interstate 90 corridor takes a path through the heart of Washington's central Cascades. Only about 40 miles wide, the central Cascade range offers the urban Seattle area its closest access to winter mountains and to the Columbia basin with its colder desert climate.

The I-90 corridor includes the reliable Denny Creek drainage and Alpental areas, as well as the seldom-formed North Bend climbs and climbing outside of Ellensburg at Umptanum Falls. While the majority of the routes found in these areas are shorter climbs and are particularly subject to the vagaries of Washington's maritime climate, ease of access is unparalleled! Because these areas are well-known and well-explored, and because of the ski areas at Snoqualmie Pass, getting information on current conditions and weather is easier here than for other areas in Washington.

When conditions are good, ice-climbing along the I-90 corridor can be an easy half-day affair, with minimal approach. However, with such easy access comes the inevitable crowding on weekends. The Alpental valley in particular can be packed with a large number of skiers, backcountry snowboarders, snowshoers, climbers, and others on a good-weather weekend. If sharing an area or a climb is unappealing to you, consider making a backup plan. When ice-climbing conditions are good along I-90, they will be excellent elsewhere.

USGS maps: Bandera, Snoqualmie Pass, Lost Lake

NORTH BEND

HAYSTACK   WI 2-, OR MIXED

This gully on the summit of Mount Si is seldom in real condition for ice climbing, but it is a fun beginner mixed route when covered with snow and/or ice.

First ascent: Unknown

Length: Two to four pitches

Avalanche danger: Minimal

Approach: Exit I-90 at exit 32, then drive north on 436th Avenue toward Mount Si for 0.4 mile. Turn left onto North Bend Way and drive 0.3 mile. Turn

Franklin Falls (photo by Krista Eytchison)

177

right onto Mount Si Road and follow it for approximately 2.4 miles. The trailhead will be on the left. Hike the Mount Si trail 4 miles to the summit.

Route: The climb begins on the northern side of the Haystack. Climb the obvious snow and ice gully to a saddle. Beginners may want to descend from here. The last 20 feet often require a bit of third-class exposed rock climbing.

Descent: Downclimb, or rappel parts of the route from small trees.

EXIT 38

BLACK ICE CRAG DRYTOOLING PARK   M3–M6

There are several routes in the Drytooling Park; many are unnamed top-roped routes first climbed by a Mountaineers Club ice-climbing course in 2000.

The area is east of what is known as the Exit 38 or Deception Crags rock-climbing area. From I-90 eastbound, take exit 38 and drive 1.7 miles to Forest Service Road 9020. Turn onto FR 9020 and drive 0.2 mile to where an overgrown jeep trail leaves the south side of the road. Hike the jeep trail through light trees to its end at a talus slope, 5 minutes from your car. There is a very rough trail along the left side of the talus slope to the base of the crag. Alternately, it is possible to walk down from the Iron Horse Trail on a nicely carved out path.

The drytooling area consists of crags above and below the railroad grade. Currently there are five sets of top-rope anchors for drytooling below the former railbed. There are plans to put up anchors above the railbed as well.

Leftmost anchor (M4): Climb a line with moss and choss left of the obvious tree.

Second from left (M3): Neat moves peeter out towards the top. This route can be easily climbed free at around 5.6.

Remaining anchors: At press time, grades for the remaining anchors were not available.

CYA   WI 4, M4

First ascent: Gene Yore, John Clouse, and Mark Anderson, December 2000 (top-roped)

Length: One pitch

Avalanche danger: Minimal. Beware of rockfall.

Approach: This route can be found at the Drytooling Park above the railroad grade. It takes a very cold winter for this to form.

Route: Ascend the mixed route. It can be top-roped by walking around the side. There are plans to put bolts in along the route so that it can be led the next time it comes in.

Descent: Rappel the route.

UNNAMED   WI 2+

First ascent: Unknown

Length: Half a pitch

Avalanche danger: Minimal

Approach: This route is 150 feet to the right of *CYA*. Fight your way through brush to get to the base of this smear. It takes a very cold winter for this to form.

Route: Ascend rambling ice, which gradually gets steeper.

Descent: Rappel the route.

RAINY DAY, MELT AWAY   WI 2

First recorded ascent: Justin Busch, date unknown

Length: Half a pitch

Avalanche danger: Minimal

Approach: This route is located just to the left of the previous unnamed climb. It takes a very cold winter for this to form.

Route: Climb up and left to a rambling WI 2 smear.

Descent: Rappel the route.

AMAZONIA   WI 3+

Amazonia is a crag in the Exit 38 (Deception Crags) rock-climbing area. This climb on the wall sees ascents during cold snaps.

First ascent: Unknown

Length: Half a pitch

Avalanche danger: Minimal

Approach: From I-90, take exit 38 and park in the large parking lot as for rock-climbing at Amazonia. Walk up to the railroad grade and walk west to the fairly distinct trail that leads up to the Amazonia area.

Route: Just left of the main Amazonia wall, ice flows over the mossy rock. Climb a short step to a rest, then move on to steeper ice above. A precarious, freehanging 30-foot pillar can also form just to the right of this route.

Descent: Rappel the route.

Rumors of Ice

In addition to the Amazonia climb, there are periodically a few ice smears that come in at the popular rock-climbing area Exit 38 (Deception Crags). The ice routes are primarily defined by the rock routes nearby them. It is possible to find ice on or around the following rock routes: between *Slippery When Wet* and *Stick Boy,* between *Hangover Helper* and *Homo Erectus,* and on *Just Dessert.*

KENT MOUNTAIN

NORTH FACE   VARIOUS MODERATES

A number of interesting moderate climbs can be found behind McClellan Butte, on the north face of Kent Mountain, up the Alice Creek drainage. The routes are either alpine in nature, like the February 1993 summit route of Dallas Kloke and C. Weidner; or are much shorter, like the 200-foot WI 2+ that can be found at approximately 3800 feet on the peak.

First ascent: North Face summit: Dallas Kloke and C. Weidner, February 1993. Ice routes: Unknown.

Length: 200–1200 feet

Avalanche danger: Serious

Approach: From I-90, take exit 42 to access Tinkham Road. Drive south on Forest Service Road 55 to the McClellan Butte Trailhead for Trail No. 1515 at 1500 feet. Ascend the trail and the Alice Creek drainage to reach the base of the north face. A map and compass is a must for people who have not been in this area before.

Routes: At 3800 feet, there are at least two WI 2–3 routes that are approximately 200 feet long. From the top of the ice routes it is possible to continue to the summit (giving your climb a more alpine flavor) via steep snow, short ice sections, and a bit of brushy rock climbing. *Special gear:* Bring rock gear and pins if a summit climb is on the agenda.

Descent: To descend the ice climbs, rappel the routes using trees, bushes, and V-threads. From the summit, walk off to the west and northwest.

DENNY CREEK DRAINAGE

With excellent access from Seattle and other urban areas, the Denny Creek drainage appears to be an excellent place for urbanites to visit. However, a word of warning: Most of these routes are in extremely avalanche-prone environments. Be aware of the snow conditions before launching up a heavily loaded drainage.

It should also be noted that with a few exceptions the routes below tend to be high-volume waterfalls, which only come in during the coldest stretches of winter. Often, there is ice plastered on the rocks next to the main falls, and periodically this can be climbed. But climbers should take heed: The combination of high-volume waterfalls and avalanche-prone slopes mean that the Denny Creek drainage is not a beginner area.

All routes are accessed from exit 47 on I-90.

FRANKLIN FALLS   WI 2–4

Upon seeing this beautiful series of ice climbs ascending falls, don't get too excited. The very end of the trail before actually attaining the climbs can be extremely tricky. One of the authors discovered just how easy it is to fall into the creek when attempting to cross snow bridges above the water. He had to hike out, frozen boots and all, without ever swinging a tool.

First ascent: Unknown

Length: 50 to 70 feet

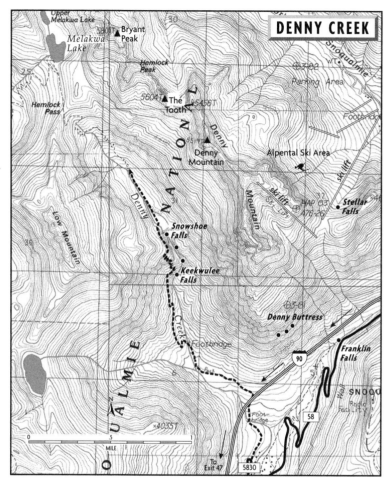

Avalanche danger: Moderate on the far left side of the falls; minimal on the right side.

Approach: From exit 47, turn toward the north side of I-90's eastbound lanes. At the T in the road, turn right and drive approximately 0.25 mile to Denny Creek Road (Forest Service Road 58). (You will cross under I-90's westbound lanes). Turn left and follow the nicely plowed road for approximately 2 miles to a bridge where the road is no longer plowed. Ski, snowshoe, or hike along the road for another mile, turning left at FR 5830. Immediately after turning, a second bridge will appear; do not cross this bridge. Turn right and follow the Franklin Falls Trail on the right side of the creek for another mile. While hiking this embankment be sure to pay attention to interesting climbs in the creekbed below. The falls are directly beneath westbound I-90.

Franklin Falls (photo by David Butler)

In good snow conditions, the total approach time from your car is about an hour. Remember that, unless the snow is very deep, it is possible to fall in the creek in the last 20 yards of the approach. It is recommended that climbers ascend the embankment to the right of the climbs and rappel to the base. If a climber falls in the creek, hike out immediately. *Coordinates*: 47°25.494' N, 121°25.892' W

Routes: After reaching the base of the falls, be wary of falling through ice or snow into the creek beneath. All routes here can be top-roped. The main falls, which seldom come in, can be climbed at WI 4. There are many routes on either side of the falls, which can be climbed at varying degrees of difficulty.

Descent: To avoid falling in the creek, it is best to climb back to the top of the falls and walk off.

KEEKWULEE FALLS   WI 3–4

This is a falls of character in two distinct sections.

First ascent: Unknown

Length: Two pitches

Avalanche danger: Serious

Approach: See the approach for Franklin Falls. Proceed to the Melawka Lake Trailhead and hike up the gentle trail into the Denny Creek drainage. The trail crosses Denny Creek twice on well-maintained footbridges before it climbs some switchbacks and into a large clearing. This clearing is at the base of a steep east-facing slope that holds significant avalanche danger. Keekwulee Falls is located where the trail reenters the trees and begins to climb steeply up along the left bank of Denny Creek. The falls form in two distinct pitches, which are separated by several hundred feet of streambed. Approach by rappelling into the

Keekwulee Falls (photo by David Butler)

drainage from large trees. It is possible to exit the drainage by climbing steep snowbanks, or the falls directly. *Coordinates*: 47°25.871' N, 121°27.081' W

Route: The lower pitch is encountered several hundred feet down the creek from the obvious main falls. It is hidden from view until at creek's edge. Climb the large-volume flow for 60 feet at WI 2 or 3, and proceed to the upper falls along the creek bed. Upper Keekwulee Falls has several lines of varying difficulty—easier on the right, harder in the center and left. Climb for half a pitch to lower-angle ice above.

Descent: Traverse left from the top of the main falls back to the trail.

UNNAMED ABOVE KEEKWULEE   WI 3+/4

First ascent: Unknown
Length: 100 feet
Avalanche danger: Minimal
Approach: Approach as for Keekwulee Falls, and continue 0.25 mile past the falls to where the trail steepens and begins switchbacking along the left bank of Denny Creek. This route can be viewed across the drainage, slightly above the main bed of the creek. Rappel into Denny Creek and leave the rope for an easy return. *Coordinates*: 47°25.945' N, 121°27.064' W

Route: Climb the steep and narrow route to the top.

Descent: Rappel from trees back into the drainage.

UNNAMED RIGHT OF DENNY CREEK   WI 4

A steep drip forms down a small rock buttress at the bottom of a small gully. This can be seen on the right side of Denny Creek.

First ascent: Unknown
Length: One pitch
Avalanche danger: Minimal
Approach: Approach as for Keekwulee Falls, and continue to where the trail steepens and switchbacks up the trail along the left bank of Denny Creek. Several switchbacks past the previous unnamed line, this route can be viewed dripping ominously from a rock buttress on the east side of the drainage, with a lone, almost limbless pine tree at its top. Rappel into the drainage, and possibly leave the rope to facilitate an easy return.

Route: Climb the line—steeper on the left and easier on the right—to the top.

Descent: Rappel the route.

SNOWSHOE FALLS   WI 3+

This is a large-volume falls that requires a long cold spell to freeze.

First ascent: Unknown
Length: 100 feet
Avalanche danger: Minimal

Approach: See approach for Keekwulee Falls. Continue up the Denny Creek drainage from Keekwulee Falls for 0.5 mile until Snowshoe Falls comes into sight, at the top of the switchbacks on the left bank of Denny Creek. *Coordinates:* 47°26.071' N, 121°27.189' W

Route: Climb the obvious falls to the top.

Descent: From the top of the climb, traverse up and left back to the trail.

DENNY BUTTRESS   VARIOUS GRADES

Not much is known about these interesting lines that loom so clearly above I-90. The climbing is varied, with rock, ice, and steep snow.

First ascent: Unknown

Length: Several pitches

Avalanche danger: Serious

Approach: It is easy to see the condition of the ice from westbound lanes of I-90, but much harder to do so from the eastbound lanes. Approach as for Keekwulee Falls, but before passing under I-90 on the trail, bushwhack right and east underneath the highway, until the very steep and avalanche-prone approach slopes come into view. Climb these steep slopes through the trees to the west, until it is possible to traverse up and right to the climbs. *Coordinates:* 47°25.526' N, 121°26.299' W

Route: Pick one of the many lines.

Descent: Rappel the route, often from improvised rock or ice anchors.

Rumors of Ice

Along the approach to Franklin Falls, there are a number of short seeps and drips in the creekbed below the trail. Some are very difficult, while others are short WI 2 gullies.

ALPENTAL

The Alpental Valley hosts perhaps the most readily accessible ice close to the Seattle area. Temperatures here at the top of Snoqualmie Pass are often significantly colder than just a few miles to the west, in the Denny Creek drainage, and the climbs form much more reliably.

This valley is perhaps one of the most intensely explored and climbed alpine areas in Washington, and sports a large number of shorter ice climbs. In good years the ice forms early, before much snowfall, and the ice climbing can be spectacular. In mediocre years the ice will form but be buried by the heavy snowfall. In bad years, temperatures will be too warm and rain will destroy most of what forms in the valley bottom, though better ice may still be found in the alpine reaches of the valley. Many of these routes have been climbed over the years, but there is so much here, and so much potential, that explorers are still rewarded with good new routes.

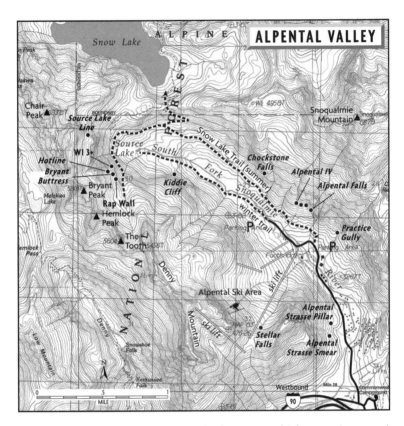

For avalanche control, the ski area (and sometimes highway maintenance) may bomb slopes surrounding Snoqualmie Pass, including slopes near Guye and Snoqualmie Peaks. They often fire artillery shells at Snoqualmie Mountain to keep the avalanche danger down. To find out when shells are scheduled to be fired, contact the Forest Service ranger station in North Bend (425-888-1421) or find the Ski Patrol at the Alpental Ski Area.

To approach the Alpental climbs, drive I-90 to Snoqualmie Pass. Take the Alpental exit, drive under the freeway onto Alpental Road, and continue a short distance to the Alpental parking lot.

ALPENTAL STRASSE PILLAR   WI 4

In very fortunate years, this long thin column forms low on a small east-facing cliff band near the junction of Alpental Strasse and the main Alpental access road. The route is visible 100 feet above the road, on the left, from several hundred feet south of the junction.

First ascent: Unknown
Length: 60 feet

Avalanche danger: Moderate

Approach: Do not park at Alpental Strasse. Instead, continue on for a few hundred feet and park in the ski area's lower parking lot. Walk or snowshoe to the base of the route in 10 minutes.

Route: Ascend the short and steep pillar to the top.

Descent: Rappel the route.

ALPENTAL STRASSE SMEAR   WI 3

In good years, a large slab opposite the hamlet of Alpental forms a nice long sheet of ice. It is found left and uphill of where the Alpental Strasse Pillar forms.

First ascent: Unknown

Length: One to two pitches

Avalanche danger: Moderate

Approach: Do not park at Alpental Strasse. Instead, continue on for a few hundred feet and park in the ski area's lower parking lot. Walk to the base of the route in 10 minutes.

Route: Ascend rambling ice slabs to the top.

Descent: Rappel the route.

PRACTICE GULLY   WI 2

The first large drainage northwest of Guye Peak is low angled with some short steps. It can be completely buried in snow in a normal winter, but forms some fun and rambling ice in a cold early season.

First ascent: Unknown

Length: Several hundred feet

Avalanche danger: Moderate

Approach: This low-angled gully is several hundred yards to the right of the first of the Alpental Falls routes. It cannot be seen from Alpental Falls or from the summer Snow Lakes Trail, but can be easily seen from the lower Alpental parking lot. *Coordinates*: 47°26.835' N, 121°25.127' W

Route: Climb short steps on rambling ice to a final 40-foot curtain of typically thin ice.

Descent: Walk off the top to the right, and then downclimb the lower sections.

ALPENTAL FALLS (A.K.A. ALPENTAL I)   WI 3

This route is easily visible from the Alpental Road just past the lower parking lot. It is the obvious flow on the right-hand side of the clearing and forms quite reliably most winters.

First ascent: Unknown

Length: Two to three pitches

Avalanche danger: Moderate to serious

Approach: Park in the Alpental Ski Area lower parking lot and ascend the summer Snow Lake Trail for 10 minutes to the first steep drainage and opening. The base of the route is at approximately 3200 feet. *Coordinates*: 47°26.853' N, 121°25.342' W

Route: Climb the first pitch to where the ice steepens. Belay from slings on shrubs to the right of the steep step, or at a bush slightly lower on the right. Climb the steep step to lower-angled ice above.

Descent: Rappel the route.

ALPENTAL II   WI 2

This route forms as a lower-angled flow, 100 feet left of *Alpental Falls*.

First ascent: Unknown
Length: 100 feet
Avalanche danger: Moderate to serious
Approach: Approach as for *Alpental Falls*.
Route: Climb low-angled ice (often thin) to an exit into shrubs.
Descent: Rappel the route.

ALPENTAL III   WI 2

This low-angled ice sometimes forms some short and fat steps, before being buried under snow later in the season.

First ascent: Unknown
Length: 200 feet
Avalanche danger: Serious
Approach: Approach as for *Alpental Falls*. This route is found several hundred feet left of the falls, past *Alpental II*, at a short steep column with a large log at the base.
Route: Climb the column (often very wet) to steps above.
Descent: Walk off the route down the main drainage to the left.

ALPENTAL IV   WI 2

This is the flow in the Alpental Falls main drainage gully, on the left side of the large opening.

First ascent: Unknown
Length: 200 feet
Avalanche danger: Serious
Approach: Approach along the summer Snow Lake Trail to the far side of the same opening where *Alpental Falls* is located, and approach the route directly.
Route: Climb short steps for a couple hundred hundred feet.
Descent: Descend the route or walk off through trees on the left.

Alpental Falls (photo by David Burdick)

STREAM DIRECT   WI 3

First ascent: Unknown

Length: 50 feet

Avalanche danger: Moderate. See note about avalanche control in the introduction for Alpental Valley.

Approach: Walk up the summer Snow Lake Trail, past *Alpental I–IV*, for approximately 10 minutes. At the second creek crossing after entering the woods, climb upstream to the base of the falls.

Route: The right side of the falls tends to ascend past some overhanging icicles at the top of an ice cone, then up more moderate 70- to 80-degree ice to the top. The left side is steeper (approximately 85 degrees) and tends to be more solid. Beware: The first 10 feet of the climb is covered by snow midseason, and as a result the route becomes shorter.

Descent: Walk off through the woods and cliffs to the right, or downclimb a short but easy mixed gully to the left.

CHOCKSTONE FALLS   WI 4

This is a route in an interesting setting with real character and an elusive grade. The last short (but vertical) WI 4 pillar is seldom in shape when the rest of the climb is not completely buried in snow, but it does come in fat most years.

First ascent: Unknown

Length: Two to three pitches

Avalanche danger: Moderate

Approach: From the lower Alpental Parking Lot, hike the summer Snow Lake Trail for approximately 1 mile. This route is easily seen from the trail in winter, just before entering the third clearing. The route's most prominent feature is the huge chockstone in the middle of the route that has to be climbed under or around in lean snow years. In heavier snow, this feature (along with the first pitch) is completely buried. The base of the route is at approximately 3600 feet. *Coordinates*: 47°27.096' N, 121°25.757' W

Route: Climb a steep, narrow curtain (often wet) for 30 feet onto low-angled but narrow ice, and proceed underneath the large chockstone. Alternately, climb steep ground to the left of the climb to bypass this first pitch. Climb up and under, or around, the bus-sized chockstone, and up a lovely open book to a final column. In heavy snow years the lower pitches tend to be steep snow.

Descent: Rappel and downclimb the route.

SOURCE LAKE LINE   WI 4/5+

This is an interesting multipitch ice climb located above Source Lake on the approach to Chair Peak. This approach has very serious avalanche hazard.

First ascent: Unknown

Source Lake Line (photo by Alex Krawarik)

Length: Two to three pitches

Avalanche danger: Serious

Approach: Hike to Source Lake from the upper Alpental Ski Area parking lot. Climb steep avalanche slopes directly above the lake, heading for Chair Peak, to the short lower-angled gully that breeches the cliff band. The climb is not visible from the lake, but is located on the right-hand side of a large rock cliff. From the upper mouth of the approach slopes it is possible to see the climb several hundred feet beyond and above to the left. *Coordinates:* 47°27.430' N, 121°27.540' W

Route: The route itself is part of an avalanche drainage gully, so exercise extreme caution. Ascend steep snow and (often rotten) ice to a belay by a fixed pin in loose rock (70 feet). In good years a steep and technical variation touches down here directly from above (WI 5+). A second pitch leads up and right half a rope length along a low-angled snowy ramp. A final steep curtain finishes in shrubs and trees.

Descent: Rappel from trees and ice anchors.

BRYANT BUTTRESS

The summer approach to the Tooth traverses the basin above Source Lake and directly under a large and wet set of cliff bands on the southeast side of Bryant and Hemlock Peaks. The first and lowest cliff band is directly above the summer trail and forms a nice 60-meter, WI 3+ route (unnamed, with a large tree at top) that is often buried after the first snows. But the Rap Wall and the Bryant Buttress climbs are found on the next cliff, 250 feet higher up the easy slopes. This area is popular with skiers and climbers alike, and can be easily approached in winter directly from Source Lake where the winter trail emerges from the short trees into the Source Lake basin.

NOT QUITE A PLUM   WI 3

This climb is found near Bryant Peak, southwest of Source Lake in the cliff bands where numerous ice climbs sometimes form.

First ascent: Justin Busch and John Giebelhausen, date unknown

Length: Half a pitch

Avalanche danger: Serious

Approach: Hike in to Source Lake from the upper Alpental Ski Area parking lot. Continue toward the southwest end of the valley.

Route: No route details are known.

Descent: Rappel the route.

HOTLINE   WI 6

If conditions are good, an 85-foot freestanding pillar can form here.

First recorded ascent: Andreas Schmidt, Sean Courage, Roger Strong, February 1999

Length: One pitch
Avalanche danger: Serious
Approach: Hike in to Source Lake from the upper ski area parking lot. Climb up the couloir toward the Tooth, and then move right several hundred feet along the base of the higher cliff band to the base of this climb.
    Route: The route is a half-pitch freestanding pillar.
    Descent: Rappel the route.

BRYANT BUTTRESS RIGHT   WI 4/4+

This is the right-hand line of the two most obvious flows on the higher cliff band, 200 feet right of *Bryant Buttress Left* and the Rap Wall. You can easily see it from Source Lake when looking up towards Hemlock Peak and the Tooth approach couloir. In some years it forms as a thin pillar; in other years it will form fatter and wider but remain steep and committing.
    First ascent: Unknown
    Length: One to two shorter pitches
    Avalanche danger: Serious
    Approach: Hike in to Source Lake from the upper ski area parking lot. Climb steep slopes above the lake towards Hemlock Peak directly to the base of the route. *Coordinates:* 47°27.239' N, 121°27.287' W
    Route: The route consists of difficult ice that steepens and thins out to a steep and narrow pillar. The route is threatened from above by avalanche-prone snow slopes.
    Descent: Rappel the route or continue up on steep snow and walk off to climber's left.

BRYANT BUTTRESS LEFT   WI 3+

    First ascent: Unknown
    Length: One to two shorter pitches
    Avalanche danger: Serious
    Approach: Approach as for *Hotline* and *Bryant Buttress Right.* This route is on the same cliff band as *Bryant Buttress Right,* only 100 feet left of it, but is not as steep and has a different, less severe character.
    Route: Climb the obvious flow for one or two pitches to steep snow above.
    Descent: Rappel the route or continue up on steep snow and walk off to climber's left.

THE RAP WALL

The next three routes are bolted, modern mixed climbs, closely spaced and each about half a pitch long. They ascend the wet wall that also forms *Bryant Buttress Left.* In good years and in early season, these routes offer real mixed climbing (like, with verglas and ice 'n' stuff!), but at other times they are drytooling practice. In general, the rock is slightly overhanging and more interesting than the routes developed at the Black Ice Drytooling Park described earlier. All the routes were developed in November 2002. Though it is possible to top-rope these routes by walking around from either side of the wall, these routes are typically led.

RZA   M7+

This is a line of seven bolts that ascends a nondescript, 80-foot wall. In winter, the first 20 feet or so of the route might be buried under snow.

First ascent: Blair Williams, Sean Courage, Merridy Rennick, Andreas Schmidt, and Roger Strong, November 2002

Length: Half a pitch

Avalanche danger: Moderate

Approach: Approach as for *Bryant Buttress Right* and continue up and left to the first bolted line, to the right of an obvious bolted overhanging roof.

Route: Climb the obvious line, passing seven bolts to the top.

Descent: Rappel the route from chain anchors at the top. If the anchors are buried, small trees offer an alternative.

CHUCK D   M7-

First ascent: Blair Williams, Andreas Schmidt, Merridy Rennick, and Roger Strong, November 2002

Length: Half a pitch

Avalanche danger: Moderate

Approach: This line is found 15 feet left of *Rza.*

Route: The climbing is very similar to *Rza.* Climb past seven bolts to the chain anchors.

Descent: Rappel the route from chain anchors at the top.

GURU   M9

This is an obvious line of bolts that ascends out an overhanging roof past three technical cruxes, about 40 feet to the left of *Rza* and *Chuck D.* In winter, the first 20 feet or so of the route might be buried under snow.

First ascent: Roger Strong, November 2002

Length: One pitch

Avalanche danger: Moderate

Approach: Approach as for *Hotline,* and continue up and left until the obvious overhanging route is seen several hundred feet further.

Route: Climb the obvious line passing seven bolts. Push through the roof to good holds after the lip.

Descent: Rappel the route from chain anchors above.

LOWER ALPENTAL VALLEY

KIDDIE CLIFF   WI 3–3+

The infamous Kiddie Cliff is an obvious cliff band found above the winter trail leading to Source Lake. The most obvious flow is on the right side of the cliff, next to the Mushroom Couloir, and is one of the most reliable climbs in the Alpental area. The variation on the left side of the main flow, with a small but obvious fir tree above, is aptly named *Oh Tannenbaum*. Other shorter pitches of ice commonly form along the cliff band.

First ascent: Unknown

Length: One pitch

Avalanche danger: Moderate to serious

Approach: From the upper ski area parking lot, follow the winter trail along the west side of the valley until it curves uphill to enter the upper Alpental Valley. Then leave the trail and continue along the base of the cliffs to the climb. *Coordinates:* 47°27.202' N, 121°26.640' W

Route: The route has three main sections: left, middle ramp, and right flow. Kiddie Cliff is the central line starting just right of the small rock cave at the base of the second tier. Ascend directly up for approximately 20 feet until the ramp is intersected. Climb up and left to a small ledge and the base of a squeeze chimney. Climb the bulge/chimney for approximately 10 feet until topping out on lower-angled ice. Continue up and right to a tree belay.

Descent: Either rappel the route with double ropes or walk off on steep ground to climber's right.

STELLAR FALLS (A.K.A. CHAIRLIFT FALLS)   WI 3–4

This particular route is inside the ski area directly to the left of the Armstrong Express chairlift. It is different from *Pan Dome Falls* in the Mount Baker Ski Area in that it is directly above a ski run. As a result, some of the ski patrol people don't look kindly on people climbing it during business hours; others, however, are fine with it. While climbing during times when the lift is operating, respect the skiers and stay out of their way. Note that Alpental Ski Area tends to be closed on Mondays after the first of the year; this is an ideal time to make an ascent, in order to avoid confrontations with skiers or the ski patrol and to protect access. Call 425-434-7669 for ski area information.

First ascent: Unknown

Length: 40 feet

Avalanche danger: Moderate

Approach: Park in the upper Alpental parking lot and hike back down the road for 0.25 mile. Cross the creek on a bridge, then walk back up the creek. If Alpental is open, cross the footbridge from the parking lot. Once across the creek, hike up the slope beside the Armstrong Express chair. Ascend easy snow to the falls. With skis and a willingness to fork over the cash, it is possible to ride the lift and then descend 3 minutes to the falls. *Coordinates*: 47°26.273' N, 121°25.689' W

Route: The falls can be top-roped by walking around to the left of the cliff band. Be sure to acquire a belay to the top of the route, as it is steep.

Descent: Rappel the route or walk off the top.

TURKEY LINE   M5+

Because of its location within the ski area (see the *Stellar Falls* route description), this route has not been bolted due to potential access issues. When and if the access issues ever change, the first ascentionists will bolt the route.

First recorded ascent: Jens Klubberud and Loren Campbell, 2002 (top-roped)

Length: One pitch

Avalanche danger: Moderate

Approach: This route is 40 feet to the right of *Stellar Falls*. The route is on overhanging rock, which is devoid of cracks.

Route: Drytool up the overhanging black rock to a small curtain of icicles. Pull onto the icicles with a gorilla grunt or a figure four and climb 15 feet of ice to the top. To date, this route has only seen top-rope ascents.

Descent: Either walk off or rappel via a small hemlock.

DENNY MOUNTAIN, NORTH FACE   WI 2–3, MIXED POTENTIAL

Denny Mountain is the peak on which the Alpental Ski Area is located. The north face routes are high enough above the ski area so as not to cause an access problem. However, if hiking to these routes, it is recommended that weekends be avoided because there are skiers everywhere on the approach. See the information in the *Stellar Falls* route description.

First ascent: Unknown

Length: One to three pitches

Avalanche danger: Moderate. You have to climb ungroomed, unskied snow with a bit of release potential. It is in an Avalanche Control Zone. Check with the ski patrol before climbing.

Approach: The best approach to these routes is to take chairlifts to the summit and ski *down* to the climbs. Ski the Adrenaline Run, which starts to the right of the Edelweiss chairlift. Descend the mountain, keeping right on Lower International until beneath the North Face of Denny Mountain. From there, hike up 30-degree snow slopes to the gully of choice. If hiking is preferred, park in the upper Alpental parking lot and make a beeline straight toward the North Face. This will take at least 2 hours.

Route: Choose one of the four gullies to climb. There is some mixed potential in the gullies depending on how the ice has set up. *Special gear:* A bit of rock gear, including a few pitons, may be helpful.

Descent: Rappel the routes.

Rumors of Ice

There is at least one report of single-pitch ice climbs that come into shape every few years about 2000 feet up the mountainside above *Alpental II*. The report indicated that there were at least fifteen routes up there.

A large tongue of ice hanging from the leftmost side of Denny Mountain can be seen from the lower Alpental parking lot and the Armstrong Express chairlift. No doubt it would be an epic mixed climb if one were to do it.

There is an interesting Grade II ramble-style climb about 0.5 mile up Snow Creek Trail, in a gully on the ridge connecting Guye and Snoqualmie Peaks. This gully follows steps of intermittent ice and snow for approximately 500 feet; you must gain slightly over 1000 feet of elevation from the trail to the first ice on the ramble. Unfortunately, this is an early-season climb, as it gets covered in snow rather quickly.

Below the ski area's International run, it is reported that there is an early-season gully that can be climbed in a series of steps for approximately three pitches. This is a wooded gully above the upper Alpental parking lot.

There are a few interesting climbs farther back from the Alpental Ski Area, out of bounds in the backcountry, though there is little information available about them.

Above Snow Lake proper are two nice climbs. Each of the climbs is approximately two pitches and can be ascended at WI 4+ and WI 5. To approach, drop over the Snow Lake divide on the way toward Chair Peak. Once again, avalanche danger is severe.

There is an interesting single-pitch climb about 2 miles up the Pacific Crest Trail toward Kendall Peak, at approximately 3800 feet. The route tends to be steep for 20 to 30 feet and then kicks back for the remainder of the pitch. The climb can be done at approximately WI 3. Avalanche danger is severe.

NOTABLE ALPINE CLIMBS IN THE SNOQUALMIE PASS AREA

CHAIR PEAK, NORTHEAST BUTTRESS   GRADE III, WI 3, 5.6

It is not uncommon for this route to be in better shape than the North Face proper. Many parties approach the mountain intent on doing the classic North Face route, only to discover that there hasn't been enough of a freeze-thaw cycle to make the route worth doing. A large number of these parties end up climbing the beautiful and highly aesthetic Northeast Buttress of Chair. It's surprising it hasn't seen more ascents, as it is a much better route than the North Face. Be aware that the Northeast Buttress can be a mixed climb in low-snow years or a climb more like the North Face in high-snow years. Because the low-snow years are what make this route interesting, the beta provided here is for those conditions.

First ascent: Unknown

Avalanche danger: Serious

Approach: Ascend the valley from the Alpental parking lot, continuing past Source Lake and up steep snow slopes to the base of Chair Peak.

Route: From the base of the ridge crest, climb the obvious S-shaped couloir. This tends to trend right and then back to the left. There is a fixed pin approximately 90 feet up. Approximately 200 feet up, there is a stout tree. Belay from the tree. This first pitch is a real rope stretcher. With ice, this pitch is usually WI 3.

The second pitch ascends the broad ridge crest toward the base of a rock gendarme on 45-degree snow. Establish a belay on the ridge or simul-climb for another 200 feet to establish a rock belay at the base of the gendarme.

On the third real pitch, begin a rising traverse to the left across the east face to the obvious steep waterfall. This pitch tends to get steeper toward the top (65–70 degrees) before encountering the falls. From the base of the gendarme a

Chair Peak (photo by Joseph Puryear)

60-meter rope provides ample space to get up and over the waterfall step to a belay at a minor rock rib. Careful routefinding will allow climbers to avoid mixed climbing on this pitch. However, the waterfall is steep—possibly overhanging—and must be met head on. The steep section is short, though, and usually WI 3.

Pitches four and five ascend 45-degree snow slopes to join the top of the North Face route and the summit pyramid.

Special gear: When it is in good form, this is a mixed route that will require an assortment of gear. Include five or six pins, a set of cams, nuts, and an assortment of screws. Short screws tend to work better on this route. A 60-meter rope is strongly suggested.

Descent: Be prepared to back up questionable anchors. As you attain the summit, the rappel anchors should be directly ahead. Two 60-meter ropes are best for the descent, but it can be done in five rappels with a single rope. Conversely, in high-snow years, much of the descent can be easily downclimbed, making one or perhaps two rappels with a single rope. At the base of the route, skirt back around the mountain to retrieve any gear that may have been left behind.

CHAIR PEAK, NORTH GROVE   GRADE III+, WI 4, MIXED

This is a relatively unknown four-pitch route on a well-known mountain. The few strong climbers who have climbed here consider this route to be very Scottish in nature. This relatively fun, moderate route sits next to an extremely futuristic unclimbed mixed line.

First ascent: Possibly Kit Lewis

Avalanche danger: Serious

Approach: Approach as for the Northeast Buttress of Chair Peak. Traverse below the popular North Face route. Pass beneath the entrance gully to the North Face and continue to traverse around the mountain for another 150 yards. An extremely steep, futuristic mixed climb on a buttress will come into view. The *North Grove* is found directly to the left of this buttress.

Route: Ascend two steep, 60-meter pitches in the slight grove to the left of the steep buttress. Expect to climb through WI 3+ and WI 4 bulges. It may be possible to climb around the bulges for an easier ascent.

Finish the climb with two more pitches of steep snow climbing. Attain the summit pinnacle on the right side. Though the climbing on this route is not too difficult, protection is scarce. It requires true patience to find and place good pro.

Special gear: Along with a standard ice rack, be sure to include a few thin pitons, a half set of cams, and stoppers. Sixty-meter ropes are recommended.

Descent: See descent for the Northeast Buttress of Chair Peak.

ABIEL PEAK, NORTH FACE COULOIR   GRADE III, WI 3

Abiel Peak is an important mountain in the Snoqualmie Pass area, and its North Face may have more ice potential than Chair Peak. There are *many* unclimbed

A climber on Chair Peak (photo by Joseph Puryear)

lines on this mountain, most of which are at least three or four pitches long. This peak could be the Ben Nevis of the Northwest.

First ascent: Dallas Kloke and C. Weidner, January 1997

Avalanche danger: Serious

Approach: Abiel Peak is located just above and to the southeast of Lake Annette. From I-90, take exit 47 and drive south, crossing a bridge. Turn left at Tinkham Road and drive 0.3 mile to a parking area. A trail from the lot ascends 1700 feet in 3.5 miles to reach Lake Annette. Ascend road 5590 for a hundred feet or so to find the start of the trail.

There are two options for this approach. The first is to simply follow the trail using snowshoes. The second is to climb up the Humpback Creek drainage to the lake. This second option is better for those who prefer to approach on skis. To climb this drainage, ascend the Lake Annette Trail to the Iron Horse Bike Trail. Turn right (west) on this trail and continue to the drainage. There will be a sign warning of avalanches. Turn left at this sign to climb the drainage. From the lake, the route can be seen just left of the center of the peak. Ascend steep timbered snow slopes to reach the base of the route.

Route: Climb the narrow ice gully ending in a hanging belay. On the second pitch, traverse somewhat diagonally and to the left, ascending two short near-vertical steps. Climb two pitches of 40-degree snow until back into the couloir. Climb the last two pitches in the couloir until near the top. Exit left at the top of the route.

Descent: Descend the broad west ridge. At 4600 feet there will be a saddle from which you must descend through timbered slopes back toward the lake.

Rumors of Ice

The North Face of Abiel Peak has many potential lines for strong ice climbers. Gene Pires and Jason Martin made an attempt on a pure ice line to the right of the center of Abiel Peak. To approach this, ascend the highest snow tongue on the north face to attain steep ice. In January 2002, the ice was rotten and full of air. During a good year this route can probably be climbed at WI 3–4.

There are a number of potential one- to two-pitch lines along the eastern central part of Abiel Peak.

There is a rock rib above Lake Annette that has a couple of potential routes.

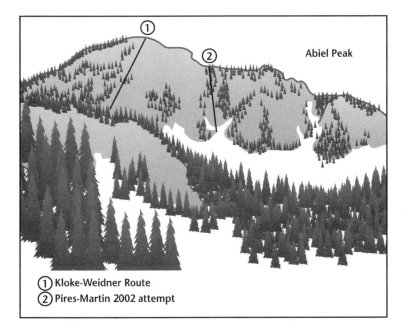

① Kloke-Weidner Route
② Pires-Martin 2002 attempt

Jason D. Martin leading on Abiel Peak (photo by Gene Pires)

ELLENSBURG

Only a few urban areas in Washington state can boast ice climbing within spitting distance of their back doors. *Umptanum Falls* is a nice little beginner route a short distance from downtown Ellensburg, which is east of Snoqualmie Pass along Interstate 90.

USGS map: Ellensburg South

UMPTANUM FALLS (A.K.A. TOOTSIE ROLL FALLS)　　　　WI 2

Umptanum Falls is a popular place for beginners. It is uncommon to meet an ice climber from Ellensburg that hasn't swung their tools on these falls at least once. Many swung there for the very first time.

First ascent: Unknown

Length: 30 feet

Avalanche danger: Minimal

Approach: From I-90, take Canyon Road (Main Street) south into Ellensburg. Follow this for a short distance to Umptanum Road (Wenas-Ellensburg Road) and turn left. Drive approximately 10 miles to a parking area with a trail sign on the left. Park so as to allow other cars room to get by; this road is busier than you might think.

The routes themselves are found in the L. T. Murry Wildlife Recreation Area and are on public land. However, the approach requires the crossing of PRIVATE PROPERTY. From the parking area, follow the creek into the woods. The trail passes by two gates. The landowners allow people to cross their property, but climbers must tread lightly. Make sure the GATES ARE CLOSED after accessing them and be sure to LEAVE NO TRACE. If there is a problem with accessing the falls across this property, it may be possible to walk outside the fence on the left side. This approach is more difficult, but important if "No Trespassing" signs are posted. Either approach takes about 20 minutes from the car.

Route: At the end of the trail, there will be a drop-off into a pool. The main falls that descends this drop is Umptanum Falls. Across the way is another interesting snowmelt-fed route that can be climbed at WI 3+. *Umptanum Falls* is an interesting albeit short climb. It is easier to access when the pool is frozen (because you can walk across the pool to the base of the falls). If the pool is not frozen, the best bet is to lower down the falls, and then climb out.

Descent: Walk off the top.

Rumors of Ice

Esmerelda Peak, Southwest Face: This is the peak north of the parking lot at the end of the North Fork Teanaway River Road (which is a turn-off road from State Route 970, east of Cle Elum). The route is on the left side of a face split by gullies. A snowmobile may be required to make the approach. Little is known about this mountain; Beckey's guide merely mentions it in passing. However, a few notable Northwest climbers have found that gullies that look rather unaesthetic in the summer can be rather interesting mixed snow, ice, and rock climbs in the winter.

A large water-ice climb was ascended in November of 2000 on the North Fork Teanaway River Road.

SOUTH CASCADES

CHINOOK PASS

Due to the winter closure of Chinook Pass and its remoteness from all major populated areas with the exception of Yakima, few ice routes have been established in the area. Perhaps the lack of exploration at the pass is explained by the lack of popular summer climbing in the area; few summer climbers are sitting around on a rock wondering if the waterfall in the distance ever freezes and prodding each other to climb it come winter.

Whatever the reason may be, there *has* been at least one major partnership developing ice climbing in Chinook Pass. Paul Soboleski and Cragg Bryant have become the keys to unlocking the secrets hiding in the area and they are responsible for a number of interesting and memorable first ascents.

Chinook Pass is east of Mount Rainier on State Route 410. Due to the winter pass closure you must approach from east of the Cascades. From Interstate 90 in Ellensburg, take the I-84 exit to Yakima. Turn right onto SR 410, going west to Chinook Pass and Naches (the sign indicates that you are heading toward White Pass and Naches). Shortly after going through Naches, U.S. Highway 12 turns off to the left. Continue straight on SR 410 toward Chinook Pass.

USGS maps: Cliffdell, Goose Prairie

PRACTICE WALL   WI 2

First ascent: Unknown
Length: 20 feet
Avalanche danger: Minimal
Approach: Heading west on SR 410, drive through the small town of Cliffdell. Approximately 29 miles from Naches, right before crossing the Little Naches River, turn right on Forest Service Road 19. The route can be found approximately 0.5 mile down FR 19, on the right.
Route: This short climb is often used as a place for new ice climbers to top-rope.
Descent: Rappel the route.

UNNAMED ON FOREST SERVICE ROAD 19   WI 3/3+, ESTIMATE

First ascent: Unknown (possibly unclimbed)
Length: 40 Feet
Avalanche danger: Minimal

Approach: Follow the approach for *Practice Wall*. This unnamed route can be found approximately 0.6 mile along FR 19.

Route: There are two flows here with no known history.

Descent: Rappel the route.

HORSETAIL FALLS   WI 3

This is perhaps the best-known climb in the Chinook Pass area. It is commonly used as a destination for some of the Mountaineers Club ice courses.

First ascent: Unknown

Length: 40 to 50 feet

Avalanche danger: Minimal

Approach: Approach as for *Practice Wall*. Drive down FR 19 for approximately 0.75 mile until you see a sign reading "Green Dot Trails"; pull out here. Look up from the road to the right at Horsetail Falls. There is literally no hiking approach.

Route: Climb the obvious line up the center of the falls, but be aware: These falls seldom freeze solid. The falls can be top-roped by hiking up and around to the left. Ascend a slope, then turn right and drop down into the drainage. There are trees to top-rope from, but they may require quite a bit of sling material, as the trees are at least 30 or so feet back from the lip.

Descent: Either rappel the route or walk off from the top.

THE GREAT WALL

This is an easily accessed area along FR 19 between Horsetail Falls and the Drowning Pool. The climbs are steep and, in some cases, very thin. Pay attention to the final moves on each of these routes; they require contemplative exit moves, particularly if the ground at the top is not frozen hard enough to accept pick placements. Be aware that two ropes are required for all rappels on this wall.

SNIVELING GULLY   WI 3–4

First ascent: Paul Soboleski and Cragg Bryant, March 2002

Length: 140 feet

Avalanche danger: Minimal

Approach: Approach as for *Practice Wall*. Park at a pullout on the left side of the road, approximately 0.9 mile along FR 19, and walk the remainder of the distance to the climbs on the Great Wall. This first climb can be found 1 mile down FR 19, on the right.

Route: The lower portion of the route ascends an easy ramp to the bottom of a wide semicircular amphitheater. Several variations exist here, with the most difficult line of ascent on the right and the grade easing toward the left. The first-ascent line led up directly beneath the large ponderosa pine tree visible from the road. *Special gear*: Bring double ropes for the rappel.

Descent: Rappel the route from the large pine tree at the top.

UNNAMED ON THE GREAT WALL   WI 4/4+ (ESTIMATE)

First ascent: Unknown (possibly unclimbed)

Length: One pitch

Avalanche danger: Minimal

Approach: Park as for *Sniveling Gully*. This route can be found approximately 1 mile down FR 19 from SR 410.

Route: This is an extremely thin route that may not have been climbed. It is somewhere between 100 and 140 feet long. *Special gear:* Bring double ropes for the rappel.

Descent: Rappel the route.

TWO FACE   WI 3+

First ascent: Cragg Bryant, possibly 2002 (top-rope)

Length: 100 feet

Avalanche danger: Minimal

Approach: Park as for *Sniveling Gully*. This climb is approximately 1.1 miles down FR 19 from SR 410.

Route: This route is formed where two rock faces in the basalt cliff intersect. To date, this climb has not been led. Gear placements are minimal at best. *Special gear:* Double ropes are required for the rappel.

Descent: Rappel from trees.

PEEKABOO   WI 3

This route is so named because, when on the route, climbers seem to be playing "peekaboo" with passing motorists.

First ascent: Cragg Bryant, possibly 2002

Length: 40 feet

Avalanche danger: Minimal

Approach: Park as for *Sniveling Gully*. *Peekaboo* is approximately 1.1 miles down FR 19 from SR 410, a few feet to the left of *Two Face*.

Route: Ascend the obvious line.

Descent: Rappel from trees.

THE DROWNING POOL

This group of three distinct falls can be considered adventure climbing, to say the least, as the approach involves a mandatory river crossing. The falls are approximately 1.5 miles down FR 19 from SR 410, on the opposite side of the river. The water is fast and slightly over knee deep. Hip waders are recommended for this crossing. In low-snow years it may be possible to park in a plowed pullout near the crossing. In high-snow years, when the road is merely a one-lane wonder, drive an additional 0.3 mile to the Quartz Creek roadhead and park, allowing space for snowmobiles to exit the side road.

Cross the river just upstream of a large logjam where a single, large log lays on the far shore (be aware that as winter storms rage, the geography of these logjams may change). Leave crossing gear once across the river—the area is aptly dubbed "The Dressing Room." Hike approximately 100 yards downstream to access the climbs, just past a snow chute, below a short basalt cliff and above the deep pool for which the area is named. Stash gear and rope up here.

The climbs listed here are in the "first" group of falls, farthest upstream. The second and third groups are a scant few dozen feet downstream.

THROUGH THE WOODS   WI 3

This was the first route to be developed in the Drowning Pool area.

First ascent: Cragg Bryant and partner, 2001

Length: 75 feet

Avalanche danger: Minimal

Approach: Begin the climb above the deep pool for which the area is named, at the far end of a snow traverse that ends where the ice begins. Beware: A fall into the deep pool could prove fatal.

Route: This route begins below a cedar tree at the top of the route. Ascend the obvious route toward the tree.

Decent: Rappel the route from the cedar tree.

BEND ME OVER THE RIVER   WI 3+

First recorded ascent: Cragg Bryant and Paul Soboleski, March 2002

Length: 150 feet

Avalanche danger: Minimal

Approach: Begin as for *Through the Woods*. Traverse above the deep pool. It is recommended that a screw be placed before and after the traverse in order for climbers to belay one another across. A small bush can be found at the far end of the traverse, just left of the start of the climb. The belayed traverse does not count as a pitch, but is required to access the routes downstream.

Route: Ascend the obvious route, trending up and right, aiming for a steep notch with a bare rock wall on the right. Ascend the notch past a bulge (crux), possibly requiring mixed climbing, to an alcove. Belay in the alcove. In fat-ice years, a second pitch may continue up from the alcove.

Descent: From the alcove, move right (upstream) a short distance and out to a sturdy shrub. Rappel from the shrub. With double ropes it is one quick rappel to the base, however you can rappel with a single rope by rappelling to the top of *Through the Woods*.

AMERICAN RIVER

UNION CREEK FALLS

WI 3+/4+

First recorded ascent: Cragg Bryant and Paul Soboleski, 2001
Length: 80 feet
Avalanche danger: Moderate to serious
Approach: This route is on SR 410 approximately 9 miles east of Chinook Pass, and 14 miles west of the FR 19 turnoff. Park at the paved pullout where there is a sign for Union Creek Falls. Follow the trail that leads to the first of the falls. Cross the small bridge and climb the drainage to the second set of falls and the base of the route. Cross the frozen pool below the falls and stash gear in the large alcove below the route on the left side. This area can be reached in approximately 1 mile from the road. *Coordinates:* 46°56.195' N, 121°21.683' W
Route: The right side of these falls can be climbed at WI 4/4+, while the left side can be climbed at a sturdy WI 3+. The right side is easily top-roped after leading the left side. Be aware that parts of these falls seldom freeze solid and communication over the noise while climbing may be an issue.
Descent: Rappel from a downed tree on the right-hand side of the falls (climber's right).

Rumors of Ice

Boulder Cave National Recreation Area hosts a number of unclimbed routes in the WI 3 range. A creek flows through a cave and carves a shallow canyon with 30-foot walls on either side. The canyon walls seep heavily and freeze solid. There are more climbs here than can be counted. It is important that visiting climbers avoid entering the cave at the head of the canyon as it is closed for bat hibernation in the winter. This area can be found just west of Cliffdell. Cross the Naches River and look for a brown sign indicating the Boulder Cave. For more information about access and bat hibernation closures, call the Forest Service's Naches Ranger Station (509-653-2205).

West Quartz Creek Falls is an amazing 150-foot free-falling flow. If this beauty ever froze solid it would be Washington's answer to *The Fang* in Colorado. This potential route is located beyond Horsetail Falls, in the hills about 2 miles above Kaner Flats, along Trail No. 952. The falls require a rappel into the canyon for access.

When approaching the Drowning Pool area, note the short wall in the trees on the right. This is an excellent place for new leaders to practice. There is an easy slope on the right that provides access to many trees for top-rope anchors above the flows.

The north side of Fifes Peak (north of SR 410, about 13 miles east of Chinook Pass) may have a bit of ice on it. To attain the peak, an early start or an overnight commitment is required.

WHITE PASS AND U.S. HIGHWAY 12

U.S. Highway 12, south of Mount Rainier, is still an area that appears to be rather unexplored by ice climbers. There are a number of interesting possibilities very close to the road. Certainly there are even more possibilities hiding just out of sight.

USGS map: Spiral Butte

CLEAR CREEK FALLS   WI 3–4

First ascent: Unknown

Length: 80 feet

Avalanche danger: Moderate

Approach: This route is 2.2 miles east of White Pass on US 12, near mile marker 154. Clear Creek Falls is the massive waterfall that drains out of Dog Lake. It is marked on the road by a scenic viewpoint sign. The route is below the highway, and potential climbers must make a rappel or two to attain the base of the falls. Do not pull the rappel line if there is any reason to suspect that the falls are out of condition or beyond a team leader's skill level. If unsure as to whether or not the falls are climbable, fix a line and bring ascenders.

Route: This is a high-flow waterfall that is seldom in perfect condition. However, it does get climbed nearly every year. Spray creates a rather thick line to the right of the main falls. It is perhaps best to climb this when the main falls becomes encased in an ice tube so that freezing spray on the climb is kept to a minimum.

Descent: The descent for this route is actually an ascent. From the top of the falls ascend the drainage until able to climb steep snow slopes back to the road. It may be possible to sling trees for protection if the snow appears to be dangerous.

Rumors of Ice

To the left of Clear Creek Falls there are two ice gullies that form up on occasion.

STROBACH MOUNTAIN

Strobach Mountain has been one of the more exciting areas to develop in Washington in recent years. The discovery and evangelization of the Strobach Mountain ice climbs can be almost singularly attributed to Yale Preston and Larry Nevers Jr., who both lived in Yakima during the discovery phase of this area's initial exploration in the late 1990s. (Preston has since moved to the greener pastures of Wyoming.) Other significant contributors include Dean and Dana Hagin and Paul Soboleski.

Despite being on the Washington ice-climbing map for several seasons, Strobach Mountain is still rarely visited, especially when compared to Leavenworth or Banks Lake. This is directly due to rumors about a hideously long approach, lack of information about the approach, and lack of information about the available climbing in general. In fact, the sheer concentration of good climbing here rivals many East Coast climbing areas, and certainly is second only to Leavenworth and Banks Lake in Washington for number and length of quality routes.

While this may come as a surprise to many climbers in Washington, we have confidence that in very little time Strobach will host a fine concentration of reliable multipitch classics. Climbers from all over Washington will come and sample what the area has to offer—long and very exposed climbs, a lengthy

First on the Left (Photo by Alex Krawarik)

season, and a lot of character. As for the approach, conditions and the time of year make all the difference. It is certainly possible that with the right timing a climber can be roping up at the base of one of the Motherlode monsters inside of an hour from leaving the car. It is equally possible that this same climber will have to endure a 3-hour ski during periods of heavier or more frequent snow. Time the climbing well, and a great outing is sure to be had.

The routes at Strobach are typically steep, multipitch affairs fed by meltwater freeze. The routes are on the east side of White Pass, on a north-facing slope, with base elevations of 4500 feet. In all but the mildest and driest of winters, the ice is reliable. Some of the area classics, such as *Sad Ce'bu* and *Sudden Change of Plan*, are completely appropriate for novice or moderate-level leaders, and should not be missed by any party. There are also some shorter routes near Dome Peak. But there is little else for novices here, with all but a handful of climbs starting in the WI 4 range and climbing right through to WI 5+.

As of the winter of 2000–01, a fair portion of the many lines have been climbed or have seen repeat ascents. These include *First Ice on the Right, Ice Dream, Sad Ce'bu, Sudden Change of Plan, Primus Sucks,* and *Dean and Dana First from Left.* All told, there are at least fourteen to twenty distinct climbs here, with the majority of them concentrated at the Motherlode area.

There is other unclimbed ice near the rock-climbing destination known as Moon Rocks, which you pass on the way to Strobach. Moon Rocks is about 5 miles west on US 12 from its junction with SR 410 and the ice is in the upper gully of the Tieton Valley, past the rock-climbing area.

USGS maps: Foundation Ridge, Tieton Basin

APPROACH

There are several approaches that have been used to reach the Strobach climbing areas over the years. While we have tried to provide easy-to-follow directions, it is essential that climbers come prepared with map and compass. The U.S. Forest Service map for Wenatchee National Forest or Green Trails No. 304, Rimrock, are both satisfactory.

Three approaches are described here: one for the Motherlode area, which stays mostly on well-marked logging roads; a more direct bushwhack route used by Preston and Nevers that lands you at Split Rock Camp; and another route used to approach the climbs nearer to Dome Peak, a mile south of the Motherlode area.

For all three approach options, drive U.S. Highway 12 from either White Pass or Yakima to the Tieton River Road, near Rimrock Lake. Turn onto Tieton River Road (plowed in winter) and proceed 2 miles, passing Goose Egg Mountain, a rocky peak on the right-hand side of the road. It is suggested that climbers always bring skis or snowshoes and a shovel. The roads described may or may not be drivable, depending on snowpack. They are maintained for snowmobile traffic during the winter, but can be impassable for all but the most burly of four-wheel-drive vehicles, even in early season.

Motherlode area: The approach to the Motherlode area of Strobach Mountain can be very straightforward, or an acute pain in the ass, depending on how drivable the roads are and whether or not you use a snowmobile. From Tieton River Road, turn onto Milk Creek Road (Forest Service Road 570). During early season and in light-snow years through December, Milk Creek Road is easily passed with a high-clearance vehicle and chains. Drive 100 yards, and make an obvious left uphill. Now climb steady switchbacks and the winding road past Kloochman Rock on the right to its junction with FR 1201. This is a T-intersection. Turn right onto FR 1201 and proceed past several large clearcuts to FR 609. At the time of this writing, FR 609 was clearly marked. Park here,

and follow FR 609 to where it terminates at a clear-cut, 0.25 mile farther. Strobach Mountain is visible directly to the south, only 30 minutes away, but the ice climbs are hidden by trees. Travel south through the forest, staying high, towards Strobach Mountain. Eventually a large boulder field will be encountered, along with views of the ice climbs. If the snow is not deep, stay on the left edge of the boulder field until able to traverse to the right, underneath the lower cliff band where the ice climbs are clearly visible. Otherwise proceed directly to the climbs.

Preston-Nevers approach: Continue on Tieton River Road past Milk Creek to FR 1202. Proceed up this road for several miles (the road is not plowed), then leave the road and bushwhack southeast through the forest to the right-hand side of the Motherlode area. The *First Ice on the Right* area is on your right (hence the name), and Dome Peak climbs are farther right.

Dome Peak area: To approach the Dome Peak climbs, drive Tieton River Road to FR 1203 and follow it to where it is gated. Park and continue to follow the road up through several switchbacks to where it comes close to Dome Peak. Several clearcuts here offer views of the climbs in this area. Bushwhacking directly to the base of these routes from the clearcuts takes about 45 minutes.

These approaches may be flagged, but it is recommended that climbers enter the area with a map and compass, or better yet, with a GPS with programmed waypoints. After successfully accessing the area once, subsequent trips to Strobach will go much more smoothly.

MOTHERLODE AREA

When Yale Preston and Larry Nevers Jr. first encountered the vast amounts of steep ice in this area of Strobach Mountain, they knew they had stumbled upon a major find. Indeed, they found the Motherlode.

This area hosts the vast majority of climbs currently documented at Strobach Mountain. The climbs are found on a lower cliff-band below Strobach Mountain's northwest face, and are separated into two distinct areas by a large, low-angled gully that is easily identified as the Separation Gully. To the left of the gully, the climbs are steep, long, narrow, and exposed. To the right of the gully, the climbs are less exposed, slightly shorter, and more protected from the wind.

To approach any climb, it is suggested that climbers bring snowshoes or skis. The boulder field below the routes can be very uncomfortable without some kind of floatation.

PRIMUS SUCKS   WI 5

First ascent: Dean and Dana Hagin, 2000
Length: Two to three pitches
Avalanche danger: Moderate

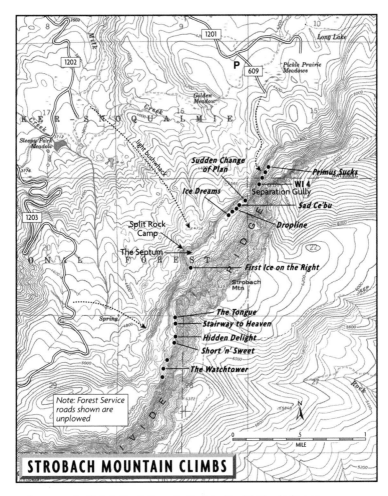

STROBACH MOUNTAIN CLIMBS

Approach: This is the leftmost climb in the Motherlode area.

Route: Climb the shorter, lower-angle, first-pitch flow to the steep, second-pitch pillar above.

Descent: Walk off climber's left or rappel the route.

THIRD ON THE LEFT   WI ?

First ascent: Unclimbed

Length: Two to three pitches

Avalanche danger: Moderate

Approach: This climb is found several hundred feet to the right of *Primus Sucks*.

Route: Climb a short, low-angle flow to the steep pillar above.

Descent: Walk off to climber's far right or rappel the route.

SECOND ON THE LEFT   WI ?

First ascent: Unclimbed
Length: Two to three pitches
Avalanche danger: Moderate
Approach: This climb is found several hundred feet to the right of *Third on the Left.*
Route: Climb a short, low-angle flow to the steep pillar above.
Descent: Walk off to climber's far right or rappel the route.

FIRST ON THE LEFT   WI 4

First ascent: Dean and Dana Hagin, possibly 2000
Length: Two pitches
Avalanche danger: Serious
Approach: This is the distinct two-pitch climb just to the left of Separation Gully. This climb has significant avalanche hazard from above.
Route: The first pitch starts with a vertical column that leads up to slightly lower-angled ice above. There are up to four variations on the second pitch, starting 100 feet above the first and climbing a variety of wider flows. Alternately, these pitches can be reached by hiking up Separation Gully.
Descent: Rappel the route or walk off to climber's right.

Gene Pires and Dave Zulinke at the base of First on the Left (photo by Jason D. Martin)

Sudden Change of Plan and Sad Ce'bu (photo by Larry Nevers Jr.)

SUDDEN CHANGE OF PLAN   WI 3+

This is the last route that Preston and Nevers climbed together at Strobach before Preston's departure to Wyoming.

First ascent: Yale Preston and Larry Nevers Jr., late 1990s

Length: Two short pitches

Avalanche danger: Moderate

Approach: This is the first climb to the right of Separation Gully.

Route: Climb the initial short curtain to the base of the real difficulties. Continue up steep, narrow ice to a short vertical section past some alders and finish on fat ice above. The slightly brushy top-out only slightly mars the overall experience.

Descent: Traverse climber's right from the top to the rappel station above *Sad Ce'bu*. Rappel *Sad Ce'bu* with double ropes.

SAD CE'BU   WI 3

This route is an area classic, with much character, some cerebral climbing, and
a very satisfying finish.

First ascent: Yale Preston and Larry Nevers Jr., late 1990s

Length: Two to three pitches

Avalanche danger: Moderate

Approach: This is the second climb to the right of Separation Gully. It shares
the same start as *Sudden Change of Plan.*

Route: This route can be climbed in two longer, or three shorter pitches.
Climb the initial short curtain to the base of a steep and sometimes fragile column. You can elect to belay here, or continue on into the cave. Ascend the fragile
column to a large cave and a belay. The cave is fairly sheltered from above and
from the wind. From the cave climb 90 feet to finish the route at a small group
of trees.

Descent: Rappel the route.

RIGHT STUFF   WI 4

First attempted by Jim Meyer of Outdoor Research, this climb forms every few
years on the rock wall just right of *Sad Ce'bu.* As of this writing, it has yet to see
a complete ascent.

First recorded attempt: Jim Meyer, date unknown

Length: Two pitches

Avalanche danger: Moderate

Approach: This is the third climb to the right of Separation Gully. It shares
the same start as *Sad Ce'bu* and *Sudden Change of Plan.*

Route: Climb the initial short curtain to the base of a long, weeping curtain. Ascend the curtain to the top.

Descent: Rappel *Sad Ce'bu.*

DROPLINE   WI 4+–5+

"Dropline" is an interim name until someone climbs this thing. This is a very
intimidating and distinctive line.

First ascent: Unclimbed

Length: One to three pitches.

Avalanche danger: Moderate

Approach: This is the third and very distinct climb to the right of Separation Gully. A dead vertical column drops, with a few rests, from a blob of alders
at the top of the cliff.

Route: Climb the initial short (sometimes mixed) corner. Climb the pillar
in one long pitch with several good rests to the top.

Descent: Traverse climber's left to the rappel station above *Sad Ce'bu,* and
rappel that route.

UNNAMED/STROBACH A   WI ?

This is a steep route to the right of *Dropline*.

    First ascent: Unclimbed

    Length: One to two pitches

    Avalanche danger: Minimal to moderate

    Approach: Approach as for *Dropline*. This route is found 100 feet to the right.

    Route: Climb the steep curtain to the top.

    Descent: Descend from trees at the top of the route, or traverse climber's left (north) and descend *Sad Ce'bu*.

Dropline (photo by Larry Nevers Jr.)

UNNAMED/STROBACH B   WI ?

This is the second steep route to the right of *Dropline*.

    First ascent: Unclimbed

    Length: One to two pitches

    Avalanche danger: Minimal to moderate

    Approach: Approach as for *Dropline*. This route is found 100 feet to the right, immediately next to the previous unclimbed route.

    Route: Climb the steep curtain to the top.

    Descent: Descend from trees at the top of the route, or traverse climber's left (north) and descend *Sad Ce'bu*.

UNNAMED/STROBACH C   WI ?

This route is a steep curtain 50 feet left of *Ice Dreams*.

    First ascent: Unclimbed

    Length: One to two pitches

    Avalanche danger: Minimal to moderate

    Approach: Approach as for *Ice Dreams* (below). This route is found just to its left.

    Route: Climb the steep curtain to the top.

    Descent: Rappel the route.

ICE DREAMS   WI 4

This is a great climb with a thin crux and an amusing finish up through the alders.

    First ascent: Larry Nevers Jr. and Yale Preston, late 1990s

    Length: One long pitch

    Avalanche danger: Minimal to moderate

    Approach: This climb is found on the far right-hand side of the Motherlode area, to the right of the Separation Gully. Walk past the other face routes and look for the only route that starts at the back of a gully.

    Route: Climb the initial short curtain to a low-angled slab, then up steep ice through a thin, narrow ice slot. Then "run" up and anchor in the alders.

    Descent: Rappel the route.

UNNAMED/STROBACH D   WI ?

This is the rightmost climb in the Motherlode area. It is unclimbed as of this writing.

    Length: One long pitch

    Avalanche danger: Minimal to moderate

    Approach: This climb is found on the far right-hand side of the Motherlode area, to the right of the Separation Gully.

    Route: Climb the rightmost flow.

    Descent: Rappel the route, or walk left and rappel *Ice Dreams*.

Ice Dreams (photo by Larry Nevers Jr.)

FIRST ICE ON THE RIGHT AREA

Approximately 0.5 mile south of the Motherlode area, the Strobach ridgeline comes down from the upper cliff bands and creates a large natural corner. This large corner is called the Septum. At the base of the Septum is Split Rock Camp, a huge boulder broken in half that provides a sheltered place to bivy. Uphill and to the south is a significant climb, *First Ice on the Right*.

FIRST ICE ON THE RIGHT   WI 4

This route includes fun climbing up a steep headwall.

First ascent: Yale Preston and Larry Nevers Jr., late 1990s
Length: One long pitch

Avalanche danger: Minimal to moderate

Approach: This climb is located 0.25 mile south of the Motherlode area, just south of the rock feature known as the Septum. As this route is set off by itself, it is hard to miss. Climbers will pass by the Split Rock Camp as they make the approach.

Route: Climb the steep headwall, followed by a short slab. After this, climb over a steep bulge, then swim up to an anchor at a tree to the right of the top.

Descent: Rappel the route.

THE WATCHTOWER AREA

Dome Peak is the major summit found along Divide Ridge, to the south of Strobach Mountain. In the vale between Strobach and Dome are several large ice climbs and much untapped potential. The largest potential climb, *The Watchtower,* features a full-pitch vertical column, which then connects to more pitches of lower-angle ice and snow. The route is obvious from the approach and can be seen from the Septum. There are three or more long, multipitch routes in this area, and many shorter ones. Like *The Watchtower,* several of the lines described below have been ambitiously named, but remain unclimbed—the challenge has been laid down. Additionally, there are some climbs on the cliffs below Dome Peak itself, but nothing is known about them as of this writing.

The climbs in this area may be approached via the Motherlode area approach. From the Motherlode area, traverse 1 mile to the south, along the lower cliff bands (easy traversing, 30–40 minutes). Conversely, it is possible to use the FR 1203 approach outlined in the introduction to this chapter.

THE TONGUE   WI ?

This is the leftmost major climb in the vicinity of *The Watchtower.*

First ascent: Unclimbed

Length: 40 feet

Avalanche danger: Minimal to moderate

Approach: From your chosen approach, look for *The Watchtower,* the most obvious and visible long, steep column in this area. *The Tongue* can be found several hundred yards to the left, below and right of a prominent tower. It is 100 feet left of another major line, *Stairway to Heaven.*

Route: Ascend the short flow through the cliff band, with a tree at the top on the right.

Descent: Rappel from the tree.

STAIRWAY TO HEAVEN   WI ?

Just right of *The Tongue* is another route that is a bit steeper and longer than its neighbor.

First ascent: Unclimbed

Length: 70 feet

Avalanche danger: Minimal to moderate

Approach: Approach as for *The Tongue*. The route is found 100 feet to the right.

Route: Climb the obvious flow.

Descent: Rappel from trees at the top.

SHORT 'N' SWEET   WI 5

This is a short, vertical column of ice.

First ascent: Jeff Street and Matt Dickman, 2002

Length: 40 feet

Avalanche danger: Minimal to moderate

Approach: Approach as for *The Tongue*. The route is a short but stout column found between *Stairway to Heaven* and *The Watchtower*.

Route: A short but stiff column leads to trees.

Descent: Rappel from trees.

HIDDEN DELIGHT   WI 3

This route rambles up a short gully.

First ascent: Jeff Street and Matt Dickman, 2002

Length: 70 feet

Avalanche danger: Minimal to moderate

Approach: Approach as for *The Tongue*. The route is a narrow gully just right of *Short 'n' Sweet*.

Route: Climb the low-angle, narrow flow to the top.

Descent: Rappel the route.

THE WATCHTOWER   WI 5/5+, ESTIMATE

An unrelenting thin column leads to more pitches of lower-angled ice above.

First ascent: Unclimbed

Length: Two to three pitches

Avalanche danger: Minimal to moderate

Approach: This route is the most obvious route in the area, a long steep column with lower steps of undulating snow and ice above. It can easily be seen from a distance. It is recognizable from Split Rock Camp and *First Ice on the Right*, and from the clearcuts on the approach to the Dome Peak climbs.

Route: Climb the stiff column in one very long pitch. Lower-angled steps lead up for several more pitches.

Descent: Rappel from trees at the very top of the route, and from ice anchors farther down. Walking off would be arduous.

UNNAMED/DOME A   WI 5

This is another steep column, only slightly shorter than its more prominent neighbor, *The Watchtower*.

The Watchtower (photo by Jeff Street)

First ascent: Unclimbed
Length: One long pitch
Avalanche danger: Minimal
Approach: This route is a thin and narrow column 100 yards right of *The Watchtower*, with a small pocket of snow and trees at the top.
Route: Climb the pillar to the top.
Descent: Rappel from trees.

MOUNT RAINIER NATIONAL PARK AND VICINITY

Mount Rainier and vicinity has long been a destination for climbers from all over the world. People climb the mountain and play in the much smaller surrounding peaks throughout the year. Skiing and mountain climbing in the area are staples for regional outdoor enthusiasts.

However, only a few ice climbers have visited the area in recent years. There was a time in the 1970s and 1980s when local guides wintered in the area and looked for ice potential, but the fruits of that exploration have been lost to modern climbers. Most of the recent ice-climbing activity has been on some of the more obvious formations, such as Skookum Falls, or on alpine routes like those found on Pinnacle Peak. It is our hope that the area's hidden potential will be rediscovered with the following routes and descriptions.

Approach via State Route 410 from the Puget Sound area for climbs near Crystal

Mountain. Climbs within Mount Rainier National Park can be reached by entering the park through the Nisqually Entrance, via Ashford and State Route 706.

USGS maps: Mount Rainier East, Sun Top

GREENWATER

SKOOKUM FALLS   WI 3–4

This is an extremely popular route with the climbers who have worked for Crystal Mountain Ski Resort over the years. Some have climbed this route many times over.

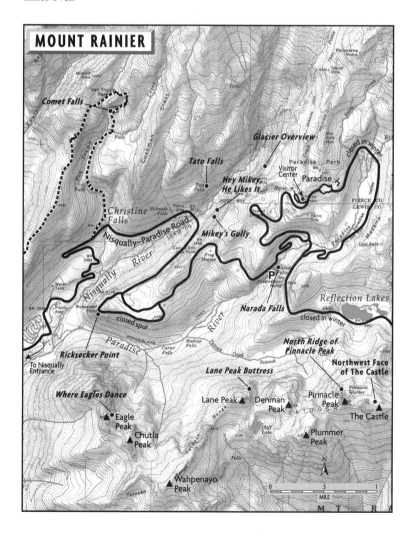

Skookum Falls (photo by Jeremy Allyn)

First ascent: Possibly Bruce White and Glen Frese, possibly mid-1970s

Length: Three pitches

Avalanche danger: Minimal

Approach: This route can be found on SR 410 about 8.2 miles east of Greenwater. Drive to this point to look at the falls before making the approach. To reach the falls, turn onto Forest Service Road 73 approximately 6.2 miles east of Greenwater. Drive this road a short distance, crossing a bridge. Park at the Skookum Falls Trailhead (Trail No. 1194). A Northwest Forest Pass is required to leave a vehicle here. Hike the trail to the base of the falls.

Routes: There are three falls that make up the Skookum Falls climbs. The one farthest to the left is a high-volume waterfall that seldom freezes solid. However, the two falls to the right have a much lower volume and freeze during cold snaps. The left falls is climbable at approximately WI 3. The other lines tend to be harder and steeper: The central falls is probably a WI 3+ and the right falls is a WI 4.

Descent: Rappel using trees on the cliff band. It may also be possible to walk off via logging roads above the falls.

Rumors of Ice

Snoquera and Goat Falls have also been climbed and can be found on SR 410 near Skookum Falls.

There is a large waterfall high above the access road to the Crystal Mountain Ski Resort. It may be viewed by parking approximately 3.1 miles up the road. It can be seen from the "35 mph" sign. This route may be accessible via skis from a chairlift in the ski area, however getting to it will probably require solid backcountry ski skills and ski skins.

MOUNT RAINIER NATIONAL PARK

There are many waterfalls inside Mount Rainier National Park. A large number of these exist at a high enough elevation that they may freeze up rather often. It has been rumored that long ago there was a small guide to water ice in the park, however its existence has never been verified and it has eluded these authors.

Overview of the Nisqually area (photo by Matt Kerns)

COMET FALLS   WI ?

First ascent: Unknown
Length: Unknown
Avalanche danger: Serious
Approach: This route can be found high above the Christine Falls drainage, which is approximately 4.3 miles beyond Longmire. Christine Falls is a high-volume waterfall. High up the drainage, two creeks meet to make the creek that eventually comes down to Christine Falls. Comet Falls can be found somewhere above the 5000-foot elevation mark in the west drainage. A summer trail ascends to the falls from the road slightly before Christine Falls. It may also be possible to access the falls from Rampart Ridge. Any way that these falls are approached is going to be long and difficult.

Route: This route has seen ascents in the distant past, but may not have been climbed since the 1970s. In any case, all information on it has been lost.

Descent: Unknown

MIKEY'S GULLY   WI 3+

First ascent: Unknown
Length: Two pitches
Avalanche danger: Moderate
Approach: From the Nisqually Bridge it is possible to see quite a way up the valley to the terminus of the Nisqually Glacier. Two interesting routes can

Mikey's Gully (photo by Matt Kerns)

be seen on the cliff band upcreek of the bridge. The route on the right is *Mikey's Gully*. Drive past the bridge and park at the nearest pullout. There is an old overgrown road that you can use to access the climbs. Climb through brambles and into the valley. Bypass a somewhat avalanche-prone snow curtain to attain the base of the route.

Route: Ascend the obvious flow.

Descent: Rappel the route. One account indicates that there is an old deadfall at the top of the route. Avoid using this as a rappel anchor.

HEY MIKEY, HE LIKES IT   WI 4+/5

First ascent: Possibly Jack Lewis, possibly 1980s

Length: One to two pitches

Avalanche danger: Moderate

Approach: Approach as for *Mikey's Gully*.

Route: The route ascends a large basaltic cliff face immediately left of *Mikey's Gully*. The ice here tends not to form well. Expect to tie off screws.

Descent: Rappel the route.

TATO FALLS   WI 3, ESTIMATE

This rambling climb is found up the Nisqually canyon beyond the Mikey climbs, on the left-hand side of the canyon.

First ascent: Unknown

Length: Two pitches

Avalanche danger: Moderate

Approach: Approach up the Nisqually canyon past *Mikey's Gully*. There is a large treed slope on the left, and this route is found in a breach about a mile up the canyon.

Route: Climb the rambling route up the low-angle streambed and falls.

Descent: Rappel the route.

GLACIER OVERVIEW   VARIOUS GRADES

First ascent: Unknown

Length: Various

Avalanche danger: Serious

Approach: This broad band of ice can be seen up the valley above *Mikey's Gully*. It is high on the right flanks of the Nisqually Glacier and is fed by water melting off the Muir Snowfield. Climbing the valley to the base of the route is a long and arduous journey. It may be possible to make this approach from Paradise. Be aware of avalanche danger, as there is 40-degree snow both above and below this area.

Routes: There are many possibilities.

Descent: Rappel the routes.

Hey Mikey, He Likes It (photo by Loren Campbell)

RICKSECKER POINT (THE BLUE ROOM)   WI 3–5

This area was named after a civil engineer who first surveyed potential road routes to Mount Rainier. Most ice climbers refer to the area as "The Blue Room." At one time this area was commonly used for climbing courses from the Evergreen State College.

First ascent: Possibly John Lawson, possibly 1980s

Length: One pitch

Avalanche danger: Minimal to moderate

Approach: Shortly after crossing the Nisqually Bridge a closed spur road will jut off to the right. This is Glacier Hill Road. Park in the pullout at the gated road. Hike this road to Ricksecker Point. The routes can be found below the road. To access them, rappel down to the base. Beware of avalanche danger at the bottom of the climbs.

Routes: Four to five routes can be found in The Blue Room. Unfortunately, because the ice is seldom great, these routes are usually top-roped—which is easily done from trees. Climbers may need to top-rope with two ropes tied together if set up with a slingshot belay. Do not rappel and pull the rope unless there is no question that the routes are in shape and climbable.

Descent: All climbs are finished on the road.

NARADA FALLS   WI 4

First ascent: Unknown

Length: One to two pitches

Avalanche danger: Minimal

Approach: Park at the Narada Falls parking area, approximately 8 miles past Longmire and about 14 miles from the Nisqually Entrance on the way toward Paradise. It is possible to rappel down into the basin to climb the falls. Before committing to this, walk across the bridge to the other side of the falls and climb down snow slopes to check the condition of the route.

Route: The falls cascades down below the bridge and parking area. The route can easily be top-roped from above. Beware, the falls have a large volume of water and seldom freeze solid. More often than not the left-hand side of the falls comes in first. The crux of the route is the initial vertical curtain, after which the route becomes WI 3. A number of climbers have reported near misses on this route, where they have sent it and then watched it fall apart. Watch the conditions closely before getting on this route.

Descent: Walk back to your car when finished.

LANE PEAK BUTTRESS   WI 3–4

First ascent: Possibly Craig John and George Sherrit, possibly 1980s

Length: One pitch

Avalanche danger: Serious

Approach: Park at the Narada Falls parking area. Ascend a steep snow slope above the restroom facilities to attain the Stevens Canyon Road (a popular cross-country ski route in winter). Follow this road to the right until able to traverse in a southeasterly direction below the serious crags of the Tatoosh Range. These routes can be found on a rock buttress beneath Lane Peak.

Routes: There are at least three routes on this buttress beneath Lane Peak. At least one of the routes begins on easy ice and ends on a WI 4 pillar. Some of the potential routes on the buttress are as short as half a pitch. You can easily make a day of climbing out of a trip to this area. *Note:* Lane Peak itself is commonly climbed in the winter via a relatively easy snow and ice gully (the gully on the extreme left) called *The Zipper*. There are variations on this alpine climb that can make it quite an interesting ice or mixed route.

Descent: Rappel the routes using a V-thread.

Rumors of Ice

There is a flow directly to the left of Narada Falls that can be climbed at WI 4. There are a few other seeps to the left that can be climbed at WI 2. There are approximately eight possible climbs in the Narada basin, many of which are quite engaging. Be aware however, that some of the lines farther down the gully may have significantly more avalanche danger than those next to the main falls.

There is a moderately large flow that forms up nearly every year on the northwest face of the Castle (in the Tatoosh Range). The route has varied in the past. At times it has been up to 200 feet long. It appears to be somewhat tiered, with bulges up to 70 degrees. More often than not, reports concerning this route have been made in March and April. It may be covered by snow earlier in the season.

Some of the small cliff bands on the Muir Snowfield tend to have small lines that form on them throughout the year.

George Dunn and another climber on Narada Falls (photo by Eric Simonson)

There is a 400-foot WI 2 at Observation Rock on the north side of Rainier. This can be approached from Spray Park. Other ice has been reported around this area.

There are a few small climbs around the base of the Carbon Glacier (on Rainier's north face). These are indeed small: At 30 to 40 feet they are only worth climbing if you are already in the area.

NOTABLE ALPINE CLIMBS IN THE MOUNT RAINIER AREA

PINNACLE PEAK, NORTH RIDGE   GRADE II, WI 2, 5.2

This is a beautiful winter alpine route with variations that can make it a beginner mixed ice route or an advanced route. In good conditions, Pinnacle Peak is hard to beat.

First winter ascent: Eric Bjornstad, John Holland, and Ed Cooper, January 1965

Avalanche danger: Serious

Approach: Park at the Narada Falls parking area and ascend the snow-covered Stevens Canyon Road toward Reflection Lakes (4854 feet). The steep North Ridge will come into view from the road. Ascend easy snow slopes toward the objective. At about 5800 feet, the snow will become steep. Beware of avalanche danger.

Route: As the approach becomes steeper and steeper, pull out the rope and tools. Continue up steep snow and ice through a gully for approximately two pitches to eventually attain a rock outcropping. Here there are two choices to attain the summit: Either climb up an exposed snow gully to the left, or climb steep free-hanging icicles to the right.

Descent: Downclimb and rappel the route. It may also be possible to downclimb and rappel into the Castle-Pinnacle saddle to make the descent.

EAGLE PEAK: WHERE EAGLES DANCE   WI 4–5, ESTIMATE

Due to the fact that this peak apparently has a named ice route on it, it is important to mention. But little is known about the route.

First ascent: Possibly Jack Lewis

Avalanche danger: Serious

Approach and route: Eagle Peak is the farthest peak to the west in the Tatoosh Range. The route ascends a thin gully that is probably located somewhere on the northeast face. Access the peak via Longmire and the Eagle Peak Trail. Ascend this trail to the east, eventually gaining the saddle between Eagle and Chutla Peaks. From this point forward, explore the area. There are many steep faces and gullies . . . . As always be aware of avalanche potential.

OUTLYING AREAS OF WASHINGTON

THE OREGON BORDER

During the coldest of cold years, a few routes form above the Columbia River on State Route 14 just east of Camas. It must be stressed that these routes only come in once every five or six years. Climbers must wait for a serious cold snap before making any kind of journey to attain an ascent of any of the routes described below.

It has been reported that the Portland climbers who first visited this area and the areas across the river in Oregon kept 5-gallon buckets of water in their yards. When there was 6 inches of ice in the bucket, they knew they could get up some of the climbs in the Gorge. When the bucket was frozen solid, they knew they could make an attempt on Hamilton Mountain or on one of the other long, committing climbs on the Oregon side. In fact, during the early years of climbing in the Gorge, it was not uncommon for the Columbia to freeze all the way across. These days, the mighty river seldom does this.

Though the described routes are only slightly off the highway, are south-facing, and seldom form, they have been included here for the sake of posterity. They have also been included because they are an indicator of the area's potential during bone-chilling years. SR 14 has quite a few possibilities and they should not be ignored.

One last note about those who came before: the climbers who put up these routes have gone on to do some amazing things. A few of the first ascentionists have sent Himalayan giants, while others continue to climb at a high standard throughout North America. At least two of these climbers have invested their lives in guiding and outdoor education.

To reach these climbs, drive Interstate 5 to the Oregon border, then drive east on SR 14. The routes can be found in the Cape Horn area, approximately 25 miles from I-5. A sign indicates Cape Horn where, on the left, there is a chain-link fence hanging over the rock. The routes listed here are on this wall above the highway. Pass the chain-link fence and park in a small pullout on the right.

Note that on the first three routes, climbers must be very careful about dropping ice onto the highway. The last three routes are both shaded and sheltered from the wind. This is a plus because when temperatures are cold enough to form ice in the Gorge, the winds may reach gale force.

USGS maps: Bridal Veil, Beacon Rock

HANGING CURTAIN   WI 3+

Scott Woolums (one of the first ascentionists) currently holds the record for times standing on the summit of Denali. He has set foot in that high and cold place thirty-two times as of winter 2002.

   First ascent: Ian Wade and Scott Woolums, 1979
   Length: 80 feet
   Avalanche danger: Minimal
   Approach: This is the leftmost route seen directly above the highway.
   Route: Ascend the obvious ice curtain.
   Descent: Rappel the route.

DODGE CITY   WI 3

   First ascent: Scott Woolums and Ian Wade, 1979
   Length: 80 feet
   Avalanche danger: Minimal
   Approach: This route is directly above the highway, to the right of *Hanging Curtain*.
   Route: Ascend the obvious pillar.
   Descent: Rappel the route.

THE PILLAR   WI 3+

   First ascent: Ian Wade and Scott Woolums, 1979
   Length: 80 feet
   Avalanche danger: Minimal
   Approach: This route can be seen directly above the highway, to the right of *Dodge City*.
   Route: Ascend the obvious pillar.
   Descent: Rappel the route.

PHANTOM GULLY   WI 3

   First ascent: Monty Mayko and Robert McGown, 1979
   Length: 300 feet
   Avalanche danger: Minimal
   Approach: This can be seen directly above the highway, to the right of *The Pillar*.
   Route: Start on lower-angled ice that slowly kicks back.
   Descent: Rappel the route.

SILVER STREAK   WI 3+

   First ascent: Monty Mayko and Robert McGown, 1979
   Length: 300 feet
   Avalanche danger: Minimal

Approach: This route can be seen directly above the highway, to the right of *Phantom Gully*.

Route: Begin on lower-angled ice that slowly kicks back.

Descent: Rappel the route.

SALMON RUN   WI 4+

First ascent: Jim Olson and Robert McGown, 1980

Length: 300 feet

Avalanche danger: Minimal

Approach: This route can be seen directly above the highway, to the right of *Silver Streak*.

Route: Ascend the obvious steep route.

Descent: Rappel the route.

HAMILTON MOUNTAIN: THE STRAND   GRADE IV–V, WI 5+/6

This route has been described as one of the greatest challenges in the area. Indeed, it may be one of the most difficult challenges in the entire state.

First ascent: Robert McGown and Mark Simpson made an attempt on this route in 1981. As of yet there has not been a complete ascent.

Length: Four to five pitches

Avalanche danger: Minimal

Approach: This peak can be found to the northeast of Beacon Rock. There are a couple of access options: The first is via Guptil Road, which is 35.5 miles east from I-5. Unfortunately, there may be access issues here as there are a number of "No Trespassing" signs posted. It may be possible to get a little closer and avoid private land by driving Guptil Road to the powerlines and then following these for a distance until it is deemed acceptable to hike. Make sure to OBTAIN PERMISSION before crossing private property.

Hamilton Mountain can also be accessed via Forest Service Road 4270, an old road leading up to a gravel quarry. The turnoff for FR 4270 is beyond Beacon Rock State Park, near Hamilton Creek. The cliff band is approximately 45 minutes uphill from the quarry.

Routes: *The Strand* is the middle line on this peak. There are two other lines on the mountain, neither of which have yet seen a complete ascent. Any prospective climbers approaching this wall should be aware that these lines are all at least Grade IV and can reach WI 6; they may be some of the hardest routes in the state.

Note: It has been suggested that climbers aspiring to send one of these lines would do well to think about rappelling a line and placing bolts for anchors. In this scenario, at least the belays would be solid—a good thing, because it's unlikely anything else would be.

Descent: McGown and Simpson rappelled from their highpoint. Beware: the rock is horrendous basalt.

Rumors of Ice

The Cape Horn area is separated into three tiers. The climbs described above are on the highest tier above the highway. Directly beneath the highway, the second tier stands alone. There has been some activity on this cliff, but little has been recorded. It may actually be possible to top-rope off the highway guardrail—if the speeding cars near the anchor aren't too scary.

The lowest tier of Cape Horn has seen some action as well. It may be approached via the Cape Horn Road, which can be accessed about a mile after Cape Horn. Park at the end of the road and walk down the railroad tracks to the lowest tier. Monty Mayko and Robert McGown made a strong attempt on the 120-foot central pillar of the lowest tier in the early 1980s. McGown was leading the WI 5+/6 pillar while large waves from the Columbia River washed over his partner. Unfortunately, the pair had to retreat in light of potential hypothermia. No complete ascents have been recorded on this lowest of tiers.

On the Oregon side of the Columbia, nearly thirty climbs have been completed above I-80. If you are already in the area, these are well worth exploring. The routes are described in the excellent guide to the area, *Portland Rock Climbs,* by Tim Olson (Wild Horse Adventures, 2001).

In a cold season additional climbs may be found on SR 14 east of Hamilton Creek.

BLUEWOOD

The Bluewood Ski Area is located in the southeastern corner of the state. There are reports of ice formations stemming from seeps above the North Fork Touchet River very near there. Under the right conditions, a very nice band of ice forms that is approximately 75 to 100 feet wide.

USGS map: Godman Spring

To get to the area, drive U.S. Highway 12 to Dayton. From Main Street, head south on Fourth Street, following the signs to the Bluewood Ski Area.

WEEPING WALL   WI 2–5

This is a great practice area that is easily accessible. Bring along ski gear for lift-served or backcountry skiing after the climbing!

First recorded ascent: Kevin Pogue, 1990
Length: 50 feet
Avalanche danger: Moderate
Approach: Head for the Bluewood Ski Area from Dayton. After 14 miles, the paved road becomes gravel. The climbs are on the left side of the road at

Climbers on the Weeping Wall (photo by Brien Sheedy)

17.4 miles, but are difficult to see approaching from this direction because they are hidden by a small hill. If you reach the Sno-Park at mile 20, you have gone too far. Turn around and proceed 2.6 miles back down the road, to where the climbs are now visible, 100 feet from the road.

Routes: This area is formed by meltwater that drops over a short cliff band above the Touchet River. On the far right-hand side is a 50-foot WI 3 flow, with bolts installed above the climb. The climbs get steeper to the left, until they become 40- to 50-foot-high freestanding pillars on the far left-hand side of the cliff band.

There are two other bolted anchors above these climbs—the first person to do these routes after a snowfall will have to dig the anchors out. Locals have attached ropes to the bolts in order to make it easier to find the anchors after a snow storm.

Descent: Rappel the routes.

Rumors of Ice

There are further reports of ice slightly south of the Oregon border along the canyon walls of the South Fork Walla Walla River.

OLYMPIC MOUNTAINS

Craig John, a longtime climber and guide, states that "there is unlimited ice potential in the Olympics if you are hardcore enough." Indeed, with the many waterfalls, steep snowfields, and large amounts of cold air, there is a great deal of potential in the Olympic Mountains for ice climbing. However, at this time there is very little information about winter ice climbing in this range.

The only areas that are currently known are alpine in nature: prepare for an alpine experience before venturing into the Olympics to climb ice.

USGS map: Mount Skokomish

MOUNT ELLINOR, NORTH FACE: ACRES OF DIAMONDS   WI 3

First ascent: George Sherrit, Craig John, and Neil Glieckman, 1980s

Length: Five to six pitches

Avalanche danger: Serious

Approach: Mount Ellinor is on the southeastern flank of the Olympics, near Lake Cushman. Approach via Forest Service Road 2419. A current map of the logging roads is essential to the approach.

Ascend the south side of the mountain to the obvious ridge. To reach the north face, climb over the ridgeline and drop down beneath the face. There will be two gullies here, one to the right and one to the left. Descend the gully to the right and cut back left to the bottom of the north face.

Route: There are many variations on this face. Descend lower to get more ice. Choose an interesting route and have at it.

Descent: Drop down an obvious gully on the east side of the mountain. Descend back to your approach tracks and your car.

LAKE ANGELES   WI 2–3

These routes are located close to Hurricane Ridge in Olympic National Park. The routes form on north-facing cliffs at Lake Angeles, which has a base elevation of 4700 feet. The ice is mostly lower-angled climbing and can be top-roped, so the area is ideal for novices and those looking to hone their leading skills.

First ascent: Unknown

Length: Various

Avalanche danger: Moderate

Approach: To get to Lake Angeles, drive 5 miles up Hurricane Ridge Road. Just before the collection station is a sign for Heather Park. Make a right, drive 500 feet to the Heather Park and Lake Angeles Trailheads, and park your vehicle. The approach to Lake Angeles climbs steeply for 3.5 miles and takes about 2 hours. When you arrive at the lake, you can approach the climbs by walking around the edge of the lake, or by going directly across if the lake is well frozen.

Routes: There are many variations on these north-facing cliffs. Also, there are some possibilities for top-roping ice climbs at the east end of the cliffs.

Descent: Rappel from ice anchors. Natural anchors are scarce.

Rumors of Ice

Mount Washington, northeast of Ellinor, may have seen a few ice ascents in the '80s. Virtually no information currently exists about possible routes.

There is a potential climb near Mount Lincoln, a peak up the North Fork Skokomish River from Lake Cushman. A rumor started with Olympic Mountaineering reports that there is a monster ice route on the mountain. However, this is the same source that believes Olympic Peninsula rock climbing is good.

On the northern slope of the Olympics, ice has been spotted in the Mount Angeles cirque, though there is no information concerning whether or not any of it has been climbed.

APPENDIX A:
UNCOMMON ASCENTS AND
FORMATIONS

Ice climbing in Washington state has an interesting history. Some formations have frozen only once or twice since the advent of modern ice-climbing techniques; others have been hard hit by the slow ebb and flow of global warming. As a result, there are a few intriguing stories (tall tales?) out there. Perhaps one day some of these mythic lines will reappear.

It has been reported that in the early 1970s, all of the gullies of Skookum Falls (north of Rainier) often formed to create a giant ice sheet. A similar occurrence took place between *Hey Mikey, He Likes It* and *Mikey's Gully* near the Nisqually Glacier terminus. Indeed there is even one report indicating that during the winter of 1972–73, water running over the road cuts on Interstate 5 between Bellingham and Seattle froze solid. Local mountain guide Pat Timson and friends actually had the opportunity to climb some of those obscure routes that winter.

It has been reported that Dallas Kloke and friends did a winter ice ascent up the flanks of Mount Erie near Anacortes. It's hard to believe, but they did not drytool the entire way. There was actually a thin layer of ice on a good portion of the route they ascended. Reportedly the most interesting section was on the Black Wall; this tends to be the most mixed section of the rock climb. . . . In other words, it is the section with a little ice.

In the frigid winter of 1996 there were reports of ice on Mosquito Lake Road outside of Bellingham. Sources indicate that the ice was indeed long enough to be climbed, but those same sources would not divulge its location.

Believe it or not, a great place to go ice bouldering is inside the Snoqualmie Pass Bike Tunnel. There are multiple flows ranging from 10 to 15 feet high inside the old train tunnel. Bring a headlamp. It's dark and spooky in there. And unfortunately, sometimes it's closed in the winter.

At the height of the ice season in 1998, the waterfall in front of Seattle's REI store froze. For some odd reason the company was less than willing to allow climbers to ascend the formation at their store.

Cascade Crags is a climbing gym located in Everett (2820 Rucker Avenue; 425-258-3431) with an indoor ice-climbing wall and a free-hanging icicle. They have actually had an ice festival at their gym.

Drytooling has become a popular sport at certain Northwest crags. Sehome Hill in Bellingham has seen the scrape of tools, and it is reported that Scott

DeCapio has played on a 5.8 route at the Cobblestone Wall on Mount Baker Highway (State Route 542). Many Bellingham locals have also scraped their tools up a 5.4 crack at Pee Wee's Playhouse, also found on SR 542. Undoubtedly many local crags have felt the bite of ice tools as of late. When exploring good areas to practice drytooling, be sure to look for those that are not too popular with rock climbers. In other words, it's best to drytool at chossy crags.

APPENDIX B:
ICE-CLIMBING INSTRUCTION

There is an unfortunate trend throughout the climbing community in which underqualified people represent themselves as instructors or guides to beginning climbers. This is a tremendously dangerous situation that has resulted in many accidents and fatalities throughout North America.

What should you look for in a qualified instructor? The safest bet is to go with a reputable guide service that has been accredited by the American Mountain Guides Association (AMGA). Accreditation by the AMGA indicates that the guides working for a given company have not only spent a significant amount of time climbing, but have had specific training concerning how to keep those they are guiding safe. In other words, the company has passed a review by the AMGA of their instruction, hiring policies, and history.

Ask anyone who represents themselves as instructors or guides what kind of training they have had. Someone who has not been ice climbing for many years should not be thought of as experienced or as an instructor.

The AMGA website contains valuable information about how to choose a mountain guide *(www.amga.com)*. The following list of questions from the AMGA website are tailored toward professional mountain guide companies and should be asked by anyone seeking instruction. (The key word here is *professional*. When seeking a guide that will provide tools and instruction to keep you safe, look for the most professional instructor available.)

- What are the company's training requirements?
- What are the company's medical training requirements?
- Does the person or guide service have insurance?
- Will the person or guide service provide a list of previous clients as references?
- How long has the person been guiding or how long has the guide service been in operation?
- Has the company had any accidents, and if so, why?
- If the trip will take place outside the guide's home base, how familiar is he or she with the destination?

Many beginning ice climbers will learn their skills from friends who purport to have sufficient knowledge to teach the sport. Below is a similar list of questions that should be asked of any individual who is not affiliated with a guide service:

- How long has the person been ice climbing?
- How many times does the person go each year?
- What kind of training does the person have?
- What kind of medical training does the person have?
- Has the person ever taught anyone how to ice climb before?
- Can the person provide a list of partners that deem him or her a safe climber?

When learning how to climb from a friend, it is important to be aware of your surroundings. If anything feels wrong, if anything feels out of place, the best thing to do is to leave.

The following is a list of reputable local guide services that offer courses in technical ice climbing. Companies are listed in order of author preference:

American Alpine Institute
1515 12th Street
Bellingham, WA 98225
360-671-1505
www.aai.cc

North Cascades Mountain Guides
HCR 74 Box A5
Mazama, WA 98833
509-996-3194
www.ncmountainguides.com

Mountain Madness
4218 SW Alaska, Suite 206
Seattle, WA 98116
206-937-8389
www.mountainmadness.com

Alpine Ascents International
121 Mercer Street
Seattle, WA 98109
206-378-1927
www.alpineascents.com

APPENDIX C:
WILDERNESS FIRST-AID
INSTRUCTION AND HOSPITALS

WILDERNESS FIRST-AID INSTRUCTION

Companies providing wilderness first-aid instruction are listed in order of author preference.

Wilderness Medicine Institute: *http://www.nols.edu.wmi*

Wilderness Medicine Associates: *www.wildmed.com*

Solo Wilderness Medicine: *www.soloschools.com*

Sirius Wilderness Medicine: *www.siruismed.com*

First Lead: *www.firstlead.com*

HOSPITALS

Bellingham
St. Joseph's Hospital North
2901 Squalicum Parkway
360-734-5400

Cle Elum
Cle Elum Medical Center
201 Alpha Way
509-674-5331

Concrete
East Valley Medical
Main Street in Concrete
911 or 360-853-8183
Not open all hours.

Ellensburg
Kittitas Valley Community Hospital
603 S Chestnut Street
509-962-9841

Enumclaw
Community Memorial Hospital
1450 Battersby Avenue
360-825-2505

Everett
Everett General Hospital
14th and Colby
425-261-2000

Leavenworth
Cascade General Hospital
817 Commercial Street
509-548-5815

Monroe
Valley General Hospital
14701 179th Avenue SE
360-794-7497

Mount Vernon
Skagit Valley Hospital
1415 E Kincaid
360-428-2165

Snoqualmie
Snoqualmie Valley Hospital
9575 Ethan Wade Way SE
425-831-2300

Twisp
Methow Valley Family Practice
Twisp River Road
541 2nd Avenue
509-997-2011
Not open all hours.

Wenatchee
Central Washington Hospital
1300 Fuller Street
509-662-1511

Vancouver
Southwest Washington Medical
  Center
400 NE Mother Joseph Place
360-256-2000

Yakima
Yakima Valley Memorial Hospital
Intersection of 28th Avenue and
  Tieton Drive
509-575-8000

SELECTED RESOURCES

BOOKS

Beckey, Fred. *Cascade Alpine Guide, Climbing and High Routes Volume 1: Columbia River to Stevens Pass*. 3d ed. Seattle: The Mountaineers Books, 1996.

——.*Cascade Alpine Guide, Climbing and High Routes Volume 2: Stevens Pass to Rainy Pass*. 3d ed. Seattle: The Mountaineers Books, 2003.

——.*Cascade Alpine Guide, Climbing and High Routes Volume 3: Rainy Pass to Fraser River*. 2d ed. Seattle: The Mountaineers Books, 1995.

Cramer, Darryl. *Sky Valley Rock*. Seattle: Sky Valley Press, 2000.

Eminger, John, and John Kittle. *The Washington Desert: A Climbers Guide*. Spokane: Serac International Press, 1991.

Cox, Steven M., and Kris Fulsaas, eds. *Mountaineering: The Freedom of the Hills*. 7th ed. Seattle: The Mountaineers Books, 2003.

Josephson, Joe. *Waterfall Ice: Climbs in the Canadian Rockies*. Calgary, Alberta: Rocky Mountain Books, 2002.

Kearney, Alan. *Classic Climbs of the Northwest*. Mukilteo, Wash.: Alpen Books Press, LLC, 2002.

Kloke, Dallas. *Winter Climbs: One Day Ascents in the Western Cascades*. Anacortes, Wash.: Mountain Goat Guide Book, 1997.

Kramar, Viktor. *Leavenworth Rock*. Leavenworth, Wash.: Snow Creek Design, 1996.

Lowe, Jeff. *The Ice Experience*. Chicago: Contemporary Books, Inc., 1979.

Nelson, Jim, and Peter Potterfield. *Selected Climbs in the Cascades, Volume I*. 2d ed. Seattle: The Mountaineers Books, 2003.

——. *Selected Climbs in the Cascades, Volume II*. Seattle: The Mountaineers Books, 2000.

Olson, Tim. *Portland Rock Climbs*. Portland, Ore.: Wild Horse Adventures, 2001.

Olympic Mountain Rescue. *Climber's Guide to the Olympic Mountains*. Seattle: The Mountaineers Books, 1988.

Serl, Don, and Bruce Kay. *The Climber's Guide to West Coast Ice*. Squamish, B.C.: Merlin Productions, 1993.

Smoot, Jeff. *Rock Climbing Washington*. Helena, Mont.: Falcon Publishing, Inc., 1999.

MAGAZINES AND JOURNALS

Bebie, Mark. "Dragontail, Northwest Face Variant." *American Alpine Journal* (63), vol. 31 (1989): 143.

Benge, Michael. "Party On: Teenagers Put Up Cascades Alpine Route." *Climbing,* no. 162 (August 1996): 48.

Cotter, Robert. "Pyramid Peak, North Face." *American Alpine Journal* (62), vol. 30 (1988): 132.

Hall-Hargis, Tom. "Bridge Creek Wall, 'Wet and Wild.'" *American Alpine Journal* (59), vol. 27 (1985): 187.

Kearney, Alan. "Table Mountain, Death Picnic." *American Alpine Journal* (61), vol. 29 (1987): 166.

Klewin, Doug. "Middle Peak of Mount Index, North Face." *American Alpine Journal* (55), vol. 23 (1981): 172.

Paul, Bart. "The Spindrift Couloir: Scrappin' it up after classes in the Washington Cascades." *American Alpine Journal* (71), vol. 39. (1997): 60–65.

Pollock, Steve M. "Drury Falls." *American Alpine Journal* (53), vol. 22, no. 2 (1980): 539–540.

Reinfurt, Steven A. "Helicopter SAR/EMS Communications and Safety." *Mountain Bulletin,* vol. XV, no. 4 (winter 2002).

Shipman, Mark, and Glen Frese. "Washington, Columbia Basin: Served Straight Up Off the Rocks." *Climbing,* no. 106 (February 1988): 34–35.

Stage, Dan. "Big Four in Winter." *Off Belay,* no. 54 (December 1980).

Sumner, William. "Mount Index, Middle-Main Peak Gully." *American Alpine Journal* (59), vol. 27 (1985): 186.

Wilson, Tim. "Dragontail, Northwest Face." *American Alpine Journal* (58), vol. 26 (1984): 162.

CLIMBERS AND CLIMBING ON THE WEB

Dave Burdick, *www.alpinedave.com*

Tim Crawford, *www.cascadeclimbers.com*

Alex Krawarik, *www.mountainwerks.org/alexk*

Larry Nevers Jr., *www.nevershome.org/climbershome.htm*

Climbing magazine online, *www.climbing.com*

Rock and Ice online, *www.rockandice.com*

INDEX TO CLIMBS

ABOUT THE AUTHORS

Jason D. Martin (photo by Andrew Shipley)

Jason D. Martin, a native Northwesterner, is a playwright, climber, and professional mountain guide. His plays have been produced internationally, with many productions in the United States and Europe. He has climbed and guided professionally throughout the Cascades, Red Rock Canyon, Joshua Tree National Park, the Sierras, Canada, and South America. Jason has completed numerous first ascents on Northwest ice and on Southwest rock. To learn more about Jason's current projects, guide work, or productions, log onto *www.dramaticwriter.com*.

Alex Krawarik, an East Coast transplant, brought his love of ice climbing from New York state when he moved to the Pacific Northwest in 1993. He has climbed extensively in the Cascades, the Canadian Rockies, and throughout North America. He has completed several first ascents on Northwest ice and rock, and works for Microsoft in his spare time.

Alex Krawarik (photo by Summer Locke)

THE MOUNTAINEERS, founded in 1906, is a nonprofit outdoor activity and conservation club, whose mission is "to explore, study, preserve, and enjoy the natural beauty of the outdoors. . . . " Based in Seattle, Washington, the club is now the third-largest such organization in the United States, with seven branches throughout Washington state.

The Mountaineers sponsors both classes and year-round outdoor activities in the Pacific Northwest, which include hiking, mountain climbing, ski-touring, snowshoeing, bicycling, camping, kayaking and canoeing, nature study, sailing, and adventure travel. The club's conservation division supports environmental causes through educational activities, sponsoring legislation, and presenting informational programs. All club activities are led by skilled, experienced volunteers, who are dedicated to promoting safe and responsible enjoyment and preservation of the outdoors.

If you would like to participate in these organized outdoor activities or the club's programs, consider a membership in The Mountaineers. For information and an application, write or call The Mountaineers, Club Headquarters, 300 Third Avenue West, Seattle, WA 98119; 206-284-6310.

The Mountaineers Books, an active, nonprofit publishing program of the club, produces guidebooks, instructional texts, historical works, natural history guides, and works on environmental conservation. All books produced by The Mountaineers Books fulfill the club's mission.

Send or call for our catalog of more than 500 outdoor titles:

The Mountaineers Books
1001 SW Klickitat Way, Suite 201
Seattle, WA 98134
800-553-4453
mbooks@mountaineersbooks.org
www.mountaineersbooks.org

The Mountaineers Books is proud to be a corporate sponsor of Leave No Trace, whose mission is to promote and inspire responsible outdoor recreation through education, research, and partnerships. The Leave No Trace program is focused specifically on human-powered (nonmotorized) recreation.

Leave No Trace strives to educate visitors about the nature of their recreational impacts, as well as offer techniques to prevent and minimize such impacts. Leave No Trace is best understood as an educational and ethical program, not as a set of rules and regulations.

For more information, visit *www.LNT.org,* or call 800-332-4100.

OTHER TITLES YOU MIGHT ENJOY FROM
THE MOUNTAINEERS BOOKS

Mountaineering: The Freedom of the Hills,
The Mountaineers
The classic mountaineering text since 1961,
Freedom has instructed and inspired more than
half a million climbers the world over.

**Medicine for
Mountaineering & Other
Wilderness Activities,**
James Wilkerson, M.D.
A classic since 1967, this book starts where
most first-aid manuals stop. Written and
edited by a team of climber-physicians, this
is the perfect companion to *Mountaineering:
The Freedom of the Hills.*

Ice & Mixed Climbing: Modern Technique,
Will Gadd
Full-color, comprehensive guide from one of the
most prominent names in climbing today.

**Climbing: Training for
Peak Performance,**
Clyde Soles
Complete fitness program
specifically tailored for all
levels of climbers.

**Climbing: Expedition
Planning,**
Clyde Soles & Phil Powers
Learn to plan, organize, and lead an expedition
of any size.

THE MOUNTAINEERS BOOKS